Student Study Guide

GLENCOE Aviation Technology Series

Aircraft
Maintenance & Repair

Sixth Edition

Prepared by
William A. Watkins
Department of Aviation Technology
Purdue University

GLENCOE
McGraw-Hill

New York, New York   Columbus, Ohio   Woodland Hills, California   Peoria, Illinois

To my parents with love and appreciation.

Student Study Guide – Aircraft Maintenance and Repair, 6/e

Imprint 2000

Send all inquiries to:
Glencoe/McGraw-Hill
8787 Orion Place
Columbus, OH 43240

ISBN 0-02-803461-9

Printed in the United States of America.

5 6 7 8 9 10 11 12 13 047 08 07 06 05 04

Contents

To the Student

Welcome to the world of aviation maintenance and repair. As with all worthwhile endeavors, however, this effort will take time and effort. You are about to embark on studies that include a variety of applications of scientific and engineering principles. After you begin your studies if you discover that you are not familiar with these basic principles, it is suggested that you first review the companion text, *Basic Aircraft Science*.

This study guide is developed to assist the user of the associated text, *Aircraft Maintenance and Repair 6/e,* by:

Providing a series of fill-in-the-blank questions that follow and identify key items in each chapter;

Demonstrating application techniques of key mathematical relationships contained in each chapter, and

Providing a means of validating an adequate knowledge of each chapter topic by offering a series of multiple choice questions.

In addition, the answers to *all* questions are included in this study guide.

It is suggested that the user first read the related chapter completely *before* attempting to complete the fill-in-the-blank questions. In this way, the completion of the fill-in-the-blank questions will both act as a review and reinforce the significance of particular discussions in the text.

The mathematical application questions, where included, should then be completed to ensure that the topic is understood. In most cases, these questions combine the most basic relationships into a single question. In some instances, questions relate to one another in order to demonstrate the interrelationships between different concepts. As a result, many mathematical application answers include short notes that anticipate common misunderstandings and explain in more detail the *Study Guide* answer.

Finally, for many users of this *Study Guide,* the primary objective is the attainment of an Airman's Certificate with an Airframe Rating. To assist in this effort, the *Study Guide* concludes each chapter with a series of multiple choice questions. These questions are designed to represent those typically found in the FAA Airframe test.

William A. Watkins

Chapter 1

1. Before attempting any activity, the aviation maintenance technician should review the

   _____ , _____ ,

   _____ , and _____

   _____ .

2. Key among the agencies concerned with hazardous materials are the _____ (CPSC),

   _____ (FDA), _____ (DOT), _____ (EPA), and

   _____ (OSHA).

3. Some Federal Air Regulations (FARs) refer to the _____ standards in their text and use these
   standards as the criteria with which the aviation industry must comply.

4. As users of potentially dangerous chemicals, the aviation industry must comply with both the

   _____ as they relate to _____ , and _____ as

   their usage relates to the _____ of its employees.

5. Hazardous materials are typically grouped into three categories: _____ ,

   _____ , and _____ .

6. FACTOR™ stands for

   a. F _____
      And

   b. C _____

   c. T _____

      Or

   d. R _____

7. The two outside letters of the acronym FACTOR, F and R (flammable and reactive), primarily become hazardous

   after some _____ , _____ , or _____ interacts
   with them.

8. _____ , when combined together with certain other materials, are capable of generating

   _____ and/or _____ , causing an explosion.

9. The inside letters of the acronym, C and T (corrosives and toxins), act _____ on the human
   body when exposure occurs.

10. Exposing the _____ , _____ , and other _____
    to reactives can cause varying degrees of harm.

11. Toxic agents cause _____ .

12. Aviation maintenance technicians should be particularly concerned when using toxic agents because it may take
    weeks, months, or even years for the poisoning to become apparent and because the toxic poisons are capable of

    using the _____ to move through the body and the _____ relationship
    may not be easily recognized.

13. Therefore, the personal safety equipment used when working with corrosive and toxic agents should be designed to _____ and/or _____ .

14. Personal safety equipment designed for use with flammable and reactive materials is designed to limit _____ or _____ .

15. The technician should be aware of the _____ on the materials found in the work area and read them carefully.

16. Flammables are materials that may easily _____ in the presence of a _____ such as _____ , _____ , or _____ .

17. They may be in any of the three physical forms: _____ ; _____ ; or _____ .

18. Frequently found flammable/combustible materials in the aviation industry include _____ , _____ , _____ , _____ , and some _____ .

19. Static electricity may produce sparks. To avoid the sparks produced by static electricity, containers should be _____ .

20. If skin or eyes should come in direct contact with a flammable, _____ immediately with _____ .

21. If contact is made through clothing, _____ wet clothing and _____ .

22. Do not attempt to remove any potentially hazardous substance with _____ .

23. Corrosive materials are those that can react with _____ and/or cause _____ .

24. Frequently found corrosives in the aviation industry include acids and bases, such as _____ and _____ .

25. Strong acids are most normally found in a _____ , whereas _____ tend to come in powdered form.

26. Never add _____ to acid.

27. Acids and bases should be stored _____ .

28. Flammable toxins and corrosive toxic materials should be _____ because the corrosive gases could _____ the flammable containers, eventually leading to a leak of flammable materials.

29. Remove any corrosives that have come in contact with your skin or eyes by _____ _____ .

30. If a corrosive chemical agent is swallowed, _____ ; _____ , and seek medical attention _____ .

31. Toxins are generally defined as any substance that can cause an _____ or _____ .

32. The effects of toxins, unlike flammables and corrosives, may appear all at once (called acute effects) or may _____ over time with additional exposure (chronic effects).

33. Some toxins may dissipate over time when further exposure is eliminated, while others _____ , even after death.

34. Frequently found toxins in the aviation industry may be grouped into eight categories:

    a. _____   e. _____

    b. _____   f. _____

    c. _____   g. _____

    d. _____   h. _____

35. The effects of sensitizers may be cumulative, so _____ levels of exposure are recommended.

36. Carcinogens may cause changes in the genetic makeup of a human cell, resulting in _____ .

37. Minimize the release of toxic agents into the environment by _____ all containers and storing them in properly ventilated areas.

38. Flammable toxins and corrosive toxic materials should be _____ .

39. If there is any doubt in your mind regarding the degree of toxicity of the substance spilled, _____ .

40. Reactive agents are those materials that _____ with other materials.

41. The reactions that may take place range from _____ to the emission of _____ and/or _____ .

42. Frequently found reactives in the aviation industry are _____ and _____ materials.

43. Oxidizers that add oxygen to situations where high levels of heat and burning are present include _____ ; _____ acid and _____ acid; and _____ .

44. Water-reactive materials react with water and form _____ gases, which are very _____ .

45. _____ are frequently caused by the use of some type of equipment that is not directly controlled by those in danger.

46. Physical hazards that are not detectable by the human senses include _____ , _____ , _____ , _____ , and _____ .

47. Aviator's breathing oxygen is considered a physical hazard if it is stored in a _____ container.

48. OSHA requires that areas where this exposure exists be _____ and that _____ to these hazards be provided the _____ .

49. Biological hazards are living organisms that may cause _____ or _____ .

50. Typically, biological hazards enter the body through _____ with contaminated objects or individuals.

51. Exposure to biological hazards for the technician would most likely occur when working on _____ aircraft or in the _____ .

52. The Hazardous Communications Standard (29 CFR 1910.1200) requires that all employees and their supervisors be informed about the _____ associated with the _____ with which they work, regardless of the _____ of the chemicals involved in the operation.

53. The Hazardous Communications Standard requirements are part of the various _____ regulations.

54. The five basic requirements of a _____ program include inventory, labeling, material safety data sheets (MSDSs), training, and written program.

55. With the hazardous-communications program, an inventory of all hazardous materials used within the work place must be _____ and _____ .

56. All _____ shall be properly labeled.

57. Material safety data sheets (MSDSs) must be obtained for all material _____ and/or _____ in the work area.

58. Material safety data sheets provide detailed information concerning the _____ , _____ , _____ , and _____ .

59. All employees must be provided _____ regarding their _____ under the right-to-know program, the _____ of these materials, the _____ , and _____ .

60. Each employer must establish a written program that must be _____ at the facility.

61. Material safety data sheets should be provided by the manufacturer for each _____ supplied by them.

62. An MSDS is divided into nine (9) sections. They are:

    a. _____   f. _____
    b. _____   g. _____
    c. _____   h. _____
    d. _____   i. _____
    e. _____

63. A chemical hazard's chemical _____ and/or _____ would be found in Section _____ , _____ , of the MSDS.

64. The _____ , _____ , and _____ of the manufacturer of a chemical hazard would be in found Section I, Product Identification, of the MSDS.

65. Any hazardous mixtures of the MSDS subject material with other solids, liquids, or gases are listed in Section _____ , _____ , of the MSDS.

66. The maximum safe exposure limits may be expressed in three types of values: _____ _____ , _____ , and _____ .

67. Exposure limits are expressed in two forms. They are a _____ and an _____ .

68. If a material is toxic, its limits are also expressed in terms of the lowest exposure that would have a toxic effect, and _____ .

69. All exposures listed on an MSDS are expressed in terms of the number of _____ for a specified volume of air.

70. Section _____ of the MSDS, _____ , lists the physical properties such as boiling point, specific gravity, vapor pressure, percent volatile, vapor density, evaporation rate, solubility in water, and appearance and odor.

71. The nature of a material's fire and explosion hazard tendencies are listed in Section _____ , _____ , of an MSDS.

72. The appropriate extinguishing agent for fires involving the material is listed in Section _____ , _____ , of an MSDS.

73. The _____ of a material is the lowest temperature at which a flammable liquid will give off enough vapor to burn.

74. The LEL is the _____ and indicates the _____ mixture (vapor to air) that will burn.

75. Section V, Reactivity Data, of the MSDS describes the ability of the material to react and _____ or _____ under specified conditions.

76. Section VI, Health Hazard Information, of the MSDS shows, among other information, the primary means of exposure, such as _____ and _____ .

77. The procedures, in a general sense, that are to be followed in case of an accidental spill or release may be found in Section _____ , _____ , of the MSDS.

78. The desired ventilation, respiratory equipment, special clothing considerations, type(s) of gloves to be used, and eye protection may be found in Section _____ , _____ , of the MSDS.

79. Section IX, Special Precautions, of the MSDS includes special _____ and _____ information.

80. A hazardous materials inventory should include the name of the hazardous materials, their _____ , and the _____ .

81. As a general rule, hazardous material labels should _____ be removed.

82. In instances where materials are received in bulk form and transferred to small containers for use, two general rules apply. First, the container should be _____ , and second, once a container is used for one hazardous substance, it should _____ .

83. The NFPA placarding system uses four (4) _____ to form _____ .

84. The top three (3) diamonds use a numbering system from one (1) to four (4), indicating the _____ .

85. In the NFPA diamond color coding scheme, the blue diamond relates to the material's _____ , flammability information is in the _____ diamond, the _____ diamond indicates the relative reactivity of the material, and any _____ may be found in the white diamond.

86. In-house labeling systems are most frequently used when the operations of the company require the _____ of hazardous materials _____ .

87. If a mixture has *not* been tested as a whole, it is to be considered hazardous if it contains more than _____ percent of any hazardous material.

88. In the case of _____ , the minimum component amount is 0.1 percent (0.1%).

89. The National Environmental Policy Act of 1969 (NEPA) established the _____ to accomplish its objectives.

90. The _____ of hazardous waste are responsible for the _____ , _____ , _____ , _____ , _____ , and _____ of the waste produced.

91. Accidental releases most typically occur when the hazardous material is in a _____ or _____ state.

92. Spillage of commonly used hazardous materials such as aviation fuels and lubricants _____ considered an accidental release of a hazardous material.

93. Prior to using a hazardous material, the aviation maintenance technician should _____ the types of accidental releases that might occur and _____ for them.

94. The EPA has established _____ procedures for accidental release of hazardous materials.

95. Whether an accidental release needs to be reported is determined by the _____ released.

Chapter 1

MULTIPLE CHOICE QUESTIONS

1. The acronym FACTOR™ may be used to assist in identifying the type of
   a. chemical hazards.
   b. physical hazards.
   c. biological hazards.
   d. flammable hazards.

2. The exposure to toxic hazards may
   a. cause immediate vomiting.
   b. cause the eyes to water.
   c. cause shortness of breath.
   d. take years to be identified.

3. In order for a material to be considered a flammable hazard, it must be in either the liquid or gaseous form.
   a. True
   b. False

4. A corrosive powder
   a. is most likely to be an acid.
   b. is most likely to be a base.
   c. must be turned into a liquid before it is hazardous.
   d. must be turned into a gas before it is considered a hazardous material.

5. When storing acids and bases
   a. acids should be stored above bases.
   b. bases should be stored above acids.
   c. acids are always to the right-most side.
   d. store them separately.

6. Nitrogen bottles used to charge landing gear struts are considered hazardous because
   a. nitrogen has a toxic nature.
   b. it is stored under pressure.
   c. it replaces the oxygen in the air.
   d. All the above.

7. Chromic acid is
   a. a flammable.
   b. an oxidizer.
   c. a biological hazard.
   d. a toxic agent.

8. As a new employee, you must be informed of
   a. all hazardous materials used by the company.
   b. all hazardous material used by the company where exposure exceeds 25 percent of the TVA.
   c. all hazardous material used by the company where exposure exceeds 50 percent of the PEL.
   d. all hazardous material used by the company where exposure exceeds 50 percent of the UTV.

9. When transferring a hazardous material from one container to another
   a. the label must be transferred from the original container to the new container.
   b. the old container must be thoroughly cleaned before it is reused.
   c. Both a and b.
   d. None of the above.

10. If you are going to use a flammable chemical and want to ensure that you have the proper extinguishing agent nearby, in what section of the MSDS would you find the appropriate information?
    a. Section I
    b. Section II
    c. Section IV
    d. Section VII

Chapter 2

1. The structure of an aircraft must be strong enough to _____ all the loads to which it might be subjected.

2. To fly, an airplane's exterior must have an _____ shape.

3. Into an airplane's shape must be fitted members having a _____ , which are capable of sustaining the forces necessary to balance the airplane in flight.

4. In general, airplanes are designed to withstand _____ times the maximum expected forces.

5. The loads imposed on the wings in flight are stated in terms of _____ .

6. Load factor is the ratio of the _____ by the airplane's wing to the actual
   _____ .

7. Another way of expressing load factor is the ratio of a given load to the _____ .

8. Aircraft may be _____ into normal, utility, or acrobatic categories.

9. The _____ is limited to airplanes intended for nonacrobatic operation and has a load factor limit of 3.8 (often referred to as the limit load factor).

10. The utility category applies to airplanes intended for limited acrobatic operations and has a load factor limit of
    _____ .

11. Acrobatic category aircraft may have a load factor limit of _____ and are free to operate without many of the restrictions that apply to normal and utility category aircraft.

12. The category in which each airplane is certificated may be readily found in the aircraft's
    _____ or by checking the _____ found in the cockpit.

13. The primary structure of the aircraft should experience no _____ when subjected to the limit load factor.

14. If the aircraft is subjected to a load in excess of the limit load factor, the overstress may cause a
    _____ of the primary structure and require replacement of the damaged parts.

15. Flight loads are also divided into two types: _____ loads and _____ loads.

16. Gust loads in general are of _____ than maneuver loads, but their direction change can be much _____ .

17. Usually the _____ govern the design of the gear attachment structure of an airplane.

18. Total reaction force divided by the weight of the aircraft is called the _____ .

19. An airplane is designed and certificated for a certain maximum weight during flight, called the
    _____ .

20. The flight operating strength of an airplane is presented on a V-N graph whose _____ scale is airspeed *(V)* and whose vertical scale is _____ .

21. The principal aircraft load-carrying structural sections or components include the _____ ,
    _____ , _____ , _____ , and
    _____ .

22. The stresses (effects of applied forces) to which structural members are subjected are _____ , _____ , _____ , _____ , and _____ .

23. _____ is the stress that tends to crush or press together.

24. _____ is the stress in a member when a force tends to elongate or stretch it.

25. Torsion is the stress of _____ .

26. Bending is actually a combination of _____ .

27. _____ is the stress developed when a force tends to cause a layer of material to slide along an adjacent layer.

28. Strain is the effect of overstressing a part or assembly to the point where a _____ takes place.

29. _____ takes place when an airplane is designed and the loads that are likely to be applied to parts or assemblies of the airplane during operation are carefully computed and analyzed by engineers.

30. It is necessary to establish a method of locating components and reference points on the aircraft. This has been satisfied by establishing _____ and _____ for the fuselage, wings, nacelles, empennage, and landing gear.

31. For large aircraft, the Air Transport Association of America (ATA) has set forth _____ in ATA-100 Specification for Manufacturers' Technical Data.

32. Longitudinal points along the fuselage of an airplane are determined by reference to a zero _____ at or near the forward portion of the fuselage.

33. The position of the datum line is set forth in the _____ or _____ for the airplane and also in manufacturer's data.

34. To locate points on the wing of an airplane, the _____ numbers are measured from the center line of the fuselage, also called the _____ .

35. The _____ is a line established for locating stations on a vertical line.

36. Component stations for individual components are given their own station _____ .

37. Zoning of large aircraft has been specified by the Air Transport Association of America in the _____ .

38. A zone is identified by one of _____ indicators, depending upon whether it is a major zone, major subzone, or simply a zone.

39. Major ATA zones consist of a standard series of numbers from _____ to _____ , and the special series numbers are in the 900 bracket.

40. Major zones are divided into major subzones by the addition of a _____ digit to the major zone number.

41. Subzones are divided by the use of the _____ digit in the three-digit number.

42. _____ are hinged sections of the trailing edge of the left and right wing, which operate in series to provide lateral control.

43. An _____ is a surface designed to obtain reaction from the air through which it moves.

44. A _____ is a heavy structural member in the fuselage to contain pressure or fluids or to disperse concentrated loads.

45. A vertical reference line or plane parallel to the center line of the airplane is called a _____ .

46. A _____ is a beam or member supported at or near one end only without external bracing.

47. The middle or central section of an airplane wing to which the outer wing panels are attached is referred to as a _____ .

48. A frame shaped to the circumference of the fuselage diameter is called a _____ .

49. The area of a small aircraft occupied by the pilot and passengers is the _____ .

50. A _____ is a movable airfoil or surface, such as an aileron, elevator, flap, trim tab, or rudder, used to control the attitude or motion of an aircraft in flight.

51. On cabin airplanes, if the pilot compartment is separated from the rest of the cabin, it is often called the _____ .

52. The hinged and removable sides of the pod or nacelle that cover the engines are referred to as _____ .

53. The _____ is a removable cover or housing placed over or around an aircraft component or section, especially an engine.

54. The hinged section of the horizontal stabilizer used to increase or decrease the angle of attack of the airplane is an _____ .

55. The _____ is the aft portion of an aircraft, usually consisting of a group of stabilizing planes or fins, to which are attached certain controlling surfaces such as elevators and rudders.

56. A _____ is a piece, part, or structure, having a smooth streamlined contour, used to cover a nonstreamlined object or to smooth a junction.

57. A term commonly applied to the vertical stabilizer (vertical fin) or any stabilizing surface parallel to the vertical center line of the airplane is _____ .

58. The _____ is a fireproof or fire-resistant wall or bulkhead separating an engine from the rest of the aircraft structure to prevent the spread of a fire from the engine compartment.

59. A hinged section of the underside of the leading edge, which, when extended, reduces air flow separation over the top of the wing is a _____ .

60. _____ are the hinged section of the trailing edge of the wing, which can be lowered and extended.

61. A circumferential structural member in the body, which supports the stringers and skin of a semimonocoque construction, is the _____ .

62. A _____ is the cross-section shape of the stringers used in the fuselage.

63. The principal longitudinal member of the framing of an aircraft fuselage or nacelle is a _____ .

64. A web that primarily seals an area in order to retain cabin pressurization is a _____ .

65. The _____ is a fore and aft member of an airfoil structure (wing or aileron) of an aircraft used to give the airfoil section its form and to transmit the load from the skin to the spars.

66. A _____ refers to any of the larger subassemblies of the airplane that are built separately, and, when joined, form the complete airplane. The airplane is broken down into smaller sections to ease production and handling problems.

67. The maximum distance, measured parallel to the lateral axis, from tip to tip of any surface such as a wing or stabilizer is called the _____ .

68. A _____ is the principal spanwise beam in the structure of a wing, stabilizer, rudder, or elevator. It is usually the primary load-carrying member in the structure.

69. A fixed horizontal tail surface that serves to maintain stability around the lateral axis of an aircraft is a _____ .

70. _____ identify locations in inches from a beginning point. Station lines in the fuselage start forward of the nose; those for the wing usually start at the center line of the fuselage.

71. A stringer is a _____ member in the fuselage or _____ member in the wing to transmit skin loads into the body frames or wing ribs.

72. A supporting brace that bears compression loads, tension loads, or both, as in a fuselage between the longerons or in a landing gear to transmit the airplane loads, is called a _____ .

73. A _____ or fin is fixed to provide directional stability.

74. A horizontal reference line or plane parallel to the ground is a _____ .

75. A _____ is a thin gauge plate or sheet that, when supported by stiffening angles and framing, will provide great shear strength for its weights.

76. The _____ is the body to which the wings and the tail unit of an aircraft are attached and which provides space for the crew, passengers, cargo, controls, and other items, depending upon the size and design of the aircraft.

77. The fuselage should be designed to satisfy two major criteria: (1) _____ _____ , and (2) efficiently tie together the powerplant, wing, landing gear, and tail surface _____ .

78. In general, fuselages are classified into three types: _____ , _____ , and _____ .

79. A _____ is an assemblage of members forming a rigid framework, which may consist of bars, beams, rods, tubes, wires, etc.

80. The lateral structures may be loosely classed as _____ .

81. The spaces between the bulkheads are called _____ .

82. In the _____ the longerons are connected with only diagonal members.

83. A _____ structure consists of a framework of vertical and longitudinal members covered with a structural skin that carries a large percentage of the stresses imposed upon the structure.

84. Between the principal vertical members are lighter _____ , or _____ , to maintain the uniform shape of the structure.

85. The longitudinal members that serve to stiffen the metal skin and prevent it from bulging or buckling under severe stress are called _____ .

86. A full monocoque fuselage is one in which the fuselage skin carries _____ the structural stresses.

87. As the diameter of a monocoque fuselage increases, the weight-to-strength ratio becomes more _____ .

88. The interior structure to which the skin or plating is attached consists of _____ , _____ , _____ , _____ , _____ , and _____ riveted, bolted, or bonded together to form a rigid structure that shapes the fuselage.

89. The skin or plating is typically _____ or bonded to the structure to form the complete unit.

90. The rear section of an aircraft is often referred to as the _____ .

91. Transport-category aircraft fuselages are generally of _____ construction, utilizing the same basic principles described for light aircraft.

92. Due to their size, transport-size aircraft use additional components such as _____ , _____ , and _____ .

93. The _____ extends along the fuselage centerline through the wheel well and under the wing center section.

94. The floor-to-skin _____ are those ties that extend longitudinally along the intersection of the floor beams and frame.

95. _____ stabilize the skin and stringers and distribute the concentrated loads.

96. _____ structural fittings are made in two parts and joined together by riveting or bonding.

97. Each part in a fail-safe design is capable of carrying the _____ required structural load of the assembly.

98. The transport fuselage contains one or more _____ assemblies.

99. The midsection contains structures to connect the _____ to the _____ and may include landing gear attachment points.

100. The afterbody or _____ is the point of attachment for the aft flight-control surfaces and, depending on the aircraft design, may also incorporate an engine installation area.

101. Normally, the exterior fuselage skins are of 2024 clad aluminum to provide a surface that

_____ .

102. Most longitudinal skin splices are of the _____ .

103. Circumferential skin splices are generally of the _____ .

104. Bonding of structural components, which is the process of joining parts by using an _____ rather than a _____ , has been used for several years and has some unique advantages over conventional mechanical fasteners.

105. In their malleable state, composite materials can be formed into an _____ of shapes and contours to support advanced aerodynamic concepts.

106. When cured, the composite structures become exceptionally _____ , _____ , and _____ -resistant.

107. Fiberglass, graphite, boron and aramid fibers, together with epoxy and other organic matrix resins, allow the designer to tailor structures to meet applied loads more effectively through _____ and more efficiently by reducing _____ where loads are light.

108. Components that are attached to the fuselage at _____ include wings, landing gear, engines, stabilizers, jackpads, and antennas.

109. For the attachment of many components, a simple _____ or _____ is used.

110. This arrangement involves cutting sheet metal to the proper size for the required _____ , shaping it to _____ , and attaching it to the fuselage in the area beneath the component being attached.

111. Some attachment points require the use of special fittings such as _____ , _____ , _____ , or _____ to be able to withstand large loads such as occur through the wing and landing gear attachment points.

112. The structure of the aircraft vertical stabilizer may be an _____ part of the aircraft fuselage, or the vertical and horizontal stabilizers may be _____ castings or reinforced bulkheads.

113. The cockpit or flight deck must be designed so that the required minimum flight crew can

_____ and _____ all necessary controls and switches.

114. For complete information concerning the requirements for the flight deck, refer to FAR Parts

_____ and _____ .

115. The seats in the passenger compartment of any aircraft must be _____ to the aircraft structure.

116. Each seat must be equipped with a _____ that has been approved by the Federal Aviation Administration (FAA).

117. No passenger door may be located in the _____ of an inboard propeller or within

_____ thereof as measured from the propeller hub.

118. The external doors on transport aircraft must be equipped with devices for locking and for safeguarding against

opening in flight either _____ by persons or as a result of _____ .

119. The openings for doors, windshields, and windows require the use of special provisions in the area to allow the

_____ to flow _____ these openings.

120. For safety in a pressurized airplane, the door is designed to act as a _____ for the door

opening, and the pressure in the cabin _____ the door firmly in place.

121. To accomplish this, the door must be _____ than its opening and must be

_____ the airplane with pressure pushing _____ .

122. Each cargo compartment must bear a _____ stating the maximum allowable

_____ of its contents.

123. Freight is generally "containerized"; that is, the freight is packed in containers designed to fit the

_____ of the fuselage.

124. A "combi" aircraft carries a combination of passengers and cargo on the same deck separated by temporary or

movable _____ .

125. The terms high-wing, low-wing, and mid-wing all describe both airplane _____ and

_____ of wing _____ .

126. Wing design can be divided into two types, _____ and _____ .

127. A cantilever wing contains all its structural strength _____ the wing structure and requires no

_____ .

128. The semicantilever design obtains its strength both by internal wing design and external support and by bracing

from _____ .

129. Conventional wings are of three general types: _____ , _____ and

_____ .

130. The monospar wing has only _____ spar, the two-spar wing has two spars as the name

indicates, and the multispar wing has more than _____ .

131. A wing spar, sometimes called a _____ , is a principal _____ member of the wing structure.

132. If a single spar is used, it is located near the _____ of the _____ .

133. If two spars are used, one is located near the _____ and the other is located near the
_____ .

134. A _____ , sometimes called a _____ , is a chordwise member of the
wing structure used to give the wing section its shape and also to transmit the air _____
from the covering to the spars.

135. To assist in holding the shape of the wing, spanwise members called _____ , or
_____ , are attached to the skin.

136. Typically in stressed-skin metal construction, the skin of the wing is riveted to the _____
and _____ .

137. The aluminum skin has high strength and is employed as a _____ load-carrying member.

138. Fuel tanks are normally located in the _____ portion of the wing.

139. In a wooden wing, the wires carrying drag loads are called _____ , and those carrying the
loads opposite drag are called _____ .

140. Transport wings consist of _____ or more main spars with _____
spars used between the _____ spars in some designs.

141. The front and rear spars provide the main supporting structure for fittings attaching the
_____ , _____ , _____ , and
_____ to the wing.

142. The auxiliary structure of the wing includes the _____ , _____ , and
_____ .

143. The leading edge of the wing incorporates leading-edge ribs, structural reinforcement members, and attachment
points for components such as _____ and _____ .

144. The trailing edge also incorporates structural members serving _____ to those of the leading
edge.

145. The trailing-edge structure normally incorporates an extensive structure to carry and transmit the loads imposed by
the operation of the _____ .

146. The wing internal structures are covered with large metal skin panels, which have _____
attached to achieve the desired structural strength of the wings.

147. Fuel tanks are included in the basic wing structure so that the wing serves as a fuel tank. This is known as an
integral fuel tank design, also referred to as a _____ .

148. Areas of the wings that do not contain fuel are termed _____ .

149. The horizontal stabilizer is used to provide _____ to the aircraft and is usually attached to
the aft portion of the fuselage.

150. If the stabilizer is designed to provide pitch trim, it normally is attached to the fuselage with a pivoting hinge as its
_____ .

151. The vertical stabilizer for an airplane is the airfoil section forward of the rudder and is used to provide
_____ stability for the aircraft.

152. On many aircraft a _____ is installed immediately forward of the vertical stabilizer.

153. The primary control surfaces of an airplane include the _____ ,
_____ , and _____ .

154. Secondary control surfaces include _____ , _____ , _____ , and _____ .

155. Landing gear must be classified as either _____ or _____ , and it may also be classified according to _____ .

156. A retractable landing gear is carried partially or completely inside the airframe structure to _____ .

157. The two most common configurations for landing gear are the _____ and _____ arrangements.

158. A conventional landing-gear configuration consists of two main landing gears located ahead of the aircraft center of gravity and a _____ .

159. _____ landing gear consists of two main landing gears located aft of the center of gravity and a nose wheel located near the nose of the aircraft.

160. The vast majority of aircraft being manufactured today, including all transport category aircraft, are of the _____ configuration.

161. An _____ is used to enclose the engine in a streamlined housing to improve the aerodynamics of the aircraft, to support and protect the engine and its components, and to direct airflow into the engine for cooling and combustion and away from the engine for proper exhaust outflow.

162. The structure employed to attach an engine nacelle or pod to a wing or fuselage may be referred to as a _____ or a _____ .

163. All engines, auxiliary power units, fuel-burning heaters, and other combustion equipment intended for operation in flight as well as the combustion, turbine, and tailpipe sections of turbine engines must be _____ from the remainder of the aircraft by means of _____ , _____ , or other equivalent means.

164. All openings in the firewall or shroud must be _____ with _____ , _____ , or _____ .

165. Firewalls and shrouds are constructed of _____ materials such as _____ , _____ , or _____ .

166. An engine mount is a _____ that supports the engine and attaches it to the fuselage or nacelle.

167. _____ usually consists of detachable sections for covering portions of the airplane, such as engines, mounts, and other parts where ease of access is important.

168. A _____ is used principally to streamline a portion of an airplane, although it may protect some small piece of equipment or merely improve the appearance.

169. On a helicopter, both the lift and thrust forces are concentrated on the _____ .

170. Early helicopter structures used primarily _____ .

171. Helicopter construction evolved to utilizing aluminum _____ and _____ designs.

172. A third type of construction utilizes _____ such as graphite, kevlar, and fiberglass combined with bonded structures.

173. The process of laying composite fibers in a curved surface without disturbing the fibers is known as _____ .

174. The natural path is the path that tape tends to follow to maintain _____ to all fibers.

175. The forward fuselage of a helicopter consists of a _____ (tub) and an _____ (cabin).

176. The lower fuselage includes the _____ fuel tanks and provides _____ support for the flooring, retractable landing gear, and cargo hook (if installed).

177. The primary purpose of the tailboom is to support the _____ and _____ of the helicopter.

178. The tail rotor is used to control the _____ of the aircraft and to counteract the _____ of the engine-transmission system.

179. A vertical stabilizer provides stability in _____ flight and relieves the _____ rotor of some of its workload in forward flight.

Chapter 2

Name _____

Date _____

APPLICATION QUESTIONS

1. If an aircraft with a gross weight of 5000 lb has a load factor of 2, what is the additional load caused by flight?

2. To what load-carrying capability would you generally expect the aircraft to be designed?

3. During normal operations, how many pounds would be applied if the aircraft was pulling 2 g's?

4. If the landing of an aircraft weighing 3000 lb results in a force of 7500 lb being applied to the aircraft at ground contact, what is the landing load factor?

Chapter 2

MULTIPLE CHOICE QUESTIONS

1. The stress of twisting is called
   a. compression.
   b. tension.
   c. torsion.
   d. shear.

2. When a location is referenced from a vertical reference line, the "zero" station is the
   a. butt line.
   b. datum line.
   c. station line.
   d. water line.

3. The control surface used to increase or decrease an aircraft's angle of attack is
   a. an aileron.
   b. an elevator.
   c. a flap.
   d. a rudder.

4. When the skin of a fuselage carries all the structural stress, the structure is referred to as
   a. a truss.
   b. a frame.
   c. monocoque.
   d. semimonocoque.

5. The structural design philosophy that allows two different paths for operational loads is called
   a. Safe-life.
   b. Duo-safe life.
   c. Fail-safe.
   d. Damage tolerant.

6. The principal spanwise load-carrying member of a wing assembly is called a
   a. spar.
   b. rib.
   c. stringer.
   d. bulkhead.

7. A wing's chordwise component that transmits the air load during flight to the main spanwise wing component is the
   a. spar.
   b. rib.
   c. stringer.
   d. bulkhead.

8. What is the purpose of a gusset or gusset plate used in the construction and repair of aircraft structures?
   a. To hold structural members in position temporarily until the permanent attachment has been completed
   b. To provide access for inspection of structural attachments
   c. To join and reinforce intersecting structural members
   d. To provide a method of adjusting the tension or location of structural members

9. Longitudinal (fore and aft) members of a semimonocoque fuselage are called
   a. spars and ribs.
   b. longerons and stringers.
   c. bulkheads and rings.
   d. ribs and formers.

10. Which statement is true regarding a cantilever wing?
    a. It employs lift wires instead of lift struts.
    b. It has nonadjustable lift struts.
    c. No external bracing is needed.
    d. It requires only one lift strut on each side.

11. Aircraft structural units, such as spars, engine supports, etc., which have been built up from sheet metal, are normally
    a. repairable, using approved methods.
    b. repairable, except when subjected to compressive loads.
    c. not repairable, but must be replaced when damaged or deteriorated.
    d. repairable, except when subjected to tensile loads.

12. Monocoque fuselages derive their principal strength from
    a. bulkheads and longerons.
    b. longerons and formers.
    c. the actual covering, metal or plywood.
    d. metal stringers.

13. Which part(s) of a semimonocoque fuselage prevent(s) tension and compression from bending the fuselage?
    a. metal stringer
    b. the fuselage covering
    c. longerons and stringers
    d. bulkheads and skin

14. Primary control surfaces
    a. rotate the aircraft around the three primary axes.
    b. are lighter in construction than secondary control surfaces.
    c. are monocoque in construction.
    d. are adjustable only in flight.

15. (1) Trim tabs are movable in flight.
    (2) Trim tabs assist in the movement of secondary control surfaces.
    Referring to the above statements,
    a. Both are always true.
    b. (1) is always true and (2) is sometimes true.
    c. (2) is always true and (1) is sometimes true.
    d. Neither statement is true.

16. The enclosure around an aircraft powerplant is referred to as a
    a. bulkhead.
    b. fairing.
    c. nacelle.
    d. pylon.

17. The structure that separates an aircraft's powerplant from the rest of the aircraft is a
    a. bulkhead.
    b. firewall.
    c. cowling.
    d. fairing.

18. If a pilot reports that the skid seemed loose on landing,
    a. the pilot is referring to the brake antiskid system.
    b. the reference was to the landing gear, if the pilot was flying a helicopter.
    c. the spoilers are most likely loose.
    d. the speed brakes do not actuate symmetrically.

19. A truss
    a. is an assemblage of load-carrying members providing the framework of a rigid body.
    b. is a supporting brace that assists in the transmission of a flight load.
    c. is a crossmember between lateral braces.
    d. cannot support a flight load when the aircraft is on the ground.

20. Bonding
    a. provides an even distribution of structural loads.
    b. is applied to structural rivets before they are installed to seal the joint.
    c. is used only on secondary control surfaces.
    d. must be applied between an aircraft's tires and the tire's rim.

Chapter 3

1. The two principal types of wood used in aircraft are _____ and _____.

2. The distinction between the two types of woods used in aircraft is based on the _____ of the wood.

3. Softwoods used in aircraft are

   a. _____   c. _____

   b. _____   d. _____

4. Hardwoods commonly used in aircraft structures include

   a. _____

   b. _____

   c. _____

5. A radial crack that cuts across the grain lines is called a _____ .

6. _____ are wrinkles or streaks across the grain line caused by mechanical stress on the wood after the annual rings had grown.

7. The weight of water contained in a wood sample compared to the weight of the wood sample if all the water was removed from it determines the _____ .

8. Generally the best wood for use in aircraft structures is _____ .

9. Aircraft woods are _____ to remove all the free water and a portion of the cell water so that the resulting moisture content is between 8 and 12 percent.

10. Aircraft wood cut so that the annual rings are parallel to the narrow dimension of the board is described as _____ or _____ .

11. The _____ of a grain line is determined by looking at the side of a board and noting the angle that the grain line makes with the edge of the board.

12. The minimum grain count for most softwoods is _____ rings per inch [2.54 cm].

13. Specifications for aircraft woods are given in Federal Aviation Advisory Circular (AC) _____ .

14. Wood composed of an uneven number of layers (plies) of wood veneer assembled with the grain of each layer at an angle of 45° to 90° to the adjacent layers is known as _____ .

15. Laminated wood differs from plywood in that each layer of wood has the grain running in the _____ direction, whereas plywood has the grain direction of each layer at a _____ to the previous layer.

16. _____ glues are manufactured from milk products, are highly water-resistant, and require the addition of sodium salts and lime to prevent attack by microorganisms.

17. _____ glues are of the urea formaldehyde, resorcinol formaldehyde, phenol formaldehyde, and epoxy types.

18. Proportions for the mixing of glue may be expressed either by _____ or by _____ .

19. The process of mixing the glue requires that the speed of mixing be slow enough so that _____ into the mixture.

20. The average working life of glues is _____ at 70°F [21°C].

21. Softwoods should not be sanded when preparing the surface for gluing because sanding fills the wood pores with wood dust and _____ .

22. There should be no more than _____ hours between the time that the surface is prepared for gluing and the gluing operation takes place.

23. The moisture content of wood when it is glued has a great effect on the _____ of glued members, the development of _____ in the wood, and the _____ of the joints.

24. A starved joint is a joint that is _____ .

25. In an _____ , the glue is applied to both surfaces to be joined, and the parts are not put together for a specified length of time.

26. If the pieces of wood are coated with glue and put together as soon as the glue is spread, the process is called _____ assembly.

27. The functions of pressure on a glue joint are to

    a. _____   c. _____

    b. _____   d. _____

28. A _____ pressure is used with thin glue and a _____ pressure is used with thick glue.

29. Solid wood is normally bent only over a very _____ radius and then only when the wood is of a _____ cross-sectional area.

30. _____ structures are used for items such as tip bows, formers, and bulkheads.

31. Plywood with a _____ curvature is often found in areas such as fairings and wing tips.

32. Soaking the wood in _____ makes the wood more flexible.

33. The wood should not be exposed to steam more than _____ hours because excessive heating causes the wood to break down structurally.

34. The forms for bending wood are usually made with a slightly _____ curvature than that required for the finished part.

35. When built-up plywood members are desired, _____ strips or sheets are bent over a form after glue has been applied to their surfaces.

36. The grain of each successive layer of veneer should be _____ to that of the adjoining layer, but in some jobs the veneer is applied on the form with the grain running at an oblique angle of about _____ from the axis of the member.

37. Solid spars use _____ wood as the primary components.

38. _____ spars can be divided into three basic types—C-beam, I-beam, and box-beam.

39. For a C-beam, the cap strips are on _____ side(s) of the spar, whereas an I-beam has cap strips on _____ side(s) of the web.

40. For a C-beam, _____ are located vertically between the cap strips at intervals to increase the strength and rigidity of the spar.

41. A _____ spar consists of a top and bottom solid-wood cap strip, plywood webs on the outside of the cap strips, with intercostals and blocks being used for strength, stiffness, and attachment of fittings.

42. If a spar has been repaired twice, it is generally considered to be _____ .

43. If the damage is in such a location that a splice is not possible without interfering with wing fittings, then it is _____ .

44. If the damage is such that the integrity of the repair will be in doubt, such as the presence of extensive decay, then the spar is _____ .

45. A wood rib is usually assembled in a _____ .

46. During assembly of wood ribs, the _____ are inserted between the blocks to hold them in the proper position for attachment of the vertical and diagonal members and the plywood gussets.

47. _____ are attached to the cap strips, verticals, and diagonals with nails and glue.

48. "Push" fit components should not have any _____ between components, and none of the components should require _____ to position them onto the jig board.

49. Once the glue has set and the rib is removed from the jig, excess glue is removed, and _____ are added to the opposite side of the rib.

50. Ribs should not be attached to a spar by nailing through the _____ , as this will significantly weaken the ribs.

51. To obtain additional gluing area when repairing leading-edge strips, the skin is _____ into the cap strip.

52. Splices to a wing-tip bow should meet the same requirements as a _____ joint.

53. During the installation of plywood skins, hold-down strips are first nailed _____ of the skin panel and then nailed _____ .

54. If a piece of paper can be laid on the surface of a plywood skin and smoothed out without wrinkling, then the plywood has a _____ curvature.

55. If the paper cannot be laid on the surface of a plywood skin without wrinkling, then the plywood has a _____ curvature.

56. If a split at the rear end of a wooden ski runner has a length not more than _____ percent of the ski length, it may be repaired by attaching, with glue and bolts, one or more wooden crosspieces across the top of the runner.

57. Wood surfaces of an airplane structure that have been repaired must be _____ to prevent the absorption of moisture, oil, or other contaminants and to prevent deterioration.

58. The interior surfaces of wooden structures such as wings and control surfaces should be thoroughly coated with at least _____ coats of spar varnish or lion oil.

59. MIL-V-6894 varnish is dopeproof and should be used when the _____ finish is to be lacquer or dope.

60. End-grain wood surfaces require _____ finish than side-grain surfaces.

61. If wood is alternately wet and dry over a period of time, it will _____ and _____ .

62. Spar varnishes of the phenol formaldehyde type (MIL-V- _____) or glycerol phthalate type (MIL-V- _____) are commonly employed for the finishing of wood structures.

63. High temperatures lead to the evaporation of _____ in coatings, and this causes brittleness and cracking.

64. Freezing of wet structures can cause _____ of fibers and cells, thus weakening the parts affected.

65. When wood is black, brown, gray, or some combination of the three colors, this is an indication of _____ and _____ .

66. Wherever a glue joint is found open or separated, the structure _____ .

67. _____ is indicated by a line or lines extending across the grain where the wood fibers have been crushed.

68. If the plywood is covered with fabric and a crack or split appears in the fabric, the fabric must be _____ so the plywood underneath can be examined for damage.

69. If the surface of the plywood is warped or wavy, defects are indicated _____ the structure.

70. Glue joints can be checked by attempting to insert one of the thinnest leaves of a feeler gauge into the joint. If the feeler gauge can penetrate the joint, the joint must be _____ .

71. In cases where a spar is laminated and bolts pass through the laminated section to attach a fitting, the bolts should be loosened to take the pressure off the area. This will allow _____ between the layers of wood to be revealed.

72. During a stress inspection, the stress is applied by pushing up, pulling down, and _____ the structure by applying pressure at the primary structures.

73. _____ from a joint indicates abrasion and breakdown of the glue joint.

Chapter 3

MULTIPLE CHOICE QUESTIONS

1. Laminated wood spars may be substituted for solid rectangular wood spars
   a. only in certain instances where the primary load is shared by one (or more) other original structural member.
   b. only if the strength deficiency is allowed for by an increase in dimension.
   c. if the same quality wood is used in both.
   d. only upon specific approval by the manufacturer or the FAA.

2. The strength of a glue joint must be equal to
   a. 75 percent of the wood strength.
   b. the strength of the wood.
   c. twice the strength of the wood in tension.
   d. 50 percent of the wood strength.

3. The strength of a well-designed and properly prepared wood spice joint is provided by the
   a. bearing surface of the wood fibers.
   b. doubler.
   c. glue.
   d. reinforcement plates.

4. Where is information found concerning acceptable species substitution for wood materials used in aircraft repair?
   a. Aircraft Specifications or Type Certificate Data Sheets
   b. Technical Standard Orders
   c. AC 43.13-1A
   d. AC 65-19C

5. A faint line running across the grain of a wood spar generally indicates
   a. compression failure.
   b. fungus growth.
   c. shear failure.
   d. decay.

6. Which statement about wood decay is correct?
   a. Decay that occurs before the wood is seasoned does not affect the strength of the finished piece.
   b. Decay that does not cause the wood to discolor or stain is not usually harmful to the strength of the wood.
   c. A limited amount of certain kinds of decay is acceptable in aircraft woods, since decay affects the binding between the fibers and not the fibers themselves.
   d. Decay, unlike some other wood defects, is not acceptable in any form or amount.

7. Pin knot clusters are permitted in wood structures provided
   a. they produce a small effect on grain direction.
   b. they are located 24 in apart.
   c. they have no mineral streaks.
   d. no pitch pockets are near.

8. Which of the following conditions will determine acceptance of wood with mineral streaks?
   a. Careful inspection fails to reveal any decay.
   b. They do not cause grain divergence.
   c. They produce only a small effect on grain direction.
   d. Local irregularities do not exceed limitations specified for spiral and diagonal grain.

9. Laminated wood is often used in the construction of highly stressed aircraft components. This wood can be identified by its
   a. increased resistance to deflection.
   b. parallel grain construction.
   c. similarity to standard plywood construction.
   d. alternate perpendicular ply construction.

10. Compression failures in wood structures are characterized by buckling of the fibers that appear as streaks on the surface
    a. at right angles to the growth rings.
    b. only in the heart wood.
    c. only in the spring wood or summer wood.
    d. at right angles to the grain.

11. The moisture content of wood at the time of gluing should be in the range of
    a. 0–4 percent
    b. 5–8 percent
    c. 8–12 percent
    d. 12–15 percent

12. Casein glue requires the addition of sodium salts and lime
    a. to prevent cracking of the glue after it is cured.
    b. to prevent attack by microorganisms.
    c. in order to have paint adhere to it.
    d. because otherwise it will not set.

13. Wood spars
    a. must be of solid construction.
    b. must be routed.
    c. may not be drilled.
    d. may be of laminated construction.

14. Wood spars may
   a. not be repaired.
   b. be repaired only once, assuming there is not question of integrity.
   c. be repaired twice, assuming there is not a question of integrity.
   d. be repaired any number of times, assuming there is not a question of integrity.

15. In order to properly inspect a laminated wood spar
   a. all gussets must be removed.
   b. all bolts should be loosened.
   c. all ribs must be removed.
   d. All the above.

Chapter 4

1. A _____ is a cut, fold, or seam made diagonally across the warp and fill fibers of a piece of cloth.

2. The chemical process used to whiten textile materials is called _____ .

3. Grade A airplane fabric is not bleached and is usually a _____ color.

4. _____ causes the nap to lay close to the surface.

5. The _____ is the ''fuzzy'' surface caused by the thousands of ends of individual fibers.

6. The fibers of a piece of fabric that are woven into the warp fabric are known as _____ .

7. _____ is a chemical process in which cotton is exposed to the action of a strong caustic solution that tends to shrink the material and give it a silky appearance.

8. The naturally bound edge of a length of fabric where the fill fibers turn around and go back through the warp fibers during the weaving process is referred to as the _____ .

9. _____ is a textile glue used to stiffen and protect fabrics and threads.

10. Thread count is the number of threads, either warp or fill, on the edge of a piece of fabric and uses a unit of measurement of _____ .

11. The threads in a woven fabric that run the length of the fabric are known as the _____ .

12. Fabric weight indicates the weight of the fabric per unit of area and is expressed in terms of

_____ .

13. Woof is synonymous with _____ .

14. Grade A mercerized cotton cloth is identified by the SAE number AMS _____ , and the specifications are set forth in _____ .

15. Approved fabric predoped with cellulose nitrate dope is numbered _____ .

16. The minimum tensile strength of approved grade A fabric in the new, undoped condition is

_____ lb/in [140 N/cm (newtons per centimeter)].

17. Grade A cotton fabric predoped with _____ dope is numbered MIL-C-5642.

18. After fabric has been used on an airplane, its minimum permissible strength is _____ percent of new strength.

19. The military specification for grade A fabric is _____ .

20. Grade A cotton may not be used on an aircraft originally covered with an _____ fabric unless approval is obtained from the aircraft manufacturer or the FAA.

21. Grade A fabric must have a thread count of _____ to _____ threads per inch in both length and width.

22. The weight of grade A fabric must be not less than _____ oz/yd² (ounces per square yard) [_____ g/m² (grams per square meter)].

23. Wing loading can be determined by dividing the maximum allowed _____ of the aircraft by the _____ .

24. Intermediate-grade aircraft fabric carries the number AMS _____ .

25. An inorganic fabric is one that requires _____ to create the fiber.

26. _____ fabrics are manufactured under the trade names of Stits Poly-Fiber and Ceconite.

27. _____ is the most widely used type of fiberglass material for covering aircraft.

28. Surface tape, also called finishing tape, is usually cut from _____ _____ .

29. The edges are pinked (cut with a saw-toothed edge) to provide better adhesion when doped to the surface and to _____ .

30. Surface tape material is used to _____ , _____ , and _____ .

31. Surface tape, if purchased separately, should have the same _____ , _____ , _____ , and _____ as the covering fabric.

32. A straight-cut surface tape has edges _____ to the warp threads.

33. A bias-cut surface tape is preferred for surfaces with _____ curvatures.

34. The warp threads found on reinforcing tapes are _____ than the _____ threads.

35. _____ is used over ribs between the lacing cord and fabric covering to prevent the cord from cutting or wearing through the fabric and to help distribute the air loads.

36. Reinforcing tape bearing the specification number _____ , or equivalent, is approved for aircraft use.

37. _____ , for either machine or hand sewing, is used to join two fabric edges together during the installation or repair of fabric covering materials.

38. _____ should be used in place of thread where a significant amount of strength is required of each stitch, such as when attaching a fabric covering to wing ribs or fuselage stringers.

39. The _____ of a thread or cord may be either right or left.

40. The term _____ twist designates a right-twist thread.

41. The words *machine, machine twist, Z twist,* and *left twist* all refer to a _____ thread.

42. Right-handed people should make seams from _____ to _____ using a _____ thread held taught with the _____ hand while each stitch is being made.

43. Left-handed people should make seams from _____ to _____ using a _____ thread held taught with the _____ hand while each stitch is being made.

44. Lacing cord is used for lacing fabric to the _____ .

45. Rib-stitching cord and rib-lacing cord are other names for _____ cord.

46. Acceptable lacing cords carry the specification numbers _____ or _____ for a linen cord and _____ for a cotton cord.

47. Waxed cords are used for attaching _____ .

48. Grommets are installed where it is necessary to _____ holes in textile materials used for _____ , _____ , or _____ .

49. After the installation of plain plastic grommets or seaplane grommets, the fabric in the grommet opening should be _____ .

50. Grommet openings should not be _____ .

51. The fabric in an inspection ring is _____ until necessary for inspection, wing or wing component installation, or other maintenance activities.

52. After the fabric is removed and access through the hole is no longer required, a _____ is installed in the hole.

53. If a wing or control surface's ribs are fabricated from wood, the only acceptable technique for installation of the wing fabric is the _____ .

54. _____ is used to coat hand-sewing threads and rib-lacing cord prior to installation.

55. The primary functions of aircraft dope are _____ , _____ , and _____ airplane fabric coverings.

56. Dope has been defined as a colloidal solution of _____ or _____ or any other substance that meets the functions of aircraft dope.

57. The most prominent pigment material associated with aircraft is _____ , which gives the dope a silver color and is used to reflect the sun's ultraviolet rays.

58. The cause of _____ is the pigment of the dope moving up into the next layer of paint, resulting in a change in the color.

59. Aircraft nitrate and butyrate dopes _____ as they dry.

60. The shrinking feature of aircraft dope is used in organic and fiberglass covering operations to aid in creating a _____ fabric finish.

61. The taughtening feature of aircraft nitrate and butyrate dopes is not desired when covering an aircraft with _____ .

62. _____ are needed in nitrate dope to provide flexibility and resistance to cracking after the dope has cured.

63. Butyrate dope is more _____ than nitrate dope and provides greater _____ of fabric.

64. Cotton and linen fabrics are subject to attacks by _____ , which will result in a reduction of their strength.

65. To combat fungus attacks, _____ were developed for addition to the dope and are applied as part of the _____ coat.

66. A military specification, _____ , requires that the first coat of a covering process with acetate butyrate dope be treated with the fungicide zinc dimethyldithiocarbonate.

67. Fungicidal dope is applied in a very _____ consistency to ensure saturation of the fabric.

68. The aluminum dope contains particles of aluminum oxide which form an aluminum layer on the surface of the fabric to reflect the _____ rays of the sun.

69. Do not confuse aluminum dope with _____ dopes that may simply be giving a silver color to the dope and do not provide the ultraviolet protection for the fabric.

70. A _____ is a thin, dopelike finish to which powerful solvents have been added.

71. Its purpose is to _____ old dope finishes, thus replacing some of the solvents and plasticizers that have been lost by evaporation and oxidation over a period of years.

72. Nitrate dope and lacquers are thinned by means of a thinner called nitrate dope and lacquer thinner. Specifications _____ or _____ meet the requirements for this product.

73. Butyrate dope must be thinned with _____ , MIL-T-6096A or equivalent.

74. _____ is a colorless liquid that is suitable for removing grease from fabric before doping and is very useful in cleaning dope and lacquer from suction-feed cups and spray guns.

75. Acetone is widely used as an ingredient in paint and varnish removers but should not be used as a _____ in dope because it dries so rapidly that the doped area cools quickly and collects moisture.

76. The absorbed moisture in the fabric then prevents uniform drying and results in _____ , which is moisture contamination of the dope.

77. _____ , or _____ , is a special slow-drying thinner used to slow the drying time of dope and other finishing products.

78. When humidity is comparatively high, rapid drying of dope causes _____ .

79. The fabric shop should be capable of being _____ off from the general aircraft maintenance area, especially when the dopes and finishing products are being applied.

80. An _____ may be used to support the airfoil in a nearly vertical position while the fabric covering is being rib-laced to the structure.

81. _____ , or "sawhorses," are needed to support wing panels in the horizontal, or flat, position.

82. The minimum strength of a fabric used to re-cover an aircraft must meet the _____ strength requirements of the covering material originally used on the aircraft.

83. When dealing with aircraft originally covered with organic materials, the detemination of fabric strength can be made by obtaining the aircraft's _____ (red-line airspeed) and wing loading.

84. The aircraft's red-line airspeed is found by looking at the aircraft operating limitations found in the _____ , _____ , or _____ .

85. If the V_{ne} is greater than _____ , then grade A cotton is the minimum fabric type that can be used on the aircraft.

86. The _____ is found by dividing the maximum gross weight of the aircraft by the wing area.

87. The maximum gross weight allowed can be found in the _____ , _____ , or _____ .

88. The wing area is the surface area of the wing as viewed from _____ and ignores _____ .

89. If the wing loading is found to be greater than _____ lb/ft^2 (pounds per square foot) [4.39 g/cm^2], then grade A cotton must be used to cover the aircraft.

90. If the wing loading is no greater than 9 lb/ft^2 [4.39 g/cm^2] and the V_{ne} is _____ than 160 mph [257.5 k/h], and the aircraft was not originally covered with some stronger fabric, then the fabric used on the aircraft must meet the standards of _____ .

91. Razorback fabric is a _____ material that is approved as replacement fabric for _____ aircraft, regardless of the type of fabric originally used.

92. Razorback fabric does not make use of an STC, but it is approved based on the requirements of FAA Advisory Circular No. _____ .

93. Razorback fabric can be identified by stamping along the _____ at regular intervals.

94. Stits Poly-Fiber products and Ceconite products are approved through _____ for use on most, if not all, production aircraft having fabric coverings.

95. Ceconite can be identified by the word "CECONITE" and the type number of the fabric (101, 102, 103, etc.) stamped on the _____ of the fabric at _____ [0.91-m] intervals.

96. Poly-Fiber materials can be identified by the stamping "POLY-FIBER D-101A (or D-103 or D-104), FAA PMA, STITS AIRCRAFT" on the selvage at 1-yd [_____ -m] intervals or two rows of three-line or six-line stamps spaced _____ [0.61 m] apart in _____ , alternating each _____ [0.46 m].

97. _____ should be in position so that after the cover is installed, the cables and wires can be pulled through the structure.

98. Any coating or finish, such as zinc chromate or spar varnish, should be covered with
_____ , _____ , _____ , or
_____ to prevent the cements, dopes, and other finishing products used on the fabric from attacking the protective coatings.

99. There are four types of machine-sewn seams: the _____ , _____ ,
_____ , and _____ .

100. The French fell and folded fell are the _____ of the four types of machine-sewn seams.

101. Hand sewing is performed by starting at _____ , folding the fabric edges under until the edges of the fabric _____ . There should be at least _____ in [12.7 mm] of material folded under with any excessive amount of material being _____ .

102. For hand sewing, the needle is pushed through the fabric no more than _____ in [6.4 mm] from the edge of the fold, through the other fold, and tied in a _____ knot locked with a _____ on each side.

103. After the initial stitch in hand sewing, a _____ is then used until the opening is closed.

104. The baseball stitches should be no more than _____ back from the edge of the fold and should be spaced no more than _____ apart along the opening.

105. When using a baseball stitch, a _____ should be included in the hand sewing at _____ -in [15.24-cm] intervals.

106. If the original thread is not long enough to completely close the seam, the stitching should be tied off with a _____ and _____ and a new thread started at
_____ .

107. Doped seams are formed by using approved _____ to attach the fabric to the structure and to attach the fabric to another piece of fabric.

108. For doped seams, the amount of minimum overlap of the fabric onto the structure or another piece of fabric varies depending upon the materials and adhesives being used, but it is in the range of _____ [5.08 to 10.16 cm].

109. The _____ method of installing a fabric cover involves making or buying a sleeve that can slide over the prepared structure.

110. The _____ method of covering involves the use of fabric as it comes off the roll. It is cut to size and folded over the structure to be covered.

111. The only restriction placed on the use of doped seams concerns _____ .

112. Unless the adhesive being used is approved for higher speed, doped seams may not be used with organic fabrics when the V_{ne} is greater than _____ mph [241.4 km/h] when using the _____ covering method.

113. Organic fabrics are _____ prior to the application of dopes by saturating the fabric with _____ .

114. Polyester fabrics are shrunk by the use of _____ .

115. Once the fabric is smooth and properly taut, the first coat of clear dope is applied. This should be a _____ coat of nitrate dope containing a _____ and applied with a _____ to assure proper penetration of the fabric.

116. With the _____ coat of clear dope, install the antitear tape, reinforcing tape, drain grommets, inspection rings, and reinforcing patches.

117. Following the application of the initial coats of dope or finishing products, the fabric covering must be attached to internal structural components by the _____ process or _____ processes.

118. The maximum rib-stitch spacing allowed for aircraft with speeds just below 250 mph [402.3 km/h] and all higher airspeed values is _____ in [2.54 cm].

119. To mark stitch spacing, start at the forward area of the rib, just aft of the leading-edge material, and mark the first stitch. The second stitch is marked at _____ of the required spacing.

120. The distance between the last two rib stitches is _____ .

121. The starting stitch is a _____ .

122. The remaining stitches are _____ knots.

123. The last stitch is a _____ knot, secured with a _____ .

124. Upon completion of rib lacing, the fabric cover should be ready for the _____ .

125. Surface tape should be applied over _____ , _____ , _____ , and _____ .

126. A coat of _____ is brushed on the areas where the tape is to be applied and then the tape is immediately placed on the _____ dope.

127. Another coat of dope is brushed over the tape and care is taken to see that _____ are worked out from under the tape.

128. If the aircraft has a V_{ne} greater than _____ mph [321.8 km/h], all surface tape placed on trailing edges should be notched at _____ -in [45.72-cm] intervals.

129. Light blocking can be determined by placing a _____ light source on one side of the fabric and looking through the other side of the fabric.

130. If light is visible, then the coating of _____ is not yet sufficient.

131. Once the aluminum coating is sufficient, at least _____ coats of pigmented dope should be applied.

132. Fiberglass coverings are visually inspected for _____ and _____ .

133. In selecting a portion of the fabric to be tested, the area where _____ is chosen.

134. The strength of the fabric is based on its _____ strength.

135. The Seyboth tester _____ the fabric and indicates the _____ of the fabric by a scale on the top of the tester.

136. The _____ tester applies pressure to the fabric and is not normally used with enough force to penetrate airworthy fabric.

137. It should be understood that the _____ on the fabric's surface may affect the punch tester's indication of fabric strength.

138. The _____ testers are considered only an approximate indication of fabric strength.

139. To test fabric strength, a sample of fabric is taken from the weakest area of the aircraft covering. Determine the weakest fabric on the aircraft by first _____ testing.

140. When using a _____ tester, all the dope is removed from the fabric.

141. The minimum tensile strength for an aircraft requiring grade A cotton is _____ lb/in [10 kg/cm].

142. For an aircraft requiring intermediate-grade cotton, the minimum strength is _____ lb/in [8.21 kg/cm].

143. Polyester fabrics should be tested to the _____ required of the original fabric covering—this may be a _____ value than for the organic materials.

144. Razorback glass fabric does not have to be tested for _____ strength.

145. Tears in a fabric covering can usually be repaired by _____ and _____ on a fabric patch.

146. The objective of a fabric patch is to restore the original _____ and _____ to the repaired area.

147. A single tear should be repaired by first removing all the _____ and _____ dope around the area to be covered with the patch and then sewing the tear using a _____ stitch.

148. The most satisfactory method of dope removal is to apply a _____ coat of dope to the area and allow it to _____ the old surface dope, which can then be removed by _____ .

149. When the cleaned surface around the tear has been sewn and the stitches locked every _____ stitches, a piece of _____ surface tape or fabric is _____ over the seam.

150. The tape or fabric patch should extend at least _____ in [3.81 cm].

151. If a tear is of the V type, the sewing should start at the _____ of the V.

152. Doped-on repair patches can be employed on all fabric-covered aircraft that have a never-exceed speed not greater than _____ mph [241.35 km/h].

153. A doped-on patch can be used for a damaged area that does not exceed _____ in [40.64 cm] in any direction.

154. The patch is cut to a size that will overlap the old fabric at least _____ in [5.08 cm] for any patch not over 8 in [20.32 cm] across.

155. For holes between _____ in [40.64 cm], the patch should overlap the original fabric by one-quarter the distance of the major dimension of the repair.

156. Where doped-on patches extend over a rib, the patch must be cut to extend at least _____ in [7.62 cm] beyond the rib.

157. If the V_{ne} of the aircraft is greater than _____ mph [241.4 km/h] and the damage does not exceed _____ in [40.64 cm] in any direction, a sewn-in patch can be used.

158. The patch is sewed in using a _____ stitch with _____ stitches every _____ to _____ stitches.

159. A surface patch, cut to cover the sewn-in patch, should extend beyond the cut edge of the fabric by at least _____ in [3.81 cm].

160. If the cut edge is within 1 in [2.54 cm] of a structural member, the surface patch must extend at least _____ in [7.62 cm] beyond the members.

161. When the damage to an aircraft fabric surface is greater than 16 in [40.64 cm], a panel should be _____ .

162. Reinforcing tape is placed over the ribs under moderate tension and is laced to the ribs in the usual manner. The rib stitches are placed _____ rib stitches.

163. If a panel repair cannot give the proper tautness by using the doped-on panel repair, a _____ panel repair can be performed.

164. A sewn-in patch should be cut that will extend _____ in [7.62 cm] beyond the ribs, to the trailing edge, and around the leading edge to the front spar on the opposite side of the wing.

165. Fabric rejuvenator is a specially prepared solution containing strong solvents and plasticizers designed to penetrate age-hardened dope and restore its _____ .

Chapter 4

MULTIPLE CHOICE QUESTIONS

Name _____

Date _____

1. It is inadvisable to dope fabric on humid days because this increases the tendency of the dope to
   a. pebble.
   b. pull and rope.
   c. run.
   d. blush.

2. When finishing a fabric surface, apply
   a. a minimum of eight coats.
   b. at least the number of coats necessary to result in a taut and well-filled finish job.
   c. the first three coats of dope by brush and the remaining five coats by spray gun.
   d. three coats of clear, two coats of aluminum, and four coats of pigmented dope.

3. A practical method of determining whether a fabric surface has been finished with nitrate (cellulose nitrate) or butyrate (cellulose acetate butyrate) dope is to
   a. press the thumb firmly against an unsupported section of the fabric and note the time required for the fabric to recover its original shape.
   b. rub a small section with lacquer thinner. Butyrate finish will not be affected, but nitrate finish will be softened.
   c. remove a 1-in-wide strip of fabric and conduct a tensile test.
   d. observe the reverse side of the fabric for evidence of blue dye (butyrate) or red dye (nitrate) that has penetrated as a result of brushing on the first two coats of dope.

4. The chief purpose of pigment (or aluminum) in dope is to
   a. make it easier to apply.
   b. make a more pleasing appearance.
   c. give a covering that has a minimum of air resistance.
   d. exclude sunlight from the fabric.

5. A correct use for acetone is to
   a. thin shellac.
   b. thin zinc chromate primer.
   c. remove grease from fabric.
   d. thin dope.

6. Fungicidal dopes are used in aircraft finishing as the
   a. first coat to prevent fabric rotting and are applied in an extremely thin consistency to saturate the fabric.
   b. first full-bodied, brushed-on coat to prevent fungus damage.

   c. finish clear coat to provide a glossy appearance and to prevent deterioration of the fabric.
   d. final full-bodied, brushed-on coat to reduce blushing.

7. The minimum allowable tensile strength of new Grade A (TSO-C15) aircraft cotton fabric in pounds per inch warp and fill is
   a. 100.
   b. 65.
   c. 46.
   d. 80.

8. When and how is finishing tape applied on a fabric-covered aircraft?
   a. Sewed or laced on before dope is applied
   b. Doped on immediately prior to the finish coat
   c. Doped on after the first or second coat of dope
   d. Doped on at the same time the last coat of dope or lacquer is applied

9. The determining factor(s) for the selection of the correct weight of textile fabric to be used in covering any type of aircraft is the
   a. maximum wing loading.
   b. speed of the aircraft.
   c. weight class of the aircraft.
   d. speed of the aircraft and maximum wing loading.

10. How many fabric thicknesses will be found in a French-fell seam?
    a. One
    b. Two
    c. Three
    d. Four

11. Prior to application of surface tape to the trailing edge of a wing or control surface, the tape should be notched at intervals to
    a. make it easier to apply to severe curvatures.
    b. increase the length of the tape's edge for better doping.
    c. prevent the entire tape from loosening in the event the tape begins to separate from the surface.
    d. prevent raveling of the tape.

12. Moisture, mildew, chemicals, and acids have no effect on
    a. glass fabric.
    b. cotton fabric.
    c. linen fabric.
    d. dacron fabric.

13. The recommended procedure for making an unsewed (doped-on) fabric patch is to
    a. cover the edges of all patches by applying pinked-edge surface tape with the second coat of clear dope.
    b. dope on the patch by means of an initial coat of clear dope thinned 50 percent to obtain sufficient softening of the dope on the underlying fabric.
    c. clean and remove all aluminum and color coats from the surface to which the patch is to be doped.
    d. clean the area thoroughly and remove all color coats, aluminum, and clear dope from the surface to be covered by the patch, using acetone only.

14. A fabric-covered surface has a damaged area that measures 16 in in one direction. How should the damaged area be repaired?
    a. Use a doped-on patch.
    b. Dope in a new panel.
    c. Use a sewn-in patch.
    d. Use a sewed-in patch with doped-on surface patch.

15. When damage to a fabric-covered surface is such that it will permit a sewn-in repair patch, what type of stitch should be used?
    a. Half hitch
    b. Modified seine
    c. Baseball
    d. Double loop

Chapter 5

1. Instructions for proper methods of applying approved finishes are provided by the _____ .

2. _____ and _____ are undercoats applied to a metal to inhibit corrosion and to provide a good base for the application of _____ , _____ , or _____ .

3. Primers should provide maximum _____ to the surface and produce a _____ foundation.

4. A _____ is a priming agent that has been thinned to a very light consistency so it will leave an extremely thin layer on the bare metal surface.

5. Wash primers conform to MIL- _____ and MIL-_____ .

6. An approved _____ is manufactured under specification MIL-P-6889A, Types I and II.

7. Zinc chromate primer, Type I, is used under _____ ; Type II is used under _____ .

8. Zinc chromate primer is commonly used on _____ , _____ , and _____ and is also suitable for _____ .

9. Zinc chromate primer is thinned with _____ to the proper consistency for spraying or brushing.

10. _____ primer is normally thinned with a petroleum thinner such as naphtha or mineral spirits.

11. Gray enamel undercoat is a _____ primer and surfacer used under _____ , _____ , or _____ .

12. Gray enamel undercoat is particularly suitable for fine sanding to provide a perfectly smooth base for the _____ .

13. An epoxy-type chromate primer, Stits Epoxy Chromate Primer EP-420, is described as a _____ , _____ , _____ , _____ , _____ primer.

14. Stits Epoxy Chromate Primer EP-420 requires the addition of a _____ in a ratio of one part catalyst to two parts primer before it is put into use.

15. CORLAR is recommended for use under IMRON _____ enamel.

16. CORLAR is a two-part primer utilized on _____ , _____ , _____ , and _____ , wherever corrosion or chemical resistance is important.

17. _____ refers to the amount of time a liquid product may be used before it sets up.

18. CORLAR has a _____ of 7 to 8 hours.

19. After CORLAR is used, spray guns, paint pots, paint hoses, and brushes must be cleaned with _____ or an approved _____ before the material has hardened.

20. Most paint finishes are made up of four basic components: _____,

_____ , _____ , and _____ .

21. The _____ provides the color and durability.

22. The _____ holds the pigment in liquid form, makes it durable, and gives it the ability to stick to the surface.

23. _____ dissolves the binder and carries the pigment and binder through the spray gun to the surface being painted.

24. _____ can have a significant effect on the paint's physical and chemical properties.

25. Additives are usually designed to _____ , _____ ,

_____ , and provide a _____ .

26. The exterior of an airplane is painted with one of two basic finishes: _____ or

_____ .

27. Lacquer dries quickly, but it usually must be rubbed with a _____ or

_____ to produce a glossy finish.

28. Enamel dries with a gloss and does not require rubbing or polishing, but it dries _____ than lacquer, and there is more of a chance for dirt and dust to settle into the wet finish and mar its appearance.

29. In general, a lacquer is a good finishing material for _____ or _____ .

30. Lacquers are also manufactured for special purposes such as fuel resistance and hydraulic-fluid resistance. The following specification numbers denote special-purpose lacquers:

Specification	Special purpose
MIL-L-6047	_____
_____	Hydraulic-fluid resistant
MIL-L-6806	_____
_____	Dull black instrument lacquer
MIL-L-19537	_____

31. _____ finishes provide a glossy, hard surface with good resistance to scratching and abrasion.

32. The disadvantages of acrylic enamel finishes include the requirement of _____ ,

_____ , and _____ when repairing any damage to the surface.

33. _____ materials provide a very high gloss surface with excellent durability, weathering resistance, and abrasion resistance.

34. Due to their resistance to chemical attack, polyurethane finishing materials are often used by aircraft manufacturers in places subject to exposure to _____ , such as areas containing Skydrol-type hydraulic fluids.

35. Polyurethane finishes normally are a two-part mixture with a catalyst added to activate the

_____ .

36. Polyurethane finishes should not be _____ .

37. _____ , also called _____ , are used to reduce the viscosity of finishing products so that they will flow properly through the spray gun and onto the surface being painted.

38. There are two variables that affect the spraying of materials: _____ and

_____ .

39. Of the two variables that affect the spraying of materials, _____ is the most crucial.

40. Hot, dry weather produces the _____ drying time.

41. _____ , _____ , or _____ weather produces
the slowest drying time.

42. A general rule to follow in selecting the proper thinner or reducer is: If the shop has _____
-drying conditions, use a slower-drying thinner or reducer.

43. In hot, dry weather, use a _____ thinner or reducer.

44. In _____ , wet weather, use a fast-drying thinner or reducer.

45. If a thinner or reducer evaporates too rapidly, the problems that can be caused are

_____ , _____ , and _____ .

46. If a thinner or reducer evaporates too slowly it will result in _____ and

_____ .

47. If the wrong thinner is used, the paint _____ , the thinner might

_____ , or the thinner may _____ .

48. Dry sanding of cellulose nitrate finishes can create _____ that can ignite nitrate fumes.

49. The use of _____ when spraying finishes is highly recommended, and with some finishing
products it is mandatory.

50. An _____ is a device that removes oil, dirt, and moisture from compressed air, regulates the
air pressure, indicates the regulated air pressure by means of gauges, and provides outlets for spray guns and other
air tools.

51. The inside diameter of a spray gun hose has the greatest effect on the _____ .

52. As the length of the hose increases, the pressure drop will also _____ .

53. The surface _____ inside an air hose will greatly influence the pressure drop.

54. A rough surface inside an air hose can cause as much as a 50 percent _____ in the pressure
drop.

55. _____ spraying is a method of spray application that does not directly use compressed air to
atomize the paint.

56. In airless spraying, _____ is used to atomize the fluid by pumping it at relatively high
pressure through a small orifice in the spray gun nozzle.

57. A pressure tank, also called a _____ or _____ , is a closed metal
container that provides a constant flow of paint or other material to the spray gun at a uniform pressure.

58. To change the rate of fluid flow from the pressure tank, the air pressure is adjusted by means of a

_____ .

59. A typical pressure feed tank consists of a _____ , _____ ,

_____ , _____ , _____ ,

_____ , _____ , _____ ,

_____ , _____ , _____ ,

and _____ .

60. _____ painting may be used with either air or airless painting systems to atomize the paint.

61. During the paint-atomization phase in electrostatic painting, a _____ electrostatic charge is placed on the paint particles as they leave the nozzle.

62. The nozzle and air cap of the conventional spray gun are designed to mix _____ with the paint stream to aid in atomization of the liquid.

63. A spray gun includes a _____ , which controls the fluid valve, a _____ , an _____ , _____ , _____ , and an _____ .

64. The balance among air pressure, airflow, fluid pressure, and fluid flow is controlled by adjusting the valves concerned to provide the desired spray _____ and _____ .

65. The first of the three basic adjustments for a good spray pattern is the _____ , which should be adjusted using the spreader adjustment valve.

66. The spread adjustment valve regulates the flow of air through the _____ .

67. The more the spread adjustment valve is open, the _____ the spray pattern.

68. The second of the three basic adjustments for a good spray pattern is the fluid-adjusting screw, which should be adjusted to match the _____ to the spray-pattern size.

69. The third of the three basic adjustments for a good spray pattern is _____ .

70. A spray gun must be held approximately _____ to _____ in [15 to 25 cm] from the surface being sprayed.

71. If the gun is held too close, it is likely to cause _____ or _____ .

72. Not releasing the trigger at the end of each pass will cause _____ to occur when the direction of spray gun movement is reversed.

73. Moving the spray gun in an arc causes _____ and _____ .

74. Manufacturers of aircraft finishes often recommend testing the viscosity with a _____ .

75. To use a Zahn viscosity cup, place the required amount of finish in the specified cup and note the time required in _____ for the finish to drain from the cup.

76. To ensure that the surface to be sprayed is clean, a _____ may be used to wipe away dust or other particles.

77. A tack cloth is a specially treated soft cloth that can be used to wipe a surface and remove all dust; it leaves _____ , _____ , or other material on the surface that would interfere with the adhesion of coatings.

78. If the spray gun is tilted, the part of the spray pattern closest to the surface will receive a _____ , and the part farthest away will get a _____ .

79. An unbalanced or distorted spray pattern indicates a _____ .

80. Wax-free paint remover is a _____ liquid and evaporates rapidly after it is applied.

81. Wax-type stripper has the consistency of _____ because of the wax which holds the solvent in contact with the paint surface long enough to lift or dissolve the old coatings.

82. _____ will not lift and wrinkle when stripper is applied, but it will soften.

83. When acrylic lacquer has softened, it should be scraped off with a _____ scraper, and then the area should be washed with _____ , _____ , or similar solvent.

84. When washing acrylic lacquer that has been softened for removal, a powerful spray gun should be used to spray the solvent into _____ , _____ , and _____ .

85. The purpose of the solvent, when washing acrylic lacquer that has been softened for removal, is to remove all traces of _____ that would otherwise be left by the stripper.

86. Paint stripper should not be allowed to come into contact with _____ , _____ , _____ , or _____ .

87. Paint-stripping agents must not be used on metal aircraft that employ _____ seams rather than riveted seams.

88. The dry stripping process utilizes a stream of _____ propelled by low-pressure (20–60 psi) air to remove materials from the surface that is to be cleaned.

89. Depth of surface removal during the dry stripping process is controlled by adjusting the _____ between the nozzle and the surface, _____ , and _____ .

90. Two common methods of hand sanding are _____ and _____ .

91. Dry sanding often results in the paper becoming _____ with the material being removed.

92. In wet sanding, periodically dipping the paper in water will _____ .

93. Of the two hand-sanding processes, _____ sanding will generally produce a smoother finish.

94. The improper application of aircraft finishes can lead to _____ corrosion (so named because it forms in fine filaments).

95. If phosphoric acid from an etching solution or wash primer is trapped under subsequent coatings before complete conversion to the phosphate film, filiform corrosion will develop under the finish coating, damaging both the _____ and the _____ .

96. To avoid this filiform corrosion, it is necessary that there be adequate _____ or in the _____ to complete the conversion of the phosphoric acid to phosphate.

97. Humidity should be such that a minimum of 0.09 lb of water is present in each pound of air [90 g per kilogram of air]. This would be accomplished with a relative humidity of _____ percent at 70°F [21.1°C] or _____ percent at 75°F [23.9°C].

98. If the humidity is not great enough to provide the required moisture, a small amount of _____ water may be added to the wash primer.

99. Another important consideration in the conversion of the phosphoric acid in the wash primer is to allow sufficient time (normally _____ to _____ min) for the conversion to take place before applying the next coating.

100. The preparation of a new aluminum surface involves thorough cleaning and treating with a _____ and/or a _____ .

101. Phosphoric acid etch is also referred to as a _____ .

102. When refinishing over an old finish on an airplane, the new finish must be _____ with the old finish.

103. Conversion coatings are applied to fresh, clean metal to aid in _____ and to _____ the surface for better adhesion of additional coatings.

104. A conversion coating for aluminum or steel can be a phosphoric acid etch, which leaves a tough, inorganic _____ on the metal.

105. The treatment of a magnesium surface requires a _____ .

106. A chromic acid etch should be _____ and the surface dried.

107. After surfaces etched with chromic acid are dry, they should be prepared for painting by applying a suitable

_____ .

108. A typical wash primer is described as a two-part butyral-phosphoric acid resin containing

_____ .

109. Wash primer may be applied directly to clean, _____, or it may be applied over the

_____ .

110. Wash primers should be applied in one very _____ wash coat.

111. A primer serves two principal purposes: _____ and _____ .

112. Zinc chromate primer complies with _____ specification and is either yellow or green in color.

113. It should be thinned to the proper consistency with _____ and applied with a spray gun on

metal surfaces which have been etched with a _____ or other _____ .

114. Application over a wash primer is not recommended unless all the chemical action of the wash primer is known to

have been completed so that _____ .

115. Two-part epoxy primers are popular for use under the _____ and

_____ coatings.

116. Epoxy primers may be used on _____ , _____ ,

_____ , or _____ .

117. For the most complete protection against corrosion, the epoxy primer is applied over a

_____ .

118. Finish coatings should be sprayed over the epoxy primer within _____ of primer application.

119. Acrylic lacquers and enamels should not be applied over an epoxy primer for at least _____

and _____ .

120. Urethane primer is a _____ primer which must be mixed a short time before use and must be

used within _____ to _____ hours after mixing.

121. If a primer or enamel craters or crawls as soon as it is sprayed on the surface, this means that it does not remain

_____ and _____ but forms small craters and ridges as if

_____ .

122. Craters or crawls are usually caused by _____ or some other contaminant on the surface.

123. Lacquers, both nitrate and acrylic, are _____ and easily applied with a spray gun, provided
that they are properly thinned with the correct reducer to meet the conditions of temperature and humidity at the
time they are applied.

124. Because of their fast-drying characteristics, lacquers quickly _____ .

125. Enamels do not dry as fast as lacquers and should, therefore, be applied in a _____ .

126. When using a spray gun, a very light dry coat is often referred to as a _____ .

127. An application of slower-drying thinners or reducers over a clear coat, when using a spray gun, is called a

_____ .

128. Double coating is often used in the application of lacquers, where a second spray coating is applied _____ after the first coat is finished.

129. To identify cellulose nitrate dope and lacquer, wipe with a cloth saturated with _____ or _____ .

130. If wiping the surface with a cloth saturated with nitrate thinner or reducer causes the paint to dissolve, it is either _____ or _____ .

131. If a synthetic engine oil, MIL-L-7808 or equivalent, does not soften the finish coat within a few minutes after application, the finish is most likely either _____ , _____ , or _____ .

132. _____ wiped onto acrylic finishes picks up pigment but does not affect epoxy or urethane finishes unless rubbed into the surface.

133. The old finish can be removed by the careful use of abrasive paper to take off the damaged coating and _____ in the edges of the damaged area with the original coat.

134. The same type materials as originally used on the aircraft should be used for the repair so that any _____ of products is _____ .

135. If acrylic lacquer is applied over an old acrylic finish, it is considered good practice to _____ the old finish.

136. An old acrylic finish may be softened with the application of acrylic thinner, either by wiping or spraying, _____ applying the finish coat.

137. _____ and _____ are normally used in laying out the trim lines.

138. The lines should _____ be laid out with a _____ or _____ because that can damage the surface or leave permanent marks.

139. The tape used should be of a type whose adhesive will _____ be attacked by the _____ in the trim paint.

140. _____ masking tape is a type of tape that is commonly used for painting.

141. Generally, compounds with coarse particles are called _____ .

142. Compounds with fine particles of pumice are called _____ .

143. Rubbing compounds are used to _____ the surface being compounded and to _____ .

144. Polishing compounds are used to smooth the finish and to bring out the _____ of topcoats, particularly with lacquers.

145. Runs and sags in painting are usually caused by _____ , _____ , or _____ .

146. Starved or thin film is the result of the gun being held _____ , being _____ , or from _____ .

147. Dry spray or texture is caused by the gun being held too _____ or by too much _____ .

148. _____ are small raised circular areas with a layer of paint over them often caused by oil or water in the air line of the spray gun.

149. Blisters or bubbles may be caused by applying a second coat of paint _____ over a fresh first coat that is still giving off large quantities of thinner.

150. _____ causes the paint to appear cloudy or milky and is caused by the paint _____ too quickly.

151. Crazing is when _____ or _____ appear in the finished surface; it is usually caused by the _____ being too cold.

152. Fish eyes are small _____ in the finish.

153. Fish eyes are caused by _____ .

154. Orange peel is the term for paint that creates an _____ like the surface of an orange peel.

155. Orange peel may be caused by _____ at the gun, the gun being held _____ , or _____ .

156. _____ is the loss of adhesion between the paint and the surface or the primer coat and may result from _____ .

157. _____ are small holes or depressions in the paint.

158. Pinholes are caused by _____ or _____ .

159. The finishing of certificated aircraft involves the application of required identification marks as set forth in _____ .

160. All aircraft registered in the United States must be marked with _____ for easy identification.

161. The identification marks must be painted on the aircraft or otherwise affixed so they are as _____ as the finish.

162. The identification marks must _____ with the background and be easily legible.

163. The letters and numbers must be made without _____ and must not have _____ that could cause confusion in identification.

164. The registration and nationality markings for United States–registered aircraft consist of the Roman capital letter _____ followed by the registration number of the aircraft.

165. When marks that include only the Roman capital letter N and the registration number are displayed on limited, restricted, or experimental aircraft, or on aircraft that have provisional certification, the words _____ , _____ , _____ , or _____ must be displayed near each entrance to the cockpit or cabin.

166. The letters used for certification identification must be not less than _____ in [5.08 cm] or more than _____ in [15.24 cm] in height.

167. Registration marks for fixed-wing aircraft must be displayed on both sides of the _____ or on both sides of the _____ between the trailing edge of the wing and the leading edge of the horizontal stabilizer.

168. If the marks are on the tail of a multivertical-tail aircraft, the marks must be on the _____ of the vertical sections.

169. Helicopters or other rotorcraft must have nationality and registration markings displayed on the _____ or _____ with the top of the marks toward the

_____ side of the fuselage and on the side surfaces of the fuselage below the window lines as near the cockpit as possible.

170. Except for special cases discussed in FAR Part 45, the height of letters must be equal and at least

_____ in [30.48] in height.

171. The width of the characters in the markings must be _____ the height of the characters, except for the number 1 and the letters *M* and *W*.

172. The letters *M* and *W* may have a width _____ the height of the letter.

173. The thickness of the strokes or lines in the letters and numbers must be _____ the height of the characters.

174. The spaces between the characters must not be less than _____ the width of the characters.

175. The space between characters is _____ in [5.08 cm].

Chapter 5

Name _____

Date _____

APPLICATION QUESTION

1. Lay out in drawing form the registration number N123Z, using a 12-in height.

Chapter 5

Name _____

Date _____

1. A wash primer is a priming agent
   a. that rinses off easily with water.
   b. that has been thinned to a very light consistency.
   c. is only used as a second priming coat.
   d. is another name for zinc chromate.

2. The purpose of a binder in paint is to
   a. hold the pigment in liquid form.
   b. prevent blushing.
   c. act as a thinning agent.
   d. improve the durability of the paint.

3. Polyurethane differs from lacquers and basic enamels in that
   a. enamels and lacquers may not be thinned.
   b. the first coat of polyurethane must be applied by a brush.
   c. polyurethane requires a catalyst.
   d. surfaces to be painted with polyurethane do not need to be clean.

4. Orange peel can be caused by
   a. overspray.
   b. too much thinner added to the paint.
   c. the thinner evaporating too quickly.
   d. water in the paint.

5. Additives that speed up a paint's cure time are referred to as
   a. loots.
   b. retarders.
   c. hardeners.
   d. flatters.

6. If a technician is having difficulty maintaining a constant pressure at the spay gun the
   a. regulator must be reset to a higher pressure.
   b. regulator must be reset to a lower pressure.
   c. the length of the air hose may need to be increased.
   d. the length of the air hose may need to be reduced.

7. Electrostatic painting
   a. may not be used on aircraft because of the potential for static electricity.
   b. electrically charges particles of paint to improve their adhesion to the metal surface.
   c. reduces the tendency for overspray.
   d. is most frequently used on aircraft fabricated from wood.

8. The normal spray pattern is
   a. a circle with a radius of 4 in
   b. an elongated oval with a height 2½ to 3 times the width.
   c. a circle with a diameter of 6 in and a slight overspray in the direction of travel.
   d. pear-shaped with the larger end on the bottom of the pattern.

9. The most important aspect of stripping paint is
   a. the complete removal of the stripper after the paint has been removed.
   b. the amount of time the stripper is allowed to remain in contact with the paint to be removed.
   c. the weight ratio of the stripper to the original paint.
   d. the type of primer to be used after stripping is complete.

10. A conversion coating aids in the prevention of surface corrosion and
    a. seals the grain of the metal or wood.
    b. enters the grain of the metal to prevent corrosion.
    c. smooths the surface of the metal.
    d. microscopically roughens the surface of the metal.

11. If a primer crawls as soon as it is sprayed on a surface
    a. the primer is too thick.
    b. the primer is too thin.
    c. there is a contaminate on the surface being primed.
    d. the primer is acting as designed; there is no problem.

12. If a rag soaked with a reducer is rubbed on a surface that has been painted with a lacquer,
    a. the rag will begin to show pigment (color) from the paint.
    b. the rag will begin to turn white and the paint a light brown.
    c. the rag will have blue streaks.
    d. the rag will show no evidence regarding the original type of paint.

13. What is the usual cause of runs and sags in aircraft finishes?
    a. Too much material applied in one coat
    b. Material drying too fast
    c. Material is being applied too fast
    d. High atmospheric humidity

14. Which defect in aircraft finishes may be caused by moisture in the air-supply line, adverse humidity, drafts, or sudden changes in temperature?
    a. Spray dust
    b. Spray mottle
    c. Blushing
    d. Sags and runs

15. To obtain a high gloss from a coat of paint, the surface would be rubbed with
    a. 400-grit dry sandpaper.
    c. 600-grit wet sandpaper.
    c. a rubbing compound.
    d. a polishing compound.

16. Which statement is true regarding paint system compatibility?
    a. Zinc chromate primer may not be used directly for touch-up of bare metal surfaces.
    b. Acrylic nitrocellulose lacquers may be used over old nitrocellulose finishes.
    c. Old wash primer coats may be overcoated directly with epoxy finishes.
    d. None of the above statements are true.

17. Which statement is correct concerning aircraft registration numbers?
    a. All registered aircraft operating in the United States must display a registration number.
    b. Restricted category aircraft operating in the United States are not required to display a registration number.
    c. All aircraft located in the United States must display a registration number.
    d. Only normal and utility category aircraft must display a registration number.

18. The letters and numbers of identification markings must be of a contrasting color and must be uniform in shape and size. The width of the characters must be
    a. one-half their height.
    b. two-thirds their height.
    c. equal to their height.
    d. five times the width of the stroke.

19. When laying out letters and numbers to display an aircraft registration number, the width of the stroke must be
    a. $1/16$ the height of the letter
    b. $1/12$ the height of the letter
    c. $1/8$ the height of the letter
    d. $1/6$ the height of the letter

20. If an aircraft is an experimental aircraft
    a. the word *experimental* must be displayed near each entrance to the cabin and cockpit.
    b. the word *experimental* must be displayed under the end of the wing.
    c. the word *experimental* must be displayed on each side of the tail.
    d. the letter *E* must follow the registration number.

Chapter 6

1. Only the _____ type of welding is used in aircraft work.

2. Typically, the types of fusion welding used by the technician are _____ , commonly called gas welding, _____ , and _____ .

3. Gas welding produces heat by burning a _____ mixture of oxygen and acetylene or other fuel as it flows from the tip of a welding torch.

4. In _____ , the heat of an electric arc is used to produce fusion of the parts.

5. Electric-resistance welding is a process whereby a _____ current is brought to the work through a heavy copper conductor offering very little resistance to its flow.

6. Inert-gas arc welding is a process in which an inert gas such as helium or argon _____ the weld area to prevent _____ of the heated metal.

7. The three types of tests commonly used to identify different materials are the _____ , _____ , and _____ .

8. The spark test may be used to recognize _____ .

9. In the spark test, samples of various metals are ground and their _____ are compared to the _____ from a piece of metal being identified.

10. The characteristics to be observed during a spark test are _____ , _____ , _____ , _____ , _____ , and _____ .

11. A chemical test distinguishes between _____ and _____ .

12. A _____ is used to identify magnesium alloys.

13. A _____ is that portion of a structure where separate base-metal parts are united by welding.

14. A _____ is a joint made by placing two pieces of material edge to edge in the same plane so that there is no overlapping.

15. There are two classifications of butt joints: _____ and _____ .

16. A _____ is a form of joint made by placing the edge of one base part on the surface of the other base part so that the surface of the second part extends on either side of the joint in the form of a T.

17. The _____ joint is acceptable for most metal thicknesses in aircraft work and also may be used for heavier metals, where the weld can be located so that the load stresses will be transverse to the longitudinal dimensions of the weld.

18. In a plain tee joint, the weld is made from each side with _____ into the intersection.

19. The _____ is a joint made by lapping one base over the other.

20. The single-welded lap joint is used for _____ , _____ , and structural shapes where the _____ .

21. The offset, or joggled, lap joint is used for sheet and plate where one side of both plates or sheets is in the _____ .

22. An edge joint is a form of joint made by placing a surface of one base part on a surface of the other base part in such a manner that the weld will be on the outer surface planes of _____ .

23. A corner joint is made by placing the edge of one part at an angle on an edge or a surface of another part so that neither part extends beyond the outer surface of the other, the structure resembling _____ .

24. The open type of corner joint is used on _____ .

25. The _____ is the exposed surface of the weld.

26. The _____ is the zone at the bottom, or base, of the weld.

27. The _____ is the distance through the center of the weld from the root to the face.

28. The _____ is the edge formed where the face of the weld meets the base metal.

29. The reinforcement is the quantity of weld metal _____ .

30. The _____ is the dimension of the weld metal extending on each side of the root of the joint.

31. The _____ is the width of the weld metal, including the depth of fusion in the base metal on each side of the joint.

32. The _____ is the metal deposited as the weld is made.

33. The three most important proportions of a weld are _____ , _____ , and _____ .

34. The depth of penetration should be at least _____ the thickness of the base metal.

35. The width of the bead should be between _____ times as great as the thickness of the base metal.

36. The height of the reinforcement should be _____ the thickness of the base metal.

37. The typical causes of improperly formed weak welds are _____ _____ ; _____ ; _____ _____ ; _____ ; _____ _____ ; and _____ .

38. If the heat remains on the metal for an excessive length of time, this will result in a reduction of such physical properties of the metal as _____ , _____ , and _____ .

39. If some element is added to the metal during the welding process, or if there is some material change in one or more of the chemical constituents, the change will usually _____ the strength of the metal.

40. The physical changes most important in welding are changes in the _____ , _____ , and _____ .

41. _____ is the quantity of a temperature that is available.

42. Heat is measured in _____ .

43. If a metal structure is unevenly heated, there will be an uneven expansion, and this will produce _____ and possibly _____ .

44. A _____ of any metal is the amount that the metal will expand per inch for each degree rise in temperature.

45. Contraction is the _____ of a substance when cooled from a high temperature.

46. If the metal is "closed" during the welding process, there is danger from _____ and
_____ .

47. To avoid damage from expansion, heat is applied to the _____ object before attempting to weld the break in the center piece.

48. _____ is the physical property of a metal that permits the transmission of heat through its mass.

49. The _____ is the speed at which a metal body will transmit heat through its mass.

50. Acetylene is a _____ , _____ gas with a distinctive odor.

51. To prevent the flame from burning back to the source of supply during welding, the acetylene, when mixed with air or oxygen, must flow from the torch at a velocity _____ than the flame spread.

52. When acetylene is compressed in an empty container to a pressure greater than _____ psi [103 kPa], it becomes unstable, and at _____ psi [202.74 kPa] pressure it becomes self-explosive.

53. As a general rule, the technician should never allow the acetylene pressure in the welding system to exceed _____ psi [103 kPa].

54. Cylinder pressures exceeding 15 psi [103 kPa] are possible because the manufacturers place a porous substance inside the acetylene cylinder and then saturate this substance with _____ .

55. A cylinder containing a correct amount of acetone can be charged to a pressure of more than _____ psi [1724 kPa] with safety.

56. The cubic feet of acetylene gas in a cylinder may be found by weighing the cylinder and subtracting the _____ weight stamped on the cylinder from the _____ weight. The difference is then _____ by the weight of acetylene, 14.5 ft^3/lb, to obtain the number of cubic feet in the cylinders.

57. It is important to avoid bringing pure oxygen into contact with _____ or
_____ .

58. To find the quantity of oxygen in a cylinder, subtract the weight of an empty cylinder from the weight of a charged cylinder, and multiply the number of pounds by _____ to obtain the cubic feet of oxygen in the cylinder.

59. An oxygen cylinder _____ (bursting disk) is contained in the nipple at the rear of the valve and consists of a thin copper-alloy diaphragm.

60. Acetylene and oxygen regulators are mechanical instruments used to _____ of the gases flowing from their _____ and to supply the gases to the torch at a _____ and _____ as required by the torch tip or nozzle.

61. Regulators on cylinders are usually equipped with _____ gauges.

62. On a two-stage regulator, a high-pressure gauge shows the pressure of the gas _____ , and a low-pressure gauge indicates the pressure of the _____ .

63. A welding torch is a device used to _____ oxygen and acetylene together in the _____ and to provide a means of directing and controlling the quality and size of the flame.

64. The needle valves of a welding torch are used to regulate the _____ of acetylene and oxygen that flow into the mixing head.

65. The purpose of the mixing head is to provide for the correct mixing of the gases for the best

_____ .

66. Welding torches may be divided into two principal types: _____ , sometimes called the

equal-pressure type, and _____ .

67. The selection of the tip size depends upon the amount of _____ and the size of the

_____ required for the _____ and _____ of the

metal to be welded.

68. The primary difference between the selection of a balanced-pressure type and an injector-type of welding torch is

the _____ .

69. If the acetylene gas used for welding is obtained from an acetylene generator, the pressure in the acetylene lines

will be _____ .

70. Balanced-pressure type torches are used where the acetylene source pressure is _____ .

71. The injector-type torch uses the _____ of the oxygen to _____ the

necessary amount of acetylene into the mixing chamber.

72. Welding tip sizes differ in the _____ , which provides the correct amount of gas mixture.

73. Velocity of the welding gases is important because it regulates the amount of _____ that will

be applied to the material to be welded.

74. The _____ of welding gases is regulated by the _____ , but the

amount of that temperature or heat is regulated by the _____ .

75. Too _____ a velocity will allow the flame to burn back into the tip and cause a ''pop,''

which will blow the flame out. This is called a _____ .

76. Care must be taken to maintain a smooth, round _____ through which the gases can emerge.

77. The acetylene hose is usually _____ in color, the threads on the fittings are

_____ , the fittings normally have a _____ around the middle of the

wrenching surface, and the word ACETYLENE may be found on the hose or the letters ACE may be found on the

fittings.

78. The oxygen hose is normally _____ in color, the fittings are _____

with _____ groove on the wrenching surface, and the word OXYGEN may be found on

some hoses or the letters OXY may be on the fittings.

79. The welding rod is used to supply the _____ required to form a joint.

80. During welding, the rod is melted into the joint, where it _____ with the molten base metal,

the metal from the rod forming a large proportion of the actual weld metal.

81. The rod must be _____ with the material being welded and be able to respond properly to

any _____ required after the weld is completed.

82. Some welding rods are coated with _____ to prevent contamination of welds, and/or are

coated with _____ to prevent the rod from _____ .

83. The diameter of the rod used is often _____ the thickness of the material being welded.

84. Welding goggles are fitted with colored lenses to keep out _____ and the

_____ and _____ rays produced during welding.

85. The tool used to light a welding torch is called _____ , _____ ,

    _____ , or _____ .

86. Never use _____ or _____ to light a welding torch.

87. _____ is generally the fire-extinguishing medium that should be immediately available to the welders.

88. When setting up the welding apparatus, the cylinder valves are _____ to clear the valve of dust or dirt that may have settled in the valve during shipment or storage.

89. The welder always stands at the _____ of, or _____ , the cylinder

    outlet to avoid being struck by dust or _____ that may be _____ by

    the cylinder's pressure; or, if the regulator is _____ , pressure may build up behind the glass

    and cause it to _____ .

90. Prior to beginning the welding process the welder should _____ .

91. The best method to test for leaks is to apply _____ to the joints with a brush.

92. Testing for leaks should never be done by using a _____ at the joints. No open flame should be allowed in the vicinity of welding equipment except for the flame of the torch.

93. When ready to open the cylinder valves, the welder should open the acetylene cylinder valve about

    _____ and open the oxygen valve _____ , slowly in both cases.

94. To light the torch, the welder opens the _____ needle valve on the torch

    _____ and then uses a _____ to light the acetylene as it leaves the tip.

95. After igniting the acetylene, the welder should slowly open the oxygen needle valve until a

    _____ cone appears near the tip of the torch.

96. This cone is surrounded by a _____ or _____ that varies in length, depending upon the size of the welding tip being used.

97. A welding flame is called _____ when the gas quantities are adjusted so all the oxygen and acetylene are burned together.

98. Theoretically, _____ volumes of oxygen are required to burn _____ volume of acetylene in order to produce the neutral flame.

99. Because part of the oxygen required to produce a neutral flame is taken from the atmosphere, it is only necessary to

    provide _____ volume of oxygen through the torch for _____ volume of acetylene consumed.

100. The neutral flame has a temperature of about _____ [3482°C].

101. A carburizing, or reducing, flame occurs when there is more _____ than

    _____ feeding into the flame.

102. An excess of acetylene is commonly used with the _____ , _____ and

    _____ .

103. An oxidizing flame results from an excess of _____ flowing through the torch.

104. An oxidizing flame is commonly used in welding _____ .

105. A _____ is a flame produced when the gases flow to the welding tip at a comparatively

    _____ .

106. If the gases flow to the welding tip at a comparatively _____, they produce a _____ that is easily recognized because it is noisy.

107. A _____ is a momentary backward flow of gases at the torch tip, causing the flame to go _____ and then immediately to _____ .

108. There are five common causes of backfires: _____ ; _____ ; _____ ; _____ ; or _____ or _____ _____ .

109. _____ is the burning back of the flame into or behind the mixing chamber of the torch.

110. Where flashback occurs, the flame _____ from the tip of the torch and does not _____ .

111. If a flashback occurs, there will be a _____ or _____ , and the flame will burn back into the torch.

112. When a flashback occurs, the welder must quickly close the acetylene and oxygen _____ to confine the flash to the _____ and let the torch cool off before lighting it again.

113. The procedure for shutting down the welding apparatus is as follows:

a. _____

b. _____

c. _____

d. _____

e. _____

f. _____

g. _____

h. _____

i. _____

114. The parts to be welded should be _____ before welding by _____ or brushing with a _____ or by some similar method.

115. All _____ , _____ , _____ , and _____ must be removed from the joint edges or surfaces to prevent them from being included in the weld metal.

116. The edges, or ends, to be welded must be prepared so that fusion can be accomplished without the use of an _____ .

117. There are three basic types of end preparations: _____ , _____ , and _____ .

118. When welding light-gauge metal, the torch is held as one might hold a _____ .

119. The torch can be held like a _____ for welding heavier work.

120. In the fusion welding process, the base material is brought to a molten state in the area of the joint, producing a _____ .

121. The puddle is moved over the joint area, allowing the molten material from one part to _____ with the other.

122. To provide reinforcement to the joint, filler material is added by _____ in the puddle.

123. The key to success in oxyacetylene welding is to _____ , making sure that the pattern used is _____ .

124. When all components of the welding process are properly balanced, the rod should remain in the puddle _____ .

125. The welder may use either the _____ , _____ , or a continuous _____ motion.

126. If too much heat is being applied to the weld area, the welder should soften the flame by _____ .

127. Another way to reduce the amount of heat applied to the weld area is to slightly _____ the distance between the torch flame and the base material.

128. The experienced welder may attempt to reduce the heat applied to the weld area by _____ the rate of travel.

129. Forehand welding, sometimes called forward welding, is a welding technique in which the torch flame is pointed _____ in the direction the weld is progressing.

130. When forehand welding, filler rod is added to the pool of melting metal _____ the torch flame.

131. _____ welding, sometimes called backward welding, is a technique in which the flame is directed away from the direction the weld is progressing.

132. In backhand welding, the welding rod is added _____ the flame and the finished weld.

133. The _____ position is the position used when the work is laid flat or almost flat and welded on the topside with the welding torch pointed downward toward the work.

134. The _____ position in welding is used when the line of the weld runs up and down (vertically) on a piece of work laid in a vertical, or nearly vertical, position.

135. The _____ position in welding is used when the line of the weld runs across (horizontally) on a piece of work placed in a vertical or almost vertical position; the welding torch is held in a horizontal or almost horizontal position.

136. The _____ position in welding is used when work is flat (horizontal) or almost flat and is welded on the lower side with the welding torch pointed in an upward direction toward the work.

137. The properly completed weld should have the following characteristics:

    a. _____

    b. _____

    c. _____

    d. _____

    e. _____

    f. _____

138. A welder can do four things to control the action of those forces that adversely affect the finished weld:

_____ ; _____

_____ ; _____ ; and _____

_____ .

139. Preheating the entire metal object before welding sets free the stored up forces and permits a more uniform

_____ when the welding job is completed.

140. In _____ , the operator welds briefly at the beginning of the seam, skips to the

_____ , then jumps to the _____ , comes back to where the first weld

ended, and repeats this staggered process until the weld is complete.

141. Another term for stagger welding is _____ welding.

142. A _____ is a rigid structure or mechanism, either wood or metal, that holds parts while they

are being worked on (drilled, sawed, welded, etc.) before assembly, or that holds the component parts while they

are being assembled or disassembled.

143. One method for reducing distortion and residual stresses is the careful _____ of the pieces to

be welded, thus providing for expansion of the base material when welding _____ joints.

144. A _____ weld is one of a series of small welds laid at intervals along a joint to hold the

parts in position while they are being welded.

145. The _____ method of welding, also called the _____ method, is a

welding technique in which the welder welds and skips intervals between tack welds with each successive pass until

the joint is completely welded.

146. When preheating is applied, the parts preheated must be also be _____ .

147. _____ is the most reliable method of relieving stress.

148. Welds should not be _____ to present a smooth appearance.

149. Welds must not be _____ with solder, brazing metal, or any other filler.

150. When it is necessary to reweld a joint, all the _____ must be removed before proceeding

with the new weld.

151. A new weld should never be made over _____ if it can be avoided.

152. A weld should never be made over a joint that was previously _____ .

153. To perform a bend test, the welder clamps the metal in a vise with the weld _____ to the top

of the jaws of the vise and slightly above the top of the vise and then strikes the _____ of

the metal with a hammer so that the metal is bent along the _____ .

154. It is strongly recommended that the appropriate type of _____ be employed when aluminum,

magnesium, or titanium parts must be joined by welding.

155. Aluminum, magnesium, or titanium and their alloys oxidize very rapidly when _____ .

156. When magnesium reaches a sufficiently high temperature, it _____ .

157. Titanium, when being welded, must be _____ protected from oxygen.

158. Designations for gas-weldable aluminum and alloys are _____ ,

_____ , _____ , and _____ .

159. Alloys 6053, 6061, and 6151 can be gas welded if provision is made for _____ after

welding.

160. Aluminum should be welded with a _____ neutral flame or a slightly

_____ flame when either acetylene or hydrogen is used for the welding gas.

161. Shielded metal arc welding utilizes an electrode filler rod and requires a special generator to provide a

_____ , _____ for the arc.

162. The electric arc is made between the _____ , which is clamped in a holder held in the hand, and the metal being welded.

163. An arc gap is made in the welding circuit by holding the tip of the electrode _____ to

_____ in [1.59 cm to 3.18 cm] away from the work.

164. The _____ of the _____ melts the metal.

165. The arc is first caused ("struck") by touching the electrode to the metal, and then the electrode is withdrawn

slightly to establish the correct _____ across which the arc flows.

166. The external welding circuit begins where the electrode cable _____ and ends

where the _____ .

167. When direct-current, straight-polarity power is used, the current flows through the electrode cable

_____ , through the holder to the _____ , and

_____ .

168. The arc stream is the electric arc created by the current flowing through air between the end of the electrode,

technically known as the _____ , and the work, more properly referred to as the

_____ .

169. As the current flows through the arc stream, a column of ionized gas called the _____ is formed.

170. The plasma is a combination of both neutral and _____ .

171. In the center of the plasma are electrons, atoms, and _____ .

172. The heat of the arc is caused by the collision of these particles at the accelerated speeds caused by

_____ as they move between the anode and cathode.

173. The temperature of the arc is most effected by three factors: _____

_____ ; _____ ; and _____

_____ .

174. A _____ forms on top of the weld and protects it during _____ .

175. The slag comes from the _____ .

176. The power supply for arc welding may be designated _____ , _____ ,

or _____ .

177. Dcsp means _____ .

178. Dcrp means _____ , where the electrode is _____ .

179. With ac power the order in which the leads from the power source are connected will

_____ .

180. _____ power provides the deepest penetration for a given amperage and is used when welding rusty surfaces and tight-fit joints.

181. _____ power produces the smoothest bead and less splatter due to the _____ penetration.

182. Thinner materials and joints with wide gaps are most frequently welded with _____ power.

183. An electrode is composed of a core of metal rod or wire material around which a _____ has been extruded and baked.

184. The core material of an electrode melts in the arc, and tiny droplets of molten metal shoot across _____ into the pool.

185. The electrode provides _____ for the joint to occupy the space or gap between the two pieces of the base metal.

186. The coating makes the _____ , _____ , _____ , and _____ _____ .

187. The _____ coding classifies electrodes by the electrode's _____ , _____ , and _____ .

188. The AWS code for mild steel electrodes is a five- or six-position identifier, which begins with a _____ .

189. The letter in the AWS code designates the _____ .

190. If the letter of the AWS code is _____ , it indicates a _____ .

191. The next two or three positions of the AWS code are numbers that identify the _____ of the core material.

192. The fourth position of the AWS code is used for tensile strength identification only if the code is _____ positions in length.

193. The next-to-last position indicates the _____ .

194. If the last digit in the AWS code is 1, it indicates _____ .

195. If the last digit in the AWS code is 2, it indicates the code composition is suitable for _____ and _____ .

196. The last digit of the AWS electrode identification code signifies the type of _____ and recommended _____ .

197. Once the arc is struck, the welder needs to maintain a gap between the material and the electrode of _____ than the diameter of the electrode.

198. A sharp crackling sound, similar to an egg frying, is an indication that the proper arc gap is _____ .

199. Electrode sticking to the material during the welding process is an obvious result of _____ .

200. Excessive splattering and poor bead quality indicate _____ .

201. The term *inert-gas welding* describes an electric-arc welding process in which an inert gas is used to _____ and _____ to prevent oxidation and burning.

202. Tungsten inert-gas (TIG) welding, classified as gas tungsten-arc welding (GTAW) by the AWS, is accomplished by means of a torch with a _____ tungsten electrode.

203. The electrode in GTAW welding is used to _____ the arc and the molten pool of metal.

204. In GTAW, filler rod is added to the pool to develop the desired _____ of bead.

205. Inert gas in GTAW is usually _____ and is fed to the weld area through the _____ on the torch.

206. The gas cup _____ the electrode and _____ the gas in a pattern to prevent the intrusion of oxygen and nitrogen from the air.

207. The inert-gas welding technique that utilizes a consumable metal electrode, which melts and is carried into the weld pool to provide the extra thickness desired, is classified _____ by the AWS.

208. Gas-metal arc welding (GMAW) is often referred to as _____ welding.

209. In GMAW, the metal _____ must be of the same material as the base metal being welded.

210. Since the electrode is consumed in this process, the electrode wire is automatically fed through the torch so that the torch may be held _____ from the work surface.

211. _____ added to argon gas is commonly used for the MIG process.

212. In plasma-arc welding, the flow of the plasma is _____ but is _____ through an orifice, resulting in _____ and _____ of heat.

213. Precautions should be taken when using certain chemical solvents such as _____ , _____ , and _____ for cleaning.

214. Some chemical solvents may break down in the heat of an electric arc and _____ .

215. Joint fit for a square-edge butt joint should always be true enough to assure _____ penetration with good fusion.

216. The single-V butt joint is used where complete penetration is required on material thicknesses ranging between _____ [9.5 and 25.4 mm].

217. When using a single-V butt joint, _____ must be used to fill in the V.

218. The double-V butt joint is generally used on stock thicker than _____ [12.7 mm], where the design of the assembly being welded permits access to the back of the joint for a second pass.

219. A flange-type butt joint should be used in place of the square-edge butt joint where some _____ is desired.

220. All tee joints require the addition of _____ to provide the necessary buildup.

221. The number of passes on each side of any joint depends upon the _____ and the _____ .

222. When 100 percent penetration is required, the _____ must be adequate for the thickness of the web material.

223. Edge joints are used solely on light-gauge material and require _____ .

224. For torches that require _____ , a _____ must be included.

225. On light-gauge material, _____ is usually used to protect the underside of the weld from atmospheric contamination resulting in possible weld porosity or poor surface appearance.

226. In addition to these functions, weld backup prevents the weld puddle from dropping through by acting as a _____ and _____ some of the heat generated by the intense arc.

227. Gas tungsten-arc welding (GTAW) can be accomplished with _____ ; _____ ; or with _____ power.

228. With gas tungsten-arc welding, _____ power is generally recommended for magnesium and aluminum alloys and castings; it also provides the best results with beryllium-copper alloys or copper alloys less than 0.040 in [1.102 cm] thick.

229. _____ power is recommended when gas tungsten-arc welding is used for stainless steel, copper alloys, nickel alloys, titanium, low-carbon steel, and high-carbon steel.

230. The oxide coating on aluminum has a _____ melting point than aluminum and interferes with the fusion of the metal.

231. With _____ power, the electrons leaving the surface of the base metal break up the oxides as they flow to the electrode.

232. During _____ of each ac cycle, when achf power is used, the electrons act in the same manner as with dcrp.

233. For any given welding current, dcrp requires a _____ than dcsp.

234. Dcsp welding will produce _____ .

235. Dcrp welding, because of the larger electrode diameter and lower currents generally employed, gives a _____ , relatively _____ weld.

236. The cleaning effect of dcrp welding results from the electrons leaving the plate or the gas ions striking the plate breaking up the surface _____ , _____ , and _____ usually present.

237. Theoretically, straight ac welding is a combination of _____ and _____ welding.

238. Because moisture, oxides, scale, and other materials on the surface of the work tend to prevent the flow of current in the reverse-polarity direction, the phenomena called _____ exists.

239. To prevent the effects of rectification, it is common practice to introduce into the welding current a _____ , _____ , _____ additional current.

240. The GTAW torch consists of the _____ and _____ to hold the _____ , the gas _____ for controlling and directing the gas _____ , the _____ , the handle through which current and gas flow, and supporting structures.

241. The filler rod must be metallurgically _____ with the metal being welded.

242. GTAW uses either _____ , _____ , or a mixture of the two gases.

243. _____ provides the smoothest arc action because the arc is more stable, it is easier to initiate, and wider variations to the length of the arc are possible.

244. _____ will raise the arc's temperature for a given arc length and amperage.

245. With GTAW, the electrode should extend beyond the edge of the gas cup _____ times the diameter of the electrode.

246. The _____ allows the gas to continue flowing through the torch for a designated time after the foot pedal is released.

247. Postflow is necessary to prevent _____ of the electrode while the electrode is _____ .

248. In arc welding with a tungsten electrode (TIG), the electrode _____ touch the work to start the arc.

249. In GTAW dc welding, the same motion is used for striking the arc; however, the electrode must

_____ the work or other apparatus in order to start the arc.

250. The arc can be struck on the workpiece itself or _____ and then carried to the starting point of the weld.

251. To stop an arc, the torch is merely _____ back to the horizontal position.

252. Arc _____ occurs when the arc shifts and wavers without apparent reason, even with the torch held stationary.

253. Arc wandering is generally attributed to one of the following causes: _____ ,

_____ , _____ , and _____ .

254. After the arc has been struck with a TIG torch, the torch should be held at about a _____ angle to the surface of the work.

255. When filler metal is required to provide adequate reinforcement, the welding rod is held at about

_____ to the work and about _____ in [2.5 cm] away from the starting point.

256. For making butt joints, the torch is held _____ to the work and the weld is usually made from top to bottom.

257. When filler rod is used in GTAW on a vertical surface, it is added from the _____ or

_____ of the puddle.

258. Multipass welding is generally required for welding material over _____ in [6.35 mm] thick.

259. The number of passes required when using multipass welding depends on the _____ ,

_____ , and _____ .

260. The first pass in multipass welding should be _____ and provide

_____ at the bottom of the joint.

261. Gas metal-arc welding (GMAW) simplistically appears to be the same process as GTAW, except that the

_____ and _____ through the torch automatically.

262. The two general techniques or processes employed when welding with MIG (GMAW) are called

_____ transfer and _____ transfer.

263. In spray-arc transfer the metal from the electrode is carried to the molten pool in fine droplets by the force of the

_____ and _____ .

264. The power source for the GMAW spray-arc process is _____ ,

_____ .

265. The shielding gas employed with spray-arc transfer is usually argon with _____ or

_____ percent oxygen for _____ of the puddle and arc.

266. When short-circuit transfer is used, the tip of the metal electrode is _____ to the metal to provide a short circuit.

267. GMAW short-circuit transfer results in a _____ , which melts the end of the electrode into the pool.

268. Typically, GMAW requires the use of _____ with a _____ .

269. With a constant voltage the power controller will automatically maintain the _____ at a level that will melt the electrode.

270. GMAW power supplies are referred to as _____ power supplies because they control the

_____ , _____ , and _____ during the welding

process.

271. For a given set of operating conditions there is a relationship between the _____ and

_____ required to establish the desired arc.

272. The relationship described in Question 271 may be graphically displayed by a straight line drawn between two such

sets of voltage-amperage relationships. The _____ of this line is the slope of the

_____ .

273. Anything that changes the resistance of the welding circuit _____ the slope of the power

source.

274. In GMAW, where a constant voltage is applied, the slope of the line is used to determine the

_____ .

275. The resultant current controls the way in which molten droplets _____ .

276. High currents typically result in droplets of molten material leaving the electrode in a

_____ ; this results in excessive _____ around the weld area.

277. _____ result in a calmer flow of molten material from the electrode to the base material.

278. The rate at which the current changes to reflect a new combination of welding variables is called

_____ .

279. By adding inductance to the welding circuit, the rate of current change is _____ and a

smoother weld can be established and maintained.

280. The "flatter" the slope of the power source line, the _____ the inductance.

281. Short arcs require _____ voltage and result in less _____ , less

_____ of the molten metal droplets, and more _____ .

282. For short arcs the slope of the power source should be set on a _____ setting, with the

_____ between the minimum setting and half of the scale.

283. The spray arc mode requires a voltage between _____ and _____ V,

needs _____ heat, and results in more fluid-metal transfer and less

_____ .

284. The slope for the spray-arc mode should be _____ , and the inductance should be in the

_____ of the inductance scale.

285. If the wire-feed rate is _____ , the electrode will eventually contact the metal.

286. If the wire-feed rate is not fast enough, the electrode will _____ into the torch cup.

287. The scratch and retreat method is designed to minimize the effect of _____ and

_____ the weld at the weld-joint ends.

288. A scratch start begins the arc _____ ; the technician then quickly moves or retreats to the

end of the joint and then proceeds, using the normal welding process.

289. A scratch start ends by moving back from the end of the joint _____ before the arc is

terminated.

290. The torch should be maintained at an angle of _____ to _____ and

moved in a _____ direction.

291. _____ is a modification of the GTAW process.

292. PAW takes advantage of the _____ by concentrating its flow through an orifice.

293. Since the temperatures of GTAW exceed those normally required by the metals being welded, the main advantages of PAW are _____ and _____ ; also, the temperature of the arc is not affected a great deal by _____ .

294. There are two welding techniques available with plasma-arc welding: the _____ technique (which is used in conventional GTAW) and the _____ technique.

295. The plasma gas, _____ , may be supplemented by an inert shielding gas.

296. In PAW the orifice gas need only be inert to _____ .

297. For PAW, the supplemental shielding gas need not be inert, but it must not _____ the properties of the weld joint.

298. Typically the orifice gas is either _____ , _____ , or an _____ mixture, depending on the _____ , the _____ , the _____ , and _____ .

299. In plasma-arc welding the workpiece may not be required to be part of the _____ .

300. The heat used in the plasma-arc process for cutting or welding is transferred to the workpiece through _____ rather than the arc itself.

301. Plasma-arc welders are classified as _____ and _____ .

302. Transfer plasma-arc welders _____ the workpiece as part of the electric circuit.

303. Nontransfer plasma-arc welders _____ the workpiece as part of the electric circuit.

304. The function of the torch orifice in PAW is to _____ and _____ the plasma gas toward the workpiece.

305. In the nontransfer application the orifice material also acts as the _____ for the electrical circuit.

306. The primary advantage of nontransfer plasma-arc welding to the technician is that the aircraft itself _____ .

307. Since the aircraft itself does not need to be part of the electrical circuit, this eliminates concerns about _____ the welded material and the _____ of current into electrical lines and instruments.

308. The electrode for PAW must be _____ and _____ .

309. In PAW welding, the tip of the electrode is _____ past the orifice cup, helping to eliminate electrode contamination.

310. The tip of the electrode is ground to an included angle between _____ and _____ , with the end being either sharp or flat.

311. A _____ system is employed in PAW; it may use either a separate power source or the welding power source.

312. An advantage of the pilot-arc system is that it is also useful in _____ the torch for the plasma arc-welding process.

313. The recommended torch angle of _____ to _____ is only slightly more steep than the GTAW torch angle.

314. A _____ technique is recommended for PAW processes.

Chapter 6

Name _____

Date _____

1. Which test below may be used by the technician to identify a type of steel?
   a. spark test
   b. chemical test
   c. flame test
   d. magnetic test

2. If two pieces of metal are welded edge to edge in the same plane with no overlap, the joint is referred to as a
   a. butt joint.
   b. tee joint.
   c. edge joint.
   d. segmented joint.

3. The distance through the center of the weld from the weld root to the weld face is called the
   a. toe.
   b. reinforcement.
   c. throat.
   d. prism.

4. The depth of penetration of a weld should be
   a. at least ¼ of the thickness of the base metal.
   b. at least ½ of the thickness of the base metal.
   c. at least ¾ of the thickness of the base metal.
   d. all the way through the thickness of the base metal.

5. Acetylene is unstable when pressurized above
   a. 5 psi
   b. 15 psi
   c. 25 psi
   d. 30 psi

6. A balanced (or neutral) flame consumes 1 volume of acetylene for every
   a. 1 volume of oxygen.
   b. 1.5 volumes of oxygen.
   c. 2 volumes of oxygen.
   d. 2.5 volumes of oxygen.

7. The selection of the size of the welding tip is determined by
   a. the type and size of torch used in the welding process.
   b. the material hardness at the beginning of the welding process.
   c. the material hardness desired at the end of the welding process.
   d. the amount of heat and the size of flame for the kind and thickness of material to be welded.

8. Acetylene hoses are
   a. red with right-hand thread fittings.
   b. red with left-hand thread fittings.
   c. green with right-hand thread fittings.
   d. green with left-hand thread fittings.

9. As a general rule the diameter of the welding rod selected should be
   a. one-quarter the thickness of the material to be welded.
   b. one-half the thickness of the material to be welded.
   c. equal to the thickness of the material to be welded.
   d. one and one-half times the thickness of the material to be welded.

10. The type of oxyacetylene flame used to weld steel should be
    a. a neutral flame.
    b. a carburizing flame.
    c. an oxidizing flame.
    d. a hot gas flame.

11. A flashback is
    a. an accelerated backfire.
    b. a technique used in igniting a torch.
    c. a technique used in starting a bead at the edge of the material.
    d. the burning back of the flame into (or behind) the mixing chamber of the torch.

12. The reason edges are sometimes beveled is to
    a. reduce the amount of heat required to weld the joint.
    b. ensure adhesion between the mating surfaces.
    c. reduce the weight of the welded joint.
    d. allow access to the bead area.

13. Which item below is an indication of a poor weld?
    a. The reinforcement gradually tapers off into the base metal.
    b. The bead exceeds ¼ of the thickness of the metal in height.
    c. The toe of the weld is abrupt.
    d. Oxides are not formed more than ½ in [12.7 mm] from the weld.

14. When replacing a weld, the old weld must be
    a. completely removed.
    b. cleaned with hydrochloric acid.
    c. filled with solder, so that its surface is smooth.
    d. free of cracks.

15. Inert-gas welding is the preferred method of welding aluminum because
    a. the welding temperature is easier to control.
    b. the aluminum will not become magnetic.
    c. the inert-gas envelope reduces the potential for oxidation.
    d. there is no flame.

16. In electric-arc welding, the arc is struck between the metal to be welded and the
    a. clamp.
    b. backing plate.
    c. electrode.
    d. ground cable.

17. In any type of electric welding, the polarity of the system is important because it determines
    a. the voltage required.
    b. the amperage required.
    c. the resistance of the welding circuit.
    d. the direction of electron flow.

18. In electric welding, which type of power supply results in the shallowest weld (all other things being equal)?
    a. direct current, straight polarity (dcsp)
    b. direct current, reverse polarity (dcrp)
    c. alternating current (ac)
    d. stagnated alternating current (sac)

19. In gas metal-arc welding (GMAW), the electrode
    a. is nonconsumable.
    b. is fabricated from tungsten.
    c. material must be compatible with the base material, since it is consumable.
    d. must be in constant contact with the base metal.

20. The major benefit to plasma-arc welding (PAW) is
    a. the decrease in power requirement.
    b. derived from the fact that there is no arc and therefore no arc wandering.
    c. that no inert gasses are required.
    d. that the weld may be accomplished with less heat.

Chapter 7

1. The steel tubing used most extensively for aircraft structures, engine mounts, and similar parts is

   _____ , also called _____ .

2. Chrome-moly is usually designated by the SAE number _____ .

3. Aircraft steel tubing is sized according to its _____ diameter and

   _____ .

4. The location where two or more pieces of tubing come together is known as a _____ .

5. If the pieces radiate out from the joint, this is called a _____ .

6. When reconstructing a structure, the joint design should _____ that of the original.

7. The feathered edges that result from close-fitting tubular structures _____ require an
   allowance for expansion during the welding process.

8. _____ are used to support and hold the various members of the steel-tube assembly in their
   proper positions while they are permanently fastened.

9. _____ welding equipment is normally used to weld steel tubing.

10. Many welders prefer to use _____ on steel tubing because the heat is more localized and
    there is no flame extension.

11. If an inert-gas process is used, check the completed structure for any residual _____ that
    might affect the aircraft magnetic compass.

12. Any residual magnetism after inert-gas welding should be removed by the use of a _____ .

13. When welding an assembly, it is desirable to _____ the components before completing any
    one weld.

14. Tack-welding involves making three or four small equally spaced _____ between each of the
    components.

15. A joint should be welded in _____ , alternating across the weld to reduce the chance of the

    tubing _____ out of alignment.

16. The method of welding fittings to tubular members depends on the _____ stress they will
    carry in operating conditions.

17. Moderately stressed fittings that are not subjected to vibration are generally made of a _____

    of sheet steel and are welded to _____ of the tube.

18. Fittings or lugs for transmitting high stresses are welded to the _____ at

    _____ one point.

19. High-stressed fittings attached to _____ of a structural unit halfway between station points

    are welded to _____ of the tube.

20. Fittings attached to the main members of tubular structures where brace members terminate are typically welded to

    the _____ .

21. The fitting may also be built up using two or three sections with _____ that extend to the

    _____ .

22. After welding, hollow steel structures may be filled with _____ or

_____ , under pressure, in order to coat the inside surface and discourage

_____ .

23. Corrosion-proofing the interior steel-tube structures can also be done satisfactorily by filling the structures with

_____ or _____ and draining before sealing.

24. Sealing only the members of steel-tube structures, by permanently closing all openings to prevent air from circulating through them, is also considered an acceptable method for protecting the interior of repaired structures,

provided that the interior of the tubing is _____ .

25. Once the structure has been welded, a _____ should be applied.

26. A very satisfactory protection for finishing the exterior of steel tubing is obtained by spraying or brushing two coats

of _____ mixed with 4 oz [113.4 g] of _____ per unthinned gallon [3.785 L]in the second coat of primer.

27. The portions of the structure coming in contact with doped fabric should be given a protecting strip of

_____ or a coat of _____ if the base finish is not already dopeproof.

28. Carefully examining all joints with a medium-power magnifying glass, at least _____ , after first removing all scale, is an acceptable method of inspection for repaired structures.

29. The structure is checked for _____ , _____ , and any indication of

_____ .

30. If bent or cracked structures are found, check around the damaged area for _____ .

31. Secondary damage may be created in some areas away from the primary damage because of the

_____ through the structure from the primary area.

32. A check for internal corrosion in tubing can be made by tapping on the tubing with a

_____ .

33. The _____ of the tubing in the _____ portions of the structure are the

most likely to corrode _____ .

34. More precise inspections of an area may be performed by _____ inspection,

_____ inspection, _____ inspection, _____

inspection, _____ inspection, and _____ inspection.

35. Replacement materials used in welding repairs should be the _____ type as the original.

36. The parts to be welded should be cut to the proper dimensions and _____ in place with clamps or fixtures to assure correct alignment.

37. The areas to be welded must be thoroughly cleaned by wire brushing, filing, or by some other method to assure a

weld free of such defects as _____ or _____ .

38. Only a _____ brush should be used, because any small amount of other metals left on the surface will weaken the weld.

39. The size of the welding torch tip is primarily governed by the _____ of the metal.

40. Burning weakens the metal and causes it to _____ when it contracts during cooling.

41. Rewelding tends to overheat the metal and leads to _____ .

42. The _____ usually is made of mild steel for welding chrome-moly steel because it flows smoothly and contributes to a uniform, sound weld.

43. If the repaired part requires heat treating, it is necessary that the welder use _____ filler rod.

44. The technician must compensate for heat _____ during the welding process.

45. As the welder approaches the edges of the material, burnaways occur more easily, so the welder should _____ the welding flame away from the material as it approaches the edge of a joint.

46. The technician should never attempt to weld over an _____ .

47. Filling the weld area with any filler material, especially those applied by heat, is _____ because not only is the area weakened, but at the same time an area of potential failure is _____ from view.

48. If there is a failure or damage in a welded area that requires rewelding, all the old welded area should be _____ .

49. Welding should never be done over a _____ or where the brazing has been _____ .

50. When steel-tube structural units and steel fittings are constructed or repaired, welders can expect to experience the effects of the material's _____ or _____ during the welding process.

51. Cracking can be prevented by reducing the strains on the weld and base metal caused by _____ of the base material itself or restriction of the normal processes of _____ and _____ .

52. Cold-rolled alloy-steel forms or heat-treated forms are _____ before welding to reduce the _____ .

53. Another practice is to relieve the stresses of alloy-steel parts after welding by heating the whole part uniformly to a temperature between _____ and _____ °F [621 to 649°C] and then allowing the part to cool _____ .

54. If a joint is held together by both riveting and welding, the _____ is completed before the _____ .

55. _____ , which is welding progressively along the joint from the beginning to the end, either continuously from start to finish or in sections, with each section tied in or joined to the next, is another method for _____ .

56. If a damaged fitting attached to a main member, where truss members terminate, cannot be removed without weakening the structural members, the part of _____ , and _____ .

57. Whenever a bent tube is straightened, the adjoining welded joints must be examined for _____ .

58. Tube-straightening procedures may be followed only if the tube is not _____ , _____ , or _____ .

59. If a dent in tubing is minor, not deeper than _____ the tube diameter, and is clear of the middle third of the tube section, it may be disregarded.

60. If the dent is large enough to require removal and the tubing is not out-of-round for any considerable distance, the dent may be _____ by _____ .

61. If there is a crack in an original weld bead, the existing bead is _____ by chipping, filing, or grinding and the crack is welded over along the _____ welded line.

62. If the crack is near a cluster joint, holes are drilled at each end of the crack to prevent the crack from _____ .

63. Split reinforcement tube is welded in place _____ the tubing over the cracked area.

64. Repair tubing should extend a distance of at least _____ times the diameter of the tubing being repaired beyond each end of the crack.

65. If a dent is not deeper than one-tenth the tube diameter and does not encompass more than one-quarter the tube circumference; if it is free from cracks, abrasions, and sharp corners; and if the tube can be substantially re-formed without cracking before the application of the patch, then a dent or hole in tubing can be repaired by applying an external patch that _____ completely surround the tubing.

66. A hole in tubing that is not longer than the _____ and does not involve more than _____ the tube circumference can be repaired by applying an external patch that does not completely surround the tubing.

67. An external patch that does not completely surround the tubing is not permitted in the _____ of the tube section and must not overlap a tube joint.

68. Splint tube repairs should be considered only for _____ , and a suitable _____ should be made as soon as possible.

69. The split-sleeve reinforcement repair is suitable for repairing _____ , _____ , _____ , and other types of damage in structural tubing.

70. If tubular members, such as fuselage longerons, have sustained local damage at a cluster, they are repaired by welding on a _____ , also called a _____ .

71. A patch plate must be of the same material and _____ as the injured tube and of a size sufficient to _____ .

72. Patch plates that extend onto the truss members should have a width equal to the _____ and a length equal to _____ .

73. Unless the damage to the member of a steel-tube structure is comparatively slight, it is usually better to _____ the injured section and to weld in either a _____ or _____ .

74. Splicing in the case of partial tube replacements may be done by using an _____ tube of the _____ diameter, in which case the replacement tube is spliced to the stub ends of the original tubing, or it may be done by using a replacement tube of the same diameter together with either _____ reinforcing sleeves.

75. If the original damaged tube includes fittings or castings that have been made especially to fit the tube, the spliced replacement tube must be of the _____ as the original tubing, and this calls for either internal or external _____ under or over the splices.

76. If no fittings or castings are attached to the original tubing, it is possible to use an _____ .

77. The two principal types of splice welds permitted in the repair of aircraft tubing are the _____ weld and the _____ weld.

78. A splice is never made by _____ welding.

79. The best form of splice welding is the _____ .

80. A fishmouth weld is a _____ used in joining two pieces of tubing end to end, in which the edges are cut to resemble a fish's mouth.

81. A _____ is a joint between two members in line with each other, in which the joining ends of one or both pieces are cut diagonally at an angle of about _____ from a center line (scarf cut).

82. A _____ is the joint made between two members of unequal diameter or width, both members being on the same general plane.

83. A welded _____ exists when the end of the smaller tube is telescoped into the end of the larger tube.

84. The cut for the _____ should be made at an angle of 30°.

85. In a fishmouth reduction splice, the length of the cut on the outside measurement of the tube is from _____ to _____ diameters of the smaller tube.

86. The fishmouth reduction splice joint has a greater length of welded seam than a _____ or _____ and does away with heating the tube to a welding temperature in a _____ .

87. The fishmouth reduction splice is used for splicing _____ of steel-tube fuselages and members of other units where tube splices of _____ are required by the construction.

88. A scarf reduction splice joint is used for splicing members of _____ and resembles the fishmouth splice to the extent that the tube is not heated to a welding temperature in a _____ .

89. The fishmouth weld is stronger than the scarf (diagonal) joint because of its resistance to _____ .

90. In a fishmouth weld, there is no single _____ of weld through the structure; hence, a straight-line _____ cannot occur if the part is subjected to _____ or _____ .

91. A cut for splicing purposes must _____ be made in the _____ of a section of tubing because aircraft tubing must withstand high bending stresses.

92. Only _____ partial replacement tube can be inserted in any one section of a structural member.

93. If a web member is damaged at a joint so badly that it is not possible to retain, at that location, a stub long enough to permit the splicing of a replacement, an _____ must be installed.

94. If a continuous longeron is damaged at a joint, the replacement-tube splices must be at locations far enough past the joint on each side to _____ the necessity of locating the splice weld _____ to the joint weld.

95. A _____ , classified as a plug weld, is a weld holding two lapped pieces.

96. Rosette welds are generally used to fuse an _____ tube with an _____ .

97. A hole diameter of a rosette weld is about _____ the tube diameter of the _____ .

98. For an inner reinforcing sleeve repair, _____ cuts are made in the damaged tubing to remove the injured portion.

99. Cuts should be located away from the _____ of the damaged section.

100. A replacement tube with a _____ and _____ equal to the original tube is cut to a length _____ in less than the removed damaged tube.

101. Two reinforcing sleeve tubes having the same _____ as the original tubing and an outside diameter _____ to the _____ diameter of the original tubing are cut long enough so that each end of a sleeve is not less than _____ tube diameters from the diagonal cuts in the _____ and the _____ .

102. Each sleeve must fit snugly inside the original tubing, leaving a clearance between sleeve and tubing of not more than _____ in [1.59 mm].

103. If holes are drilled to assist in the installation and positioning of the inner-sleeve reinforcement tubes, the technician should _____ over the drilled holes.

104. Inner-sleeve reinforcement repairs have the advantage of presenting a _____ outside surface for the repaired section.

105. Splicing using larger-diameter replacement tubes involves using a replacement tube large enough to _____ over the original tubing.

106. Splicing with larger-diameter replacement tubes can be used only where there is sufficient undamaged tubing at each end of the section so that one stub end has a minimum of _____ tube diameters of length and the other stub end a minimum of _____ diameters of tube length.

107. When splicing using larger-diameter replacement tubes, the original tubing is cut _____ across at each end.

108. The larger-diameter replacement tube must have the same _____ as the original tube and should have an inside diameter just large enough to slip over the stub ends of the original but not be more than _____ in [1.59 mm] larger than the outside diameter of the original tube.

109. A _____ end should be cut on each end of the replacement tube with an angle of _____ from the centerline.

110. The tube should be of such a length that each end will extend a minimum distance of _____ tube diameters over the stub at each end.

111. The use of a partial replacement tube of the same diameter as the original is referred to as an _____ repair.

112. An outside-sleeve repair requires more welding than an inner-sleeve or larger-diameter tube repair and is therefore usually the _____ desirable repair method.

113. When replacing a cluster at a station, before the original cluster is cut, the structure should be _____ in order to maintain the _____ .

114. Sleeves cut to fit the truss members should be slipped over the ends of the truss members _____ the longeron weld is made.

115. When repairing a tubular structure at a built-in fuselage fitting with a tube (sleeve) of larger diameter than the original, it is permissible to _____ the longeron fitting holes to a larger diameter to enable the longeron fitting bracket to fit over the larger-diameter tubing.

116. Four methods that have been proven reliable and are accepted by the Federal Aviation Administration for certificated aircraft are briefly described as:

    a. a section of _____ that is one gauge thicker than the original tube serves as the splicing reinforcement;

    b. a _____ is welded over the original tube to reinforce the splice;

    c. an _____ of streamline tubing is used as a reinforcement; and

    d. steel plates are used in a _____ to reinforce the splice.

117. Welded engine mounts are particularly vulnerable to damage by _____ , largely because of the vibration to which they are subjected.

118. Engine-mount repairs are accomplished in the same manner as other tubular-steel repairs; however, replacement tubes should be large enough to _____ the original tubing.

119. Repairs to engine mounts must be governed by accurate means of _____ .

120. Minor damage, such as a crack adjacent to an engine attachment lug, may be repaired by _____ and extending a _____ lug past the damaged area.

121. Engine-mount rings that have been extensively damaged should _____ be repaired.

122. When it is necessary to make a repair of a fabric-covered, steel-tubing fuselage without the removal of large sections of fabric, care must be taken to see that the fabric is not damaged by _____ or _____ .

123. When the fabric is rolled back, it should not be _____ or _____ .

124. Airplane parts that cannot be welded include _____ , _____ , and _____ that have been _____ .

125. All members that depend on heat treatment for their original physical properties should be _____ after the welding operation.

126. Exhaust manifolds for reciprocating engines and exhaust cones and noise suppressors for turbine engines are usually constructed of _____ , _____ , or other high-temperature alloy. Welding of cracks in these parts is most satisfactorily accomplished by means of _____ .

127. Before repairing a crack or break, the metal on the inside and outside must be _____ and _____ , and the crack must be _____ .

128. When fuel and oil tanks are repaired, either by inert-gas or oxy-fuel welding, it is most important that the tank be thoroughly _____ of any fuel or oil fumes before the welding is begun.

129. The correct procedure for purging fuel and oil tanks is to wash the tank with hot water and a detergent and then allow _____ to flow through the tank for about _____ .

130. The welding of fuel tanks, whether they be constructed of aluminum, stainless steel, or titanium, should be done by the _____ method if possible.

131. When baffle plates are riveted to the fuel tank shell, the rivets are headed _____ to make them liquid tight.

132. If a fuel tank is repaired by gas welding, it is extremely important to remove all _____ after a repair in order to prevent corrosion.

133. To remove the welding flux, the tank is washed inside and outside with great quantities of hot water as soon as welding is completed and then drained. It is then either immersed in 5 percent _____ or _____ acid or filled with this solution and also washed on the outside with the same solution. The acid is left in contact with the weld about _____ and then rinsed carefully with clean, fresh water.

134. The efficiency of the flux-removal cleaning process is tested by applying some acidified 5 percent _____ solution to a small quantity of rinse water that has been used for the last washing of the weld. If a _____ is formed, the cleaning has _____ been done thoroughly, and the washing must be repeated.

135. Cracks in aluminum and aluminum-alloy cowlings are repaired by _____ , if possible, and all welds must have enough penetration to provide a small bead on the lower side.

136. In soldering, if the filler metal has a melting point of more than 800°F [426.67°C], the process is called _____ or _____ .

137. The soldering processes depend on _____ to draw the solder into the joint, so soldered joints require _____ .

138. When the entire copper point of a soldering device is covered with melted solder, it is considered _____ .

139. The flame of the torch used for either soft or hard soldering should be either a _____ or _____ to limit the potential for oxidation.

140. Sweat soldering is a method of soldering in which the parts to be soldered are first _____ (coated with solder), and then the melted solder is drawn between the surfaces to be soldered by capillary attraction with the application of heat.

141. _____ are chemical compounds that assist in cleaning the surface of the joint area of oxides, prevent the formation of oxides during the soldering process, and lower the surface tension of the solder.

142. Lowering the surface tension of the solder improves its _____ (or sticking) properties.

143. The use of acid fluxes is _____ approved for aircraft work because of the corrosive effects of such fluxes.

144. The fluxes recommended for aircraft work are _____ and _____ flux.

145. Excess paste flux should be _____ after the soldering is completed.

146. In soft soldering, the sealing and securing of a joint between two metal pieces is accomplished with solder that consists of an alloy of _____ .

147. Common solders are referred to using two numbers, the first number being the percentage of _____ and the second number being the percentage of _____ .

148. The solder does _____ actually _____ with the metals being joined but bonds to them on the surface.

149. The metals commonly soldered are _____ , _____ , _____ , _____ , _____ , and _____ .

150. Only _____ aluminum alloys may be hard soldered.

151. _____ is the process of hard soldering most frequently used in aviation on gasoline- and oil-pipe joints and similar joints.

152. Silver soldering is suitable for _____ , _____ ,

_____ , and _____ parts.

153. Brazing, with a _____ rod used for ''soldering'' the joint, is also a form of hard soldering.

154. The term *eutectic* describes _____ metals.

Name _____

Date _____

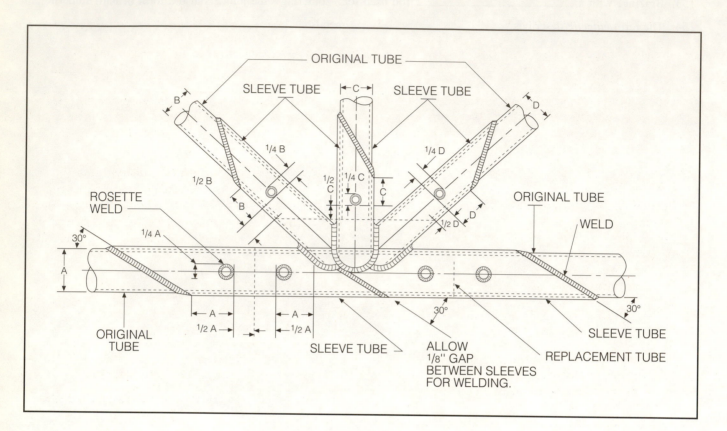

1. Using the criteria set forth in the sketch above and assuming the following dimensions:

   A = 1 in

   B = ⅞ in

   C = ¾ in

   the diameter of rosette weld D is ⅛ in

   Calculate:

   a. the size drill (include number drills) for the rosette weld for tube A.

   b. the distance between the rosette welds on the reinforcement tube for tube A.

   c. the distance between the closest end of the scarf weld on tube B and the replacement tube B.

   d. the diameter of the original tube D.

Chapter 7

Name _____

Date _____

MULTIPLE CHOICE QUESTIONS

1. The use of electric-arc welding techniques on ferrous metals may result in the metal becoming magnetized. Magnetism should be removed by
   a. striking the welded area with a hammer no less than six blows.
   b. zinc-chromating the welded area.
   c. the use of a degausser.
   d. rewelding the area with the opposite polarity used during the initial weld.

2. After a welded repair is complete, the weld should be cleaned of all oxides, visually inspected, and should have a corrosion preventative applied. The visual inspection
   a. need not require any magnification.
   b. should be accomplished with a magnifying glass of at least 4 power.
   c. should be accomplished with a magnifying glass of at least 6 power.
   d. should be accomplished with a magnifying glass of at least 10 power.

3. If a wire brush is used to clean an area for oxyacetylene welding of chrome-moly material
   a. it should be a hard bristle brush so as not to scratch the material.
   b. it should be an aluminum wire brush so as not to scratch the material.
   c. it should be a steel wire brush so that foreign metals will not be left on the material to be welded.
   d. the area must be treated with acid to clean all foreign matter from the weld area.

4. If a joint is both riveted and welded
   a. the rivet should be installed before welding.
   b. the welding should be accomplished before riveting.
   c. the rivet should be installed before welding and then replaced after welding.
   d. it must be replaced with a new factory joint.

5. All dents in tubing must be filled with weld in order to
   a. provide a smooth outside surface.
   b. increase the strength of the dented area to an equal or greater strength.
   c. ensure uniform loading of the structural member.
   d. The above statement is false; dents are not filled with weld.

6. When designing a welded patch repair the patch should extend
   a. to a length equal to the damaged area.
   b. at least 1 in beyond each end of the damaged area.
   c. at least 1½ times the diameter of the damaged tube beyond each end of the damaged area.
   d. at least 1½ in beyond each end of the damaged area.

7. As a general rule all repairs to damaged tubing
   a. must be in the middle third of the tube length.
   b. must not be in the middle third of the tube length.
   c. may be permanently repaired using a clamped-tube reinforcement, providing the reinforcement tube is heat-treated.
   d. are major repairs.

8. A reduction joint
   a. should not be used on aircraft.
   b. must be butt-welded.
   c. is required when the tubes to be welded are of different diameters.
   d. requires an internal reinforcement plate.

9. When cutting an angle for splice welds, the angle should be
   a. 15°
   b. 30°
   c. 45°
   d. 90°

10. Butt welds of tubing are not generally recommended because
    a. they are too hard to inspect.
    b. the heat is concentrated in a localized area.
    c. reinforcement must be internal.
    d. too much carbon buildup will exist in the weld area.

11. A fishmouth weld is generally preferred to a scarf weld because
    a. the fishmouth has more weld area.
    b. in a fishmouth weld there is no single straight line welded through the structure.
    c. a fishmouth adds more material to the joint, making it stronger.
    d. The above statement is not true; scarf welds are preferred to fishmouth welds.

12. The diameter of a hole for a rosette weld should be
    a. equal to the wall thickness of original material.
    b. equal to the wall thickness of reinforcement material.
    c. ¼ of the diameter of the internal tubing.
    d. ¼ of the diameter of the external tubing.

13. The purpose of a rosette weld is to
    a. allow a means of transmitting loads between structural members.
    b. ease the stress buildup during the expansion experienced during welding.
    c. maintain the relative positions of the tubes.
    d. provide a location for the expended gases experienced during welding to escape, thus preventing excessive pressure buildup.

14. Generally the closest distance allowed between the closest edge of a reinforcement to the edge of the internal tubing is
    a. the diameter of the internal tube.
    b. 1½ times the diameter of the internal tube.
    c. 2 times the diameter of the internal tube.
    d. 2½ times the diameter of the internal tube.

15. When replacing a weld cluster
    a. the structure should be braced sufficiently to ensure that the correct alignment is maintained.
    b. the longeron section should be replaced first.
    c. rosette welds should not be used.
    d. only fishmouth joints are acceptable.

16. Heat-treated structural components
    a. may not be welded.
    b. may be welded only if they are in the middle half of the component.
    c. must have the bead of the weld filled (smoothed) with braze.
    d. must be heat-treated after welding.

17. Structural materials that obtain their strength through cold working
    a. may not be welded.
    b. may be welded only if they are in the middle half of the component.
    c. must have the bead of the weld filled (smoothed) with braze.
    d. must be cold worked after welding.

18. Exhaust system components should be welded using
    a. oxyacetylene.
    b. electric arc.
    c. a form of inert-gas welding.
    d. a brazing technique.

19. In order to solder a joint correctly,
    a. the materials must be sufficiently close to take advantage of capillary action.
    b. the material must be spaced at least as far apart as the filler material is in diameter.
    c. an acid flux must be used to ensure proper etching of the contact surfaces.
    d. the filler material must contain 5 percent magnesium.

20. 40–60 common solder is composed of
    a. 40 percent lead and 60 percent silver.
    b. 40 percent tin and 60 percent lead.
    c. 40 percent silver and 60 percent tin.
    d. 40 percent lead and 60 percent tin.

Chapter 8

1. There are two general groupings of sheet-metal components in aircraft construction: _____ and _____ components.

2. Structural components are those components of the aircraft that _____ the forces exerted on the aircraft from one location to another or _____ the forces during flight.

3. Nonstructural components are those components that _____ transmit or absorb the forces of flight.

4. The philosophy of safe-life design was to test the various components to failure and to use as a component's airworthy maximum life _____ of the average life, when tested to destructive failure.

5. In fail-safe construction each component was designed to be able to _____ of adjacent components should their _____ fail.

6. Damage-tolerant design philosophy accepts the existence of minor flaws in components, _____ , and establishes an _____ designed to identify these flaws before they become critical to the aircraft's airworthiness.

7. Engineers almost always apply a _____ to their design to provide a margin of safety to compensate for material variances, design errors, product misuse, and other unforeseen variances from the norm.

8. By adding the desired safety factor to 1 and then dividing the result into the maximum strengths, the _____ strength limits may be calculated.

9. The _____ is the ratio of the allowable (ultimate) force divided by the applied (design) force less 1.

10. _____ is the load applied over a given area.

11. When a material is formed, the _____ applied to the material to form it must _____ the material's _____ to being formed.

12. This resistance to being formed may be considered a type of _____ .

13. _____ is a special type of compression loading.

14. _____ is measured by establishing a ratio between the increase in length that results from a stress divided by the original length of the material.

15. The accumulation of stresses over time results in a weakening of the material called _____ .

16. Each time a material experiences strain, even if the stress applied does not exceed its elastic limit, there is a minor _____ of the deformation experienced.

17. Scratches and cracks are referred to as _____ .

18. Scratches lessen the _____ of the material and as the area lessens, stress _____ .

19. Holes concentrate stress by a factor of _____ , other symmetrical patterns, by a factor of _____ , and nonsymmetrical patterns, by approximately _____ times the stress applied in the immediate area of the cause.

20. As the _____ from the cause of stress increases, the factors cited in Question 19 are

    _____ .

21. The number of cracks generated during the drilling process for rivets may be reduced by first drilling the hole

    slightly undersize and finishing the hole to the proper size with a _____ .

22. Holes create a _____ change to the cross-sectional area of the material.

23. When the cause of an increase in corrosion is applied stress, this phenomenon is called

    _____ .

24. Structural fasteners, which include various types of rivets and bolts, are used to _____ the

    forces applied from _____ piece of material _____ .

25. In the case of a repair patch, the load is transferred from the _____ to

    _____ and _____ to the _____ , then to the

    _____ , which return the load to the _____ .

26. Screws are normally _____ considered structural fasteners.

27. In repair design, the addition of holes to the structure will reduce the _____ capability of the
    original material.

28. For materials in _____ the maximum load is equal to the UTS of the material.

29. Material in _____ may carry a maximum load of approximately 70 percent of the UTS.

30. Therefore, components subject to torsion can be assumed to be able to withstand loads no greater than

    _____ .

31. When loads are applied to joints secured by fasteners, there are six types of load-carrying capabilities that must be

    taken into consideration: _____ , _____ ,

    _____ , _____ , _____ ,

    and _____ .

32. The fastener's ability to resist a shear load is directly dependent upon the _____ of the
    fastener.

33. Each material has a maximum _____ load-carrying capability, based upon the type,
    thickness, and width of the material.

34. In determining the tensile load-carrying capability of the material, the number of _____
    required must be considered.

35. For a given material type and thickness, the ability of the sheet material to resist the tearout load is a function of

    the _____ between the edge of the material and edge of the fastener hole.

36. The resistance to bearing loads of a given type of material is a function of the _____ , which
    is the diameter of the hole times the thickness of the material.

37. _____ is the cross-sectional area of the fastener, which is calculated with the formula $\frac{\pi \times d^2}{4}$.

38. The _____ of a sheet is the width of the sheet where the load is applied times the thickness
    of the sheet.

39. _____ is the total area of the sheet that will have to be torn if the rivet is to be separated
    from both splice sheets.

40. The _____ is the cross-sectional area of a hole where the slicing plane passes through the
    center of the hole and is perpendicular to the direction of the applied force.

41. Fastener shear load is the cross-sectional area of the fastener times the _____ of the rivet material.

42. _____ is the _____ of the sheet material times the tensile area.

43. _____ is the ultimate shear strength of the sheet times the total area that must be torn out in order to shear both of the splice sheets.

44. _____ is the bearing area of the sheet times the ultimate bearing strength of the sheet.

45. The composition of the metal, its temper, and its thickness determine the _____ radius that may be successfully generated in the part through bending without adversely affecting the material.

46. Radius bends require _____ material than do right-angle bends.

47. When a piece of sheet metal is bent, the material on the outside of the bend is in _____ and stretches; the material on the inside of the bend is in _____ and shrinks.

48. Where the two forces of tension and compression meet within the metal, the plane is called the _____ .

49. Empirically it has been shown that the actual neutral axis is approximately _____ percent through the thickness of the metal, measuring from the inside of the bend.

50. When describing a bend in aviation, the term *bend radius* is used and refers to the _____ .

51. The distance of the bend allowance depends on the _____ , the _____ , and the _____ .

52. The bend begins and ends at the _____ , and the length of the neutral axis between the two lines is the _____ .

53. The _____ is the number of degrees the material must be bent from its flat position to obtain the desired configuration.

54. The _____ is equal to 180° less the bend angle.

55. A _____ is an angle of bend of less than 90°.

56. The _____ of a part are given from the end of the metal part to the outer mold point.

57. The _____ is the intersection of the outer mold lines after the part is bent.

58. The _____ is the angle formed by the mold-lines and is the same as the _____ .

59. The _____ is the distance from the mold point to the bend tangent lines.

60. *X-distance* is also called _____ .

61. Subtracting the setback from the mold-line dimension results in the _____ of the mold-line dimension.

62. Since the tangent point is at right angles to the moldline, the simple trigonometric tangent function (cotan (*x*) = adjacent/opposite) can be used to calculate the _____ .

63. The distance from the center point of the radius and the outer moldline is the sum of the _____ and the _____ .

64. Charts that give the factor tan (bend angle/2) are called _____ charts.

65. Substituting the K-factor for the tan (bend angle/2), the equation for setback becomes _____ .

66. When looking up the K-factor for a bend angle, find _____ on the chart and read the K-factor in the _____ .

67. In a flat-pattern layout, the length of any leg is the length of the _____ less its _____ .

68. In flat-pattern layout, the minimum width of the material required to produce the part is called the _____ .

69. In flat-pattern layout, the minimum length is called the _____ .

70. The _____ of a circle is defined by the equation $C =$ _____ .

71. Since the _____ is considered to be _____ through the thickness of the material, the circumference of the neutral axis becomes $C = 2\pi \times$ _____ .

72. To calculate the bend allowance (BA), a factor for the _____ of the radius arc that actually exists needs to be added, where N equals the _____ ; the following equation is applicable: $BA = 2\pi \times (R + 0.5T) \times$ _____ .

73. The empirical bend allowance formula is derived by substituting _____ for 0.5T and eliminating all _____ values from the equation.

74. Bend-allowance _____ are derived from the empirical formula.

75. To protect the undersurface of the material from any possible damage in layout work, it is often advisable to place a piece of heavy paper, felt, or plywood between the material and the _____ .

76. _____ of various kinds are applied to a metal surface for layout work so that the pattern will stand out clearly while the technician is cutting along the drawn or scribed lines.

77. Among the fluids or coatings used are _____ , _____ , _____ , and _____ .

78. Zinc chromate _____ be removed from a part after the layout and forming are completed.

79. Bluing fluid does not protect metal against corrosion or serve as a binder for paint; hence it _____ from the part with alcohol or other suitable solvent.

80. Flat white paint will come off when _____ is applied.

81. Copper sulfate solution, through a chemical action, deposits a coating of copper on the _____ or _____ .

82. Copper sulfate solution _____ used on aluminum or aluminum-alloy surfaces.

83. A reference edge provides a line from which various _____ can be made, thus increasing the uniformity and accuracy of the work.

84. When possible, these reference edges should be edges of the _____ .

85. When cutting tools are not available, or when it is not practical to establish a reference edge, _____ should be drawn or scribed, preferably two lines at right angles.

86. Reference edges and reference lines may be better understood if they are regarded as _____ used in the construction of angles, parallel lines, and intersecting lines required in the layout.

87. The finished part should have no _____ or _____ whatsoever.

88. All scratched layout marks should be able to be cut away from the _____ .

89. The use of a black lead (graphite) pencil for marking on sheet metal should be done carefully so that _____ are made on the metal that makes up the finished part.

90. The hammers shown are used for smoothing and forming sheet metal and are commonly called _____ .

91. A _____ tool is used to remove metal from small areas by cutting out small pieces of metal in confined areas.

92. A _____ is a small, circular saw, the shank of which can be inserted in the chuck of a drill motor or drill press.

93. Small holes may be punched in sheet metal with a _____ .

94. A _____ is used in commercial sheet-metal work and is also used for some hand-riveting operations in aircraft work.

95. The rivet gun is equipped with a _____ designed to fit the head of the rivet being driven.

96. The rivet set is inserted into the _____ of the rivet gun and is held in place by means of a _____ .

97. The _____ must _____ be in place to prevent the rivet set from leaving the rivet gun and causing injury to anyone who may be in the vicinity.

98. When operating the rivet gun, the set should always be placed against a _____ stationary object such as a piece of wood or aluminum.

99. Rivet guns are available in various sizes, starting with _____ , the smallest, which is used for rivets of 1/16 and 3/32 in.

100. The _____ of a rivet set is the part inserted into the rivet gun.

101. Rivet sets designed for use with universal- or brazier-head rivets have a _____ to fit over the rivet head.

102. The actual force applied during the riveting operation is a function of the _____ setting and the _____ of the throttle.

103. A _____ is a smooth steel bar made up in a variety of special shapes and sizes and used to form a head on the shank of a rivet while it is being driven by a rivet gun.

104. The face of the bar, placed against the shank of the rivet, _____ .

105. A common rule of thumb is that the bucking bar should weigh approximately _____ less than the number of the rivet gun with which it is being used.

106. _____ are steel blocks whose diameters or widths can be adjusted.

107. The tool designed to hold sheets of metal together is called a _____ .

108. When the sheet fastener pliers are released, the _____ are drawn back over the _____ , causing the wires to separate and grip the sides of the drilled hole.

109. A _____ is a tool used to locate the position of holes to be placed in replacement or repair material relative to existing holes in aircraft structures or skin when the hole locations may not be more directly transferred.

110. A _____ is used to cut rivets to the proper length for a particular installation.

111. _____ are used to cut and square sheet metal.

112. This scale on a squaring shear is _____ to the cutting blades.

113. _____ resemble regular squaring shears except that the housing is constructed so that the sheet may pass completely through the machine, thus making possible the cutting of any desired length.

114. _____ are used to slit sheets in lengths where the squaring shears are too narrow to accommodate the work.

115. The frame of the _____ is made so that sheets of any length may be cut and the metal may be turned in any direction, allowing irregular lines to be followed or notches to be made without distorting the metal.

116. _____ are used for slitting sheet metal and cutting irregular curves and circles.

117. A _____ is used to cut short, straight lines on the inside of a sheet without cutting through the edge.

118. _____ is especially useful in cutting internal curved patterns where the radius is small.

119. The nibbling machine operates on the shearing principle and leaves _____ .

120. A _____ is a tool commonly used to turn narrow edges and to turn rounded locks on flat sheets of metal to receive stiffening wires.

121. A _____ machine is a machine designed to bend flanges either on flat sheets or on stock that has previously been formed into a cylindrical shape.

122. The _____, also called a _____, is a machine used to make simple bends in flat sheet-metal stock.

123. When properly set up, the distance between the radiused end of the radius bar and the pivot point of the bending leaf is equal to the _____ .

124. The _____ differs from the cornice brake in that the upper jaw is composed of fingers that can be positioned or removed from the upper leaf of the brake, allowing the forming of boxes, pans, and similar shapes without having to distort existing sides to make the final bend.

125. The _____ is used to form sheet metal into cylinders of various diameters.

126. A _____ is a short-throated rotary device used on circular work to turn a narrow edge (flange) or to score a crease.

127. The _____ is used to turn beads on pipes, cans, buckets, etc., both for stiffening and for ornamental purposes.

128. The _____ is used to make one end of a pipe joint smaller so that several sections may be slipped together.

129. The _____ is a three-speed, motor-driven combination of the burring, turning, wiring, elbow-edging, beading, crimping, and slitting machines.

130. The _____ of a metal-cutting band saw must have hard-tempered teeth that will cut through hard metal without excessive wear or breakage.

131. A _____ is a type of small anvil having a variety of forms; it can be set in a bench plate and used to bend and shape sheet metal to the desired form by hand or by hammering.

132. A _____ is a bench- or floor-mounted machine designed to rotate a drill bit and press the sharpened point of the bit against metal in order to drill a hole.

133. A _____ is a pattern from which the shape and dimensions of a part may be duplicated.

134. Aviation snips either cut _____ , in an arc to the _____ , or in an arc to the _____ .

135. Since a bend begins at the bend tangent line, this line will be positioned _____ the center of the radius of the radius bar on the brake.

136. The _____ is located a distance equal to the radius from the bend tangent line and when the material is placed in the brake, the sight line is _____ the nose of the radius bar.

137. The _____ uses the same basic concept as the sight line but is one material thickness from the sight line and is aligned with the edge of the bed of the brake.

138. If a production machine, such as a press brake, is used, the reference line used to position the part is called a _____ and is located between the two bend tangent lines.

139. When holes are to be drilled in any of the legs or flanges of a part before the part is bent, the hole centerline dimensions are treated the same as _____ .

140. If the material annealed prior to forming, it must be returned to the appropriate hardness by _____ .

141. If possible, a bend in sheet metal should be made _____ .

142. Normally, the grain of clad aluminum sheet runs _____ with a full sheet.

143. The manufacturer's identification letters and numbers are _____ with the grain.

144. When a reinforcing angle is attached to metal sheet across a splice, it is usually necessary to _____ the angle.

145. Making curved flanges involves the _____ or _____ of the flange.

146. To make a curved _____ flange, it is necessary to shrink the flange metal.

147. The fabrication of parts involving compound curves, when done by hand, is accomplished by _____ .

148. After a rivet is inserted through the holes in a piece of metal, a _____ is formed on the end opposite the manufactured head.

149. In the NAS-523 rivet code, the upper left quadrant designates the _____ , the upper right quadrant specifies the _____ of the rivet and the required _____ of the manufactured head of the rivet, the lower left quadrant provides _____ , and the lower right quadrant gives the _____ and indicates whether a _____ may be used as an alternative method.

150. There are three steps to preparing the fastener hole: _____ , _____ , and _____ .

151. Generally, the harder the material, the _____ the drill-point angle.

152. Drill speed determines the rate at which the _____ of the drill is moving across the material being cut.

153. When harder materials are drilled, _____ speeds are required.

154. In drilling larger holes of ³⁄₁₆ in [4.76 mm] or more, it is wise to drill a _____ hole first.

155. For holes that must be held within extremely close tolerances, a _____ is normally used.

156. When beginning to drill a hole, hold the drill _____ to the material being drilled and _____ the drill and motor so that the drill will not move away from the correct position and damage the adjacent material.

157. It is common practice to start the drill by placing it in position and turning it _____ before turning on the electric or air power to operate the motor.

158. Removal of burrs from drilled holes may be accomplished with a manufactured _____ , a _____ using a very light cut, or other tool that will clear the edges of a drill or punched hole.

159. When using the 7-rule, the first dash number of a rivet is added to the first number of the drill size to equal _____ .

160. To install countersunk rivets, it is necessary to provide a _____ in the surface of the skin so that the head of the rivet is flush with the surface.

161. The surface depression is made by means of a _____ when the skin is sufficiently thick and by _____ when the skin is thin.

162. A sheet of metal should never be countersunk through more than _____ .

163. _____ for countersunk rivets is a common practice when using a relatively thin skin such as 0.016 to 0.025 in [0.41 to 0.64 mm] in thickness.

164. When thin skin is attached to a heavier structural member, the heavy member is _____ and the skin is _____ into the countersunk depression.

165. A process wherein the sheet metal is caused to flow to the shape of dies is called _____ .

166. The rivet gun air pressure should be adjusted so that the bucked head of the rivet will be properly shaped, using as _____ of the rivet gun as possible.

167. The bucking bar is held firmly against the end of the _____ of the rivet while the rivet gun with the correct set is applied to the manufactured head.

168. The preferred length of the rivet shank exposed after installation through the rivet hole is _____ .

169. Although the desired height of the bucked head is _____ , a minimum height of _____ will be accepted.

170. After the rivet is driven sufficiently to fill the countersunk hole completely, the excess of rivet material projecting above the surface of the skin may be removed with a small rotary mill called a _____ .

171. Rivets are removed by drilling through the manufactured head with a drill _____ than the shank of the rivet to a depth _____ than the _____ .

172. A pin punch the same diameter as the hole may be used to _____ the head off.

173. After the head of the rivet is removed, the shank may be pushed or driven out with a _____ .

174. If the hole is too large, it should be drilled to the correct size for the _____ rivet to be used.

Chapter 8

Name _____

Date _____

APPLICATION QUESTIONS

1. Assuming a desired safety factor of at least 25 percent and a design shear load of 40 000 psi, what is the minimum ultimate shear strength of the material to be used in fabrication?

2. If the design tensile strength is 50 000 psi and the ultimate tensile strength of the material used in fabrication is 75 000 psi, what is the margin of safety?

3. 2024-T3 has an ultimate tensile strength of 59 000 psi; assume a safety factor of 25 percent is applied.
   a. What is the maximum load that may be applied to a sheet 0.040 in thick and 1 in wide?
   b. If a scratch 0.004 in deep exists in the material, what is the maximum load that may be applied before failure?
   c. What percentage of the designed safety factor is exhausted because of the 0.004-in scratch?

4. Four (4) AN470AD3-4 rivets are used in a piece of aluminum 0.040 in thick in a 1-in-wide lap joint with 2D edge distance.
   a. What is the fastener shear area?
   b. What is the tensile area of the sheet without holes?
   c. What is the tensile area of the sheet with holes?
   d. What is the tearout area of the joint?
   e. What is the bearing area for a rivet hole?

5. The ultimate shear strength of 2117-T3 is 30 000 psi. The tensile strength of clad 2024-T3 is 59 000 psi. The shear strength of clad 2024-T3 is 37 000 psi. The bearing strength of clad 2024-T3 with 2D edge distance is 121 000 psi.
   a. What is the shear strength of the rivet?
   b. What is the tensile strength of the sheet without holes?
   c. What is the tensile strength of the sheet with holes?
   d. What is the maximum tearout load the joint can experience without failure?
   e. What is the maximum load that may be applied to the sheet before bearing failure is experienced?

6. Assume a bend radius is 1/8 in and the material thickness is 0.040 in in the drawing shown.
   a. What is the distance B?
   b. What is the distance $A + B$?

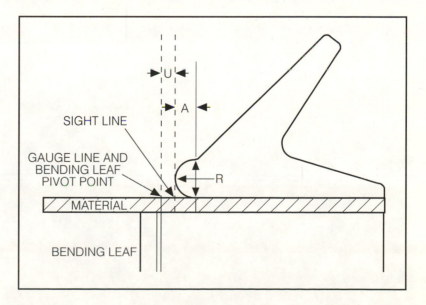

7. Calculate the flat-pattern layout for the drawing shown.

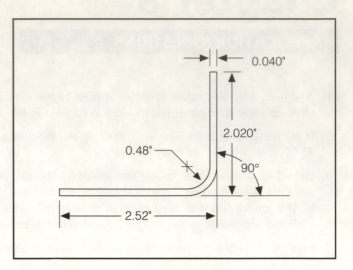

8. Calculate the flat-pattern layout for the drawing shown.

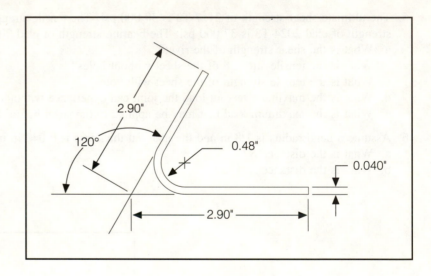

9. Calculate the flat-pattern layout for the drawing shown.

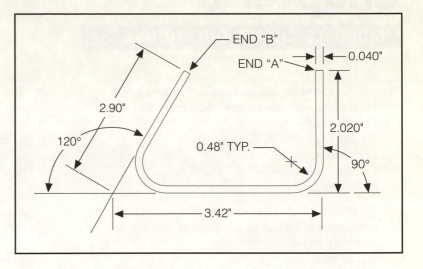

10. What is the distance in a flat-pattern layout from end A to the center of the 0.25-in D hole.

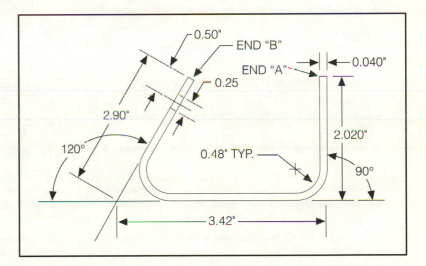

Chapter 8

Name _____

Date _____

1. The structural design philosophy that anticipates failure and specifies an inspection criteria to identify the failure is
   a. safe-life.
   b. fail-safe.
   c. damage-tolerant.
   d. on-condition.

2. A ratio of the ultimate strength of a material of a component to its design requirement less 1 is the
   a. safety factor.
   b. design tolerance.
   c. useful load.
   d. margin of safety.

3. Strain
   a. is a load applied over a given area.
   b. is the amount a material changes in length as a result of the application of a stress.
   c. always results in a permanent deformation.
   d. is the stress multiplied by the safety factor plus 1.

4. Fatigue
   a. is an accumulation of the effects of multiple stresses.
   b. can be eliminated through application of ultrasound.
   c. affects the strength of a material by increasing its hardness.
   d. is a function of the margin of safety used in an aircraft's design.

5. Scratches are considered stress risers because they
   a. decrease the cross-sectional area over which a load is applied.
   b. increase the cross-sectional area over which a load is applied.
   c. decrease the load applied.
   d. increase the load applied.

6. Stress risers
   a. are independent of one another.
   b. are eliminated through the use of stop-drilling.
   c. have a multiplying effect, which decreases the closer two stress risers are to one another.
   d. have a multiplying effect, which increases the closer two stress risers are to one another.

7. As the number of rivets in an area increases, the
   a. shear load-carrying capability decreases.
   b. tensile load-carrying capability of the sheet decreases.
   c. the repair becomes stronger.
   d. tearout load increases.

8. The load-carrying capabilities of a rivet of a given material are a function of the
   a. style of head of the rivet.
   b. the diameter of the rivet.
   c. the width of the bucked head.
   d. the height of the bucked head.

9. By multiplying the ultimate tensile strength of a material by the material's lowest cross-sectional area the
   a. maximum sheet tensile load is determined.
   b. maximum sheet tearout load is determined.
   c. maximum sheet shear load is determined.
   d. maximum sheet bearing load is determined.

10. The bearing area of a rivet hole is a function of
    a. the material of the rivet.
    b. the number of rivet holes in a single plane.
    c. the diameter of the hole times the material thickness.
    d. the shear load applied to the rivet.

11. The neutral axis of a bend is
    a. a line created by the points where the compressive load of the bend equals the tension load.
    b. specified on the inside radius on modern aircraft drawings.
    c. the same as the setback.
    d. a function of the K-factor.

12. Bend allowance refers to the
    a. force required to bend a material over a $\frac{1}{8}$-in radius bar.
    b. design tolerance of the bend in terms of degrees.
    c. amount of material in a flat-pattern layout that must be allocated to make a bend.
    d. safety factor that must be applied to ensure that the material will not fail when making a bend.

13. Setback is the
    a. distance the radius bar of a cornice brake must be inboard of the brake's transverse line.
    b. distance between the bend tangent line and the mold point.
    c. amount of material allocated to the lowermost leg of a radiused part.
    d. distance between the mold point and the center of the bend radius.

14. K-factor charts calculate
    a. the setback.
    b. the kinetic energy required to form a bend.
    c. the number of allowable kinks in a bend.
    d. the mold-line dimension.

15. The use of pencils for marking on sheet metal parts should be avoided because
    a. they harden the sheet.
    b. they are too easily erased.
    c. they may leave graphite on the surface of the material.
    d. paint will not adhere to graphite.

16. The radius of a universal rivet set is
    a. slightly greater than that of the appropriate rivet head.
    b. equal to that of the appropriate rivet head.
    b. slightly less than that of the appropriate rivet head.
    d. None of the above are true because there is no radius to a universal head rivet.

17. The distance between the bend tangent line of a radius bar on a properly set up cornice brake and the pivot point of the brake is
    a. the sum of the radius of the radius bar and the setback calculated for the bend.
    b. the radius of the radius bar less the inside radius of the bend.
    c. the radius of the radius bar less the setback calculated for the bend.
    d. the radius of the radius bar plus the thickness of the material to be bent.

18. The proper dill for an AN470AD3-4 rivet is a no.
    a. 40 drill.
    b. 30 drill.
    c. 21 drill.
    d. 11 drill.

19. A material would be dimpled instead of countersunk to accept an MS20426 rivet when
    a. the material used is softer than the original.
    b. the material thickness is greater than shank length of the rivet.
    c. the material thickness is less than the height of the countersink head.
    d. None of the above, because an MS426 rivet is a universal head rivet and does not require countersinking.

20. The minimum acceptable dimensions, where D equals the diameter of the rivet shank, for an upset end of a rivet are
    a. height $0.65D$, width $1.0D$.
    b. height $0.50D$, width $1.5D$.
    c. height $0.65D$, width $1.5D$.
    d. height $0.50D$, width $1.0D$.

Chapter 9

1. The most obvious form of NDI is the visual check, which may be performed with the _____ or assisted by _____ .

2. The most frequently used magnification level employed in aviation is 10 power, designated as _____ .

3. It is advisable in general visual-type inspections to observe the aircraft _____ the cleaning process is begun as well as after the cleaning.

4. Inspection of a metal structure is easily accomplished by means of _____ inspection; the dye penetrates and then seeps out of cracks; when a _____ is applied to the joint the crack is revealed as a _____ .

5. In _____ inspection a liquid containing a fluorescent material is applied to the part to be inspected and is allowed to penetrate cracks, laps, and other discontinuities. The part is then washed with a suitable solvent and dried and a _____ is applied to draw the penetrant to the surface. Using an ultraviolet light, cracks and other flaws are revealed as fluorescent markings.

6. In _____ inspection a magnetic powder is applied to a _____ part; this is an efficient, practical, and nondestructive method that will reveal tiny cracks and other flaws in a part.

7. After the magnetic-particle inspection the magnetization must be neutralized with an _____ .

8. _____ inspection uses radioactive cobalt "bombs" to X-ray joints at almost any location.

9. Ultrasonic inspection techniques apply _____ to the part being inspected.

10. In an _____ inspection, electrical currents are generated in the part by means of electromagnetic waves.

11. The FAA states in Advisory Circular 43.13-1A & 2A and throughout its other related publications that the technician must comply with the provisions of the aircraft manufacturer's Structural Repair Manual if applicable and, _____ , refer to AC43.13-1A & 2A and MIL-HDBK-5, *Metallic Materials and Elements for Flight Vehicle Structure*, as _____ for the repair design.

12. If the repair is a _____ , it must be approved by the FAA, through the use of the FAA's Form 337.

13. The primary purpose of a repair to sheet-metal parts is to return the damaged area to its _____ .

14. A patch typically consists of _____ joints, one to _____ the load and another to _____ the load.

15. One type of repair that does not alter the basic aerodynamics of the original material is the use of a _____ and reinforcement plate (sometimes called a _____).

16. The plug is used to maintain the surface plane and _____ carry any loads.

17. The reinforcement plate is the medium by which the _____ .

18. The classifications of aircraft damage are _____ , _____ , and _____ .

19. Negligible damage is damage that _____ affect the airworthiness of the aircraft.

20. Repairable damage is damage that might affect the airworthiness of the aircraft and could result in a loss of function of a component or system _____ .

21. Replacement damage is damage that cannot be _____ and where repairing is specifically _____ .

22. Before any attempt to make a repair is undertaken, the technician should first attempt to identify the _____ and nature of the damage.

23. If the cause of the damage is due to normal operations, consideration needs to be given to increasing the appropriate _____ of the structure.

24. Although strength is an important attribute, the technician must be careful _____ to equate _____ with _____ .

25. In certain situations the _____ of the structure may play an important role in determining the strength of an aircraft component.

26. Any repairs not approved by the manufacturer must be approved by _____ .

27. The presence of a repair design or philosophy in AC43.13-1A & 2a does _____ imply FAA _____ in any specific application.

28. Whenever possible the technician should use material of the _____ type and thickness as the original material.

29. In replacing rivets, the _____ size should be used if this size will properly fit and fill the holes.

30. If the original size no longer fits the hole, it should be drilled or reamed for the _____ .

31. The rivet diameter for a sheet-metal joint should be approximately _____ times the thickness of the _____ or somewhat larger for thin sheets.

32. The space between rivets in a single row is called _____ , and the distance between rows of rivets is called _____ .

33. _____ is the distance between the center of the rivet shank and the nearest edge of the material.

34. Rivets at the ends of the rivet rows must meet edge distance requirements in _____ directions.

35. The minimum spacing for aircraft rivets specified by the FAA in AC43.13-1A & 2A is _____ times the diameter of the rivet shank, except for two row repairs, which should be _____ times the diameter of the rivet shank.

36. The minimum edge distance is _____ times the diameter of the rivet shank; however, it is recommended that the edge distance be not less than _____ times the rivet shank diameter when the rivet is of the _____ type.

37. It is general practice to limit the maximum pitch (space between rivets in a single row) to _____ times the thickness of the sheet metal.

38. The width of the repair should be _____ that of the damaged area.

39. In a fastener-secured repair, _____ all cracks.

40. In a fastener-secured repair, _____ all corners.

41. The thickness of the patch material used in a repair should be at least _____ that of the original material.

42. Rivet patterns should be designed so that the rivet rows are _____ with the crack(s) and _____ with the relative load vector.

43. The effective load vector may be assumed to be directly _____ to a line drawn between the ends of the crack.

44. Rivet spacing should be _____ in all directions (symmetrical) so that concentrations of the load are not permitted.

45. Repairs should be _____ .

46. After the minimal rivet diameter is established, lay out the rivet repair as though a rivet _____ than the minimal rivet diameter were actually going to be installed.

47. The _____ installation, however, would be made with the originally calculated _____ .

48. The number of rows used in a joint is determined by the _____ of the joint repair, the diameter of the _____ , the _____ rivet spacing, the _____ , and the _____ for the repair.

49. To determine the length of a rivet row, the assumed edge distance is subtracted from the width of the joint _____ .

50. Dividing the length of the rivet row by the rivet spacing yields the number of spaces that are available within the row. However, because the row begins and ends with a hole, there is _____ more hole required than spaces.

51. The number of rows is the total number of fasteners required divided by the maximum number of fasteners in a row rounded to the _____ .

52. To develop equal spacing between fasteners in a row, divide the _____ of the row by the _____ the row.

53. The use of the proper size and spacing of rivets and their proper installation determines whether a riveted assembly will withstand _____ .

54. It is important for the technician to note that _____ designed using these data must be _____ via FAA Form 337 before the repair design may be considered airworthy.

55. Although these tables are considered approved data in support of a repair design, they are _____ approved for all conditions.

Questions 56 through 70 deal with using the mechanical properties of repair materials to determine the basic repair design. Individuals interested only in design based on the use of AC 43.13-1A & 2A tables should proceed to Question 71.

56. The maximum load that the sheet can withstand at the rivet joint is equal to the _____ of the sheet.

57. If the rivet's _____ capability is less than that of the sheet-bearing load, the _____ will shear before the sheet.

58. If the rivet's shear load–carrying capability is greater than that of the _____ load, the _____ will fail before the rivet.

59. The objective of establishing a minimum edge distance and rivet spacing is to ensure that the sheet material does not _____ before _____ failure; to do this, the tearout load of the sheet must be equal to or greater than the bearing load.

60. Increasing the edge distance _____ the tearout capabilities of the joint.

61. The strength of a riveted joint is based on the _____ strength of the _____ to be used and the _____ strength of the sheet metal.

62. The tensile strength of a sheet of a particular piece of material depends on the _____ of the sheet that is _____ to the plane in which the load is applied.

63. The cross-sectional area of a sheet with holes is the _____ of the sheet less the _____ of each rivet hole affecting the cross-section.

64. The _____ is multiplied by the ultimate tensile strength of the material to determine the tensile strength of the sheet.

65. In situations where more than one pattern of rivet holes exist, the row with the _____ (the _____ rivets) would be used to determine the tensile strength of the rivet joint sheet.

66. The number of fasteners required to transfer the load from one sheet to another is equal to the tensile load of the sheet at the joint divided by the _____ or the _____ , whichever denominator is _____ .

67. Remember that the number of rivets calculated is the number of rivets required to transfer the load from one piece of material to another at a _____ . This makes the actual number of rivets required for a typical patch with two lap joints _____ the number calculated.

68. The width of a patch must be _____ than the width of the damaged area if material of the same type and thickness is used for the patch.

69. The tensile-strength capability of the patch is the _____ of the patch times the _____ .

70. The width of the patch must exceed the width of the patch by at least the _____ plus the rivet spacing for those fastener holes _____ .

71. Before using AC 43.13-1A & 2A to determine the number of rivets required [refer to Table 9–3 in the text], the rivet _____ and _____ and the thickness of the _____ sheet must be known.

72. Referring to AC 43.13-1A & 2A, Figure 2.28 [Table 9–3 in the text],

    a. the leftmost column refers to the _____ of the material expressed in inches.

    b. each row under the thickness header specifies a standard _____ .

    c. the rightmost column refers to the use of _____ .

    d. the header for the five middle columns refers to the _____ and _____ of the rivet.

    e. each column under the center general header specifies a _____ .

    f. the bottom of the figure indicates general usage _____ and _____ .

    g. the number in each cell [intersection of a row and a column] is the number of rivets required _____ of width in the joint.

73. The number of rivets calculated using AC 43.13-1A & 2A, Fig. 2.28 [Table 9–3 in the text], is the number of rivets required _____ .

74. The rivets in each _____ of rivets actually transfers a _____ .

75. The first row of rivets transfers _____ , with decreasing loads being transferred by each subsequent row of rivets.

76. Each rivet transfers its _____ capabilities until the load remaining to be transferred is _____ than the capabilities of the rivet.

77. The patch material needs to carry only the _____ that is transferred.

78. The patch material thickness required at the first row only needs to be thick enough to support the load _____ by that row.

79. When more than two sheets make up a fastener joint, there are _____ .

80. Since the load planes are adjacent, separated only by one material thickness, a portion of the load applied to one plane _____ into the next plane.

81. In most materials' handbooks, including MIL-HDBK-5E, the shear strengths for _____ are established.

82. These two-plane shear strengths are _____ than the single-plane shear strength; therefore the technician should consult these handbooks for the proper values.

83. If the cause of the repair is insufficient load transmission under normal flight operations, the technician should consult the _____ .

84. If the mechanical property being calculated exceeds its mechanical properties, the _____ should be used in all subsequent equations.

85. _____ rivet should be placed in a line _____ with the vector that represents the _____ .

86. Where specific instructions for sheet-metal structural repairs are not available in the manufacturer's manuals, which should always be the _____ of the technician in determining the type of repair to use, publications such as AC _____ published by the FAA and _____ may be used for the development of a repair design for unique applications.

87. Whenever specific instructions for a major sheet-metal structural repair are not available in the manufacturer's manuals, the technician _____ obtain FAA approval for the repair by submitting _____ .

88. The prudent technician will make it a habit to obtain approval _____ beginning the installation of major sheet-metal structural repairs.

Chapter 9

Name _____

Date _____

APPLICATION QUESTIONS

1. If you wish to substitute 2024-T3 clad for a piece of 0.040-in-thick 2024-T3 bare, what is the minimum thickness you should use?

2. If two sheets of aluminum, one 0.040 in thick and the other 0.063 in thick, are to be riveted together, using the general guideline, what is the recommended rivet diameter?

3. It is determined that three rows of MS20426AD4 rivets are to be used in a lap joint. What is the minimum overlap of the joint sheets?

4. If you wish to ensure that the joint in Question 3 is repairable, what is the desired overlap?

5. Using Table 9–3 in the text or AC 43.13-1A & 2A, Fig. 2.28, how many rivets are required to fabricate a 2-in-wide lap joint with an upper wing surface stringer, using MS20426AD4 rivets in 0.032-in material?

6. Using Table 9–3 in the text or AC 43.13-1A & 2A, Fig. 2.28, how many rivets are required to fabricate a 2-in-wide lap joint with an upper wing surface stringer, using MS20470AD4 rivets in 0.032-in material?

7. Using Table 9–3 in the text or AC 43.13-1A & 2A, Fig. 2.28, how many rivets are required to fabricate a 2-in-wide scab patch, using MS20470AD4 rivets in 0.040-in material?

Chapter 9

Name _____

Date _____

1. NDI and NDT
   a. are designed to verify the existence of a certain attribute.
   b. verify that no cracks exist in an aircraft component.
   c. ensure that no internal stresses exist in an aircraft component.
   d. are designed for use on powerplant systems only.

2. Ultrasonic inspection employs
   a. the use of electromagnetic waves and electrical current.
   b. the generation of magnetic fields.
   c. the echoing of sound waves.
   d. the phasing of alternating current.

3. The design of major structural repairs not included in the aircraft's maintenance or structural repair manuals must be
   a. approved by the aircraft manufacturer.
   b. approved by a technician with an inspection authorization.
   c. submitted on Form 337 and approved by the FAA.
   d. included in the maintenance logbook at the next annual inspection.

4. The primary function of a fastener in a lap joint is to
   a. hold down the uppermost layer of the repair.
   b. stop air from entering between the layers of a patch.
   c. transmit the loads from one layer of the patch to another.
   d. provide an aerodynamically clean profile around the damaged area.

5. If the plug of a surface patch has one-fourth the surface area of the doubler and both are the same type and thickness of material, functionally the plug carries
   a. four times the load of the doubler.
   b. the same load as the doubler.
   c. one-fourth the load of the doubler.
   d. no load.

6. If the original sheet is clad, nonclad material of the same type may be substituted
   a. providing it is 50 percent thicker than the original.
   b. providing it is at least the same thickness as the original.
   c. providing it is 50 percent thicker than the original and there is supplemental corrosion protection.
   d. providing it is at least the same thickness as the original and there is supplemental corrosion protection.

7. As a general rule the diameter of a rivet should be
   a. equal to the total thickness of the joint material.
   b. equal to twice the thickness of the thinnest sheet of the joint material.
   c. equal to three times the thickness of the thickest sheet of the joint material.
   d. equal to four times the thickness of the thinnest sheet of the joint material.

8. According to AC 43.13-1A & 2A, the minimum rivet spacing is
   a. edge distance equal to $2D$, pitch and gage equal to $3D$, except for rivet patterns of two rows where pitch and gage of $4D$ is the minimum.
   b. edge distance equal to $2D$, pitch and gage equal to $4D$, except for rivet patterns of two rows where pitch and gage of $3D$ is the minimum.
   c. edge distance equal to $3D$, pitch and gage equal to $3D$, except for rivet patterns of two rows where pitch and gage of $4D$ is the minimum.
   d. edge distance equal to $3D$, pitch and gage equal to $4D$, except for rivet patterns of two rows where pitch and gage of $3D$ is the minimum.

9. The general rule for determining the width of a repair is that it should be
   a. equal to the width of the damaged area.
   b. equal to 1.5 times the width of the damaged area.
   c. equal to 2 times the width of the damaged area.
   d. equal to 2.5 times the width of the damaged area.

10. If the original rivet hole is elongated or damaged in some other manner, the rivet used to replace the original rivet must be large enough to remove all the damaged area and maintain the hole's roundness,
    a. regardless of the resultant rivet spacing.
    b. but if the resultant rivet spacing is less than that specified in AC 43.13 the rivet must be replaced by a standard airframe bolt (AN3 through AN20).
    c. but if the resultant rivet spacing is less than that specified in AC 43.13 the rivet must be replaced by a huckbolt.
    d. but if the resultant rivet spacing is less than that specified in AC 43.13 the repair will most likely have to be replaced.

11. The minimums dimensions established by the FAA in AC 43.13
    a. should be used for dimensional layout of a repair.
    b. should be exceeded by a factor of 1.25 to provide extra strength.
    c. may be exceeded by the amount necessary to make a repair repairable.
    d. do not account for the thickness of the material.

12. Rivet layout patterns
    a. should be as close as possible to increase the joint's shear strength.
    b. should be as far apart as possible to increase the joint's tensile strength.
    c. should be symmetrical to reduce the potential for load concentrations.
    d. are not critical providing AC 43.13-1A & 2A minimums are maintained.

13. In calculating the shear strength of a rivet, the diameter used is
    a. the standard diameter of the rivet.
    b. one standard size smaller than the standard rivet size actually used.
    c. the size of the rivet hole (example: no. 40 drill diameter for a −3 rivet).
    d. one standard size larger than the standard rivet size actually used.

14. To maximize the load-carrying capability of a fastener joint, the shear strength of the rivet should be as close to the
    a. bearing strength of the sheet as possible.
    b. tearout strength of the sheet as possible.
    c. tensile strength of the sheet as possible.
    d. shear strength of the sheet as possible.

15. To maximize the load-carrying capability of a fastener joint, the bearing strength of the sheet should be as close to the
    a. shear strength of the rivet as possible.
    b. tearout strength of the sheet as possible.
    c. tensile strength of the sheet as possible.
    d. shear strength of the sheet as possible.

16. As a general rule, if MS20426 rivets are used the edge distance should be
    a. 2D.
    b. 2.5D.
    c. 3D.
    d. unaffected.

17. Using the charts in AC 43.13-1A & 2A, the number of rivets required for a patch repair should be
    a. factored by 1.0, because no adjustments are needed.
    b. factored by 1.5, because the patch material should be one half the thickness of the original material.
    c. factored by 2.0, because the load transfer of a patch repair consists of two joints.
    d. factored by 4.0, because there are four sides to the repair.

18. The purpose of a stacked doubler is to reduce the weight of a repair. It does this by
    a. adding reinforcements in the proper areas.
    b. layering the patch metal in such a way that only the strength required is used to calculate a layer's thickness.
    c. adding the inverse proportional stress to the dynamic stress.
    d. factoring the hardness of the metal and the coefficient of conductivity to determine the minimum thickness required.

19. The maximum design loads used in the development of a rivet pattern for the repair of an existing rivet joint
    a. may be determined by analyzing the current rivet pattern.
    b. must be attained from the FAA.
    c. must be attained from the aircraft manufacturer.
    d. may be found in the aircraft's Type Certificate Data Sheet.

20. Which statement(s) below is (are) false?
    a. The strength of a joint is solely a function of rigidity.
    b. The strength of a joint may be determined to some degree by the flexibility of the material.
    c. Existing rivet patterns may be duplicated in laying out a rivet repair.
    d. The cause of the discrepancy must be considered in designing a repair.

Chapter 10

1. _____ plastics are plastic compounds or solutions that require the application of heat to set up properly, or "harden."

2. Thermosetting materials include many _____ that fall under the broad plastic classifications and many materials that can also be called _____ .

3. _____ materials are those that soften with the application of heat.

4. This characteristic allows this type material to be used to form _____ items such as windshields and landing-light covers.

5. This type of material includes _____ such as Plexiglas.

6. There are two general classifications of clear plastics used in aircraft: _____ and _____ .

7. Acrylic materials, such as Plexiglas, are the more modern materials and have _____ acetate materials in most usages.

8. Acrylic plastics used in aviation applications must comply with the appropriate military specification: MIL-_____ for standard acrylics; MIL-_____ for craze-resistant acrylics; and MIL-_____ for heat-resistant acrylics.

9. The two materials can be identified by their _____ and _____ characteristics and by their reaction to certain chemicals and solvents.

10. When viewed edge-on, acrylic material appears _____ or the color of the tinting if the material is tinted.

11. Acetate material appears _____ when viewed edge-on.

12. When burned, acrylic has a _____ and gives off an aroma described as fairly pleasant or fruit-like.

13. Acetate burns with a _____ and a strong, _____ .

14. If a sample of acrylic material is rubbed with a cloth moistened in acetone, the plastic turns _____ .

15. Acetone _____ acetate but _____ .

16. If zinc chloride is placed on acetate, it turns the material _____ , but it has no effect on _____ .

17. To protect the surface of a plastic sheet, it is covered with a _____ .

18. If the masking paper adhesive has dried out and will not peel off of the surface easily, _____ can be used to moisten the paper.

19. If naphtha is used to remove old masking tape, once the masking is off, wash the area with _____ to remove any residue of the naphtha.

20. Plastic sheets should be stored in _____ or _____ .

21. When cutting plastics, keep in mind that _____ on an area will cause the plastic to crack.

22. Chipping can be avoided somewhat by feeding the plastic _____ through the cutting blade.

23. Any heat buildup in the cutting area of a plasic _____ into the surrounding material but is held in the cutting area, causing the plastic to melt and flow onto the cutting blade and preventing further cutting of the material.

24. To counteract the flow of plastic onto the cutting blade, some sort of _____ may have to be used when cutting plastics.

25. Cooling can be achieved by the use of an _____ aimed at the cutting area or by a _____ if the operation allows the use of a fluid without electrical or other dangers existing.

26. The smoother the cutting operation, the _____ chance there is of chipping or cracking the plastic.

27. The cutting teeth should either be _____ to allow for clearance between the side of the cutting tooth and the workpiece, or the teeth should be set to provide _____ .

28. The _____ and _____ relationship for the type of plastic and cutting teeth is important to maintain in order to prevent melting the plastic and compacting of the cutting chips.

29. To make short, straight cuts in plastic, _____ a deep line across the material to be cut, place a rod or some type of edge directly _____ the scribe line, and then press evenly and quickly down on _____ of the scribe line.

30. For drilling completely through plastic materials, the bit should be reprofiled to have an included angle of _____ and the rake angle should be cut to _____ .

31. For drilling partway through plastic, shallow holes with _____ ratios of 3:1 or less should be drilled with a bit having a tip angle of _____ .

32. If the depth-to-diameter ratio is 3:1 or greater, the tip angle should be _____ .

33. When drilling thin plastic, it should be backed up with a wood block to prevent chipping or breaking of the plastic as the drill bit _____ .

34. When drilling plastic, the drill motor should rotate at as _____ a speed as possible using only _____ pressure on the bit.

35. When cold-forming thermoplastic material, the plastic can be bent if the radius of the bend is at least _____ times the thickness of the material.

36. For most applications, _____ is used to soften the material and form it to the desired shape.

37. Plastic may be formed by the use of a _____ , _____ , _____ , or _____ .

38. An _____ is convenient to use when a small piece of plastic must be formed, such as when making a surface or plug patch for a contoured surface.

39. A _____ is used to heat a straight line on the plastic so that it can be bent along that line.

40. Once plastic is shaped in a heated air chamber, it is allowed to cool _____ and then trimmed to the _____ .

41. If, during the forming process, any of the material involved in the form _____ forming temperature, cold-forming results.

42. If the material is formed outside the cold-forming parameters, _____ will result in the part.

43. A _____ is used to soften small areas of a plastic piece so that it can be shaped to fit a particular installation.

44. Acrylic plastic comes in either a _____ or _____ condition.

45. Unshrunk plastics are subject to _____ during the hot-forming process.

46. Plexiglas G is an _____ .

47. When preparing plastic surfaces to be joined by cementing, they must be cut to the proper shape, formed as necessary, and checked to be sure that all surfaces and edges to be joined are in _____ contact.

48. The edges do not need to be roughed for cementing of plastics, since the bonding is caused by actually _____ the pieces together _____ .

49. The specific cement used with a plastic varies depending on the _____ .

50. A cement syrup can be made by mixing _____ with the _____ .

51. The plastic cementing syrup is sometimes desirable, since it is easier to handle than the liquid cement, especially when working on _____ and on the _____ .

52. Cement is applied on the _____ mating surface, and the two parts are then held in contact until the cement has set under moderate pressure.

53. The pressure used to hold the pieces together when cementing plastics should be just enough to assure _____ , about 1 psi [6.9 kPa].

54. Excessive pressure when cementing plastics could result in distortion, since the cement works by _____ the materials and allowing the surfaces to intermingle.

55. Once the cement has dried, the strength of the joint can be increased by applying _____ to the joint area.

56. By heating the joint, the solvents in the plastic move outward into the surrounding material, causing the joint to _____ .

57. Annealing relieves _____ , provides greater _____ and improves the plastic's _____ .

58. Annealing should be accomplished _____ cementing, particularly if a machining-type operation was performed in preparation for cementing.

59. Annealing also should be the _____ finishing operation performed before the part is ready to install.

60. All polishing and other final finishing processes should be completed _____ annealing.

61. The annealing of acrylic plastics consists of _____ (heating) the material at an elevated temperature and then cooling it _____ .

62. The best way to clean plastic surfaces is by flowing _____ across the surface and then using the hand to gently remove any particles adhering to the surface.

63. When using a cloth to clean plastic, always use a _____ , not a shop rag, even if it is clean.

64. Commercial plastic-cleaning materials often include a _____ and an _____ that reduces the static buildup on the plastic.

65. Commercial waxes that do not contain cleaning grit can be used to _____ clean plastic surfaces.

66. Commercial plastic waxes will fill in some of the _____ that appear on plastic and _____ to some degree.

67. Machines should not be used when polishing, as their _____ of operation may _____ the plastic and cause distortion.

68. Solvents such as lacquer thinner, benzine, carbon tetrachloride, acetone, and other similar materials _____ be used on plastic sheet because they will penetrate the surface and cause _____ .

69. Crazing is the formation of a network of _____ in the surface of the material.

70. There are three techniques to remove paint from plastics: _____ , _____ , and _____ .

71. A commonly used generic solvent for paint removal is _____ .

72. When the paint removal is complete, care must be taken to remove all the _____ from the plastic. Residual amounts of paint remover could cause _____ when other surface treatments are used.

73. Trialene soap may be used when removing _____ from Plexiglas or paint that has been in place for an extended period.

74. If a plastic component does not fit properly into the structure, mark the edges that need to be trimmed. The edge should then be trimmed with a band saw, hand file, or belt sander to within about _____ in [6.35 mm] of the trim line and then the fit should be rechecked.

75. After the plastic material is fitted, a _____ may have to be used to heat local areas and adjust the contour slightly to reduce any _____ caused by the flexing required to fit properly.

76. Once the new windshield or window is fitted, it should be removed and a _____ should be attached to the edges that will be in the channel.

77. The fitted piece should fit a minimum of _____ in [2.86 cm] into the channel, but it must be at least _____ in [3 .18 mm] from the bottom of the channel to allow for _____ of the plastic material. (The exact dimensions vary from one aircraft to another.)

78. Holes for the installation of bolts, screws, and fittings should be _____ in [3.18 mm] larger in diameter than the bolt or screw to be installed to allow for _____ of the plastic panel.

79. The bolts and nuts are tightened until _____ snug and then backed off _____ to allow for expansion and contraction.

80. When inspecting plastic components the surface abrasion should be checked, and, if not deep, this abrasion can be removed by an abrasion removal process such as the _____ .

81. If excessive crazing is found during the inspection of a plasic windshield or window, it should be _____ .

82. Any damage that is in the pilot's normal area of vision and that cannot be restored to a clear vision area is cause for _____ of the plastic component.

83. If the crack is not in the normal vision area, the crack should be _____ and _____ .

84. A surface patch of the _____ as the original material should be cut to extend beyond the edges of the crack at least _____ in [1.91 cm] and formed to lay _____ on the surface contour. The edges of the patch should be _____ and the patch spread with adhesive and positioned on the surface of the panel being repaired.

85. When a hole is found in a plastic windshield or window, any cracks radiating from the holes should be _____ .

86. If a plug patch is to be installed in a plastic windshield or window, the hole should be trimmed out to a circle or oval that _____ .

87. For the plug patch, a plug is cut from material _____ than the original material. The plug is cut to the proper size and the taper is _____ than that of the prepared hole. The plug is _____ into the hole to allow the plug to match the edges of the hole. After the plug has cooled, it is removed, _____ is applied, and the plug is installed in the hole.

Chapter 10

MULTIPLE CHOICE QUESTIONS

1. Which is an identifying characteristic of cellulose acetate plastics?
   a. They burn with a steady, clear flame.
   b. If you rub and blow on acetone, it will turn blue.
   c. When heated or burned, it has a very pleasant odor.
   d. Zinc chloride will turn the plastic milky.

2. Which is an identifying characteristic of acrylic plastics?
   a. When heated or burned, it has a very repugnant odor.
   b. Zinc chloride will have no effect on it.
   c. It has a yellowish tint when viewed from the edge.
   d. Acetone will soften plastic, but will not change its color.

3. If an aircraft's transparent plastic enclosures exhibit fine cracks that extend in a network over or under the surface or through the plastic, this is called
   a. creeping.
   b. fatiguing.
   c. stretching.
   d. crazing.

4. When installing transparent plastic enclosures that are retained by bolts extending through the plastic material and elastic stop nuts, the stop nuts should be
   a. tightened to a firm fit plus one full turn.
   b. tightened sufficiently to make a waterproof seal.
   c. tightened to a firm fit and then backed off one full turn.
   d. tightened to a firm fit.

5. Which is considered good practice concerning the installation of acrylic plastics?
   a. When nuts and bolts are used, the plastic should be installed hot and tightened to a firm fit before the plastic cools.
   b. When rivets are used, adequate spacers or other satisfactory means to prevent excessive tightening of the frame to the plastic should be provided.
   c. When rivets or nuts and bolts are used, slotted holes are not recommended.
   d. When using nuts and bolts, the plastic should be installed cold and each nut tightened to a firm fit before the plastic warms up.

6. The coefficient of expansion of most plastic enclosure materials is
   a. greater than both steel and aluminum.
   b. greater than steel but less than aluminum.
   c. less than either steel or aluminum.
   d. approximately the same as aluminum.

7. If no scratches are visible after transparent plastic enclosure materials have been cleaned, their surfaces should be
   a. buffed with a clean cloth dipped in a mixture of turpentine and chalk.
   b. polished with an automobile cleanser applied with a damp cloth.
   c. buffed with a clean, dry cloth.
   d. covered with a thin coat of wax.

8. What is the most common method of cementing transparent plastics?
   a. The heat method
   b. The soak method
   c. The splice method
   d. The bevel method

9. When holes are drilled completely through Plexiglas,
   a. a standard twist drill may be used.
   b. a combination drill should be used.
   c. a specially modified twist drill should be used.
   d. a wood drill may be used.

10. For a plug patch of plastic materials,
    a. the thickness of the plug material should be less than the thickness of the original material.
    b. the thickness of the plug material should be equal to the thickness of the original material.
    c. the thickness of the plug material should be greater than the thickness of the original material.
    d. Either a or b above may be considered correct.

Chapter 11

1. In its simplest form, a composite is a combination of two or more materials joined permanently together so that the strength of the combined materials is _____ than any of the component materials.

2. The use of mechanical fasteners, such as screws, bolts, and rivets, as a means of transferring the aircraft's structural loads, requires that _____ be drilled or punched into the structural members and skins weakening them.

3. A bonded structure eliminates _____ due to the creation of holes and evenly distributes the load along the entire surface of the assembly.

4. A bonded structure is an assembly that is _____ together and does not use mechanical fasteners to give the assembly its strength.

5. The construction process in a bonded structure uses specially formulated adhesives that are

   _____ .

6. Curing is a process that prepares, preserves, or finishes material by a _____ or

   _____ process.

7. Materials are exothermically cured when the chemicals involved in the process combine in a manner such that the heat produced is a result of the _____ between the _____ and not from an external source.

8. The exothermic bonding technique is also called _____ .

9. The _____ process uses elevated temperatures to cure the adhesives while in a vacuum or under specific pressures.

10. Composite assemblies consist of a fiber reinforcement material _____ in a resin

    _____ .

11. If specific instructions are not found in the manufacturer's manuals, a minor repair may be made in accordance with the standard practices set forth in FAA Advisory Circular _____ describing riveted repairs.

12. The final finish applied over a composite structure or repair is _____ enamel.

13. A composite is an _____ material that has been created by the _____ assembly of two or more materials to obtain specific characteristics or properties.

14. Unlike metal alloys, which are _____ , the component materials in composites

    _____ their individual identities.

15. Composite structures are those aircraft components that are manufactured using _____ materials combined with a specially formulated medium called a _____ .

16. A _____ resin is a type of resin that once cured, cannot return to the uncured, or soft, state.

17. _____ resins may be repeatedly softened with heat, even after they are originally cured.

18. When a matrix is added to fibrous material as part of the material's manufacturing process, it is

    _____ .

19. _____ properties are the most critical properties of a composite and are controlled by the _____ of the reinforcement fibers and the ability of the matrix to _____ from one fiber to another.

20. The load-carrying properties of a fibrous composite are greatest when the load applied runs in the _____ as the fibers.

21. Loads that do not run parallel to the reinforcement fibers must, at least in part, be _____ through the _____ , which typically has the _____ load-carrying capability.

22. The greater the ratio of reinforcement fibers to matrix, the _____ the strength of the composite.

23. Advantages of composite materials include: _____ , _____ , _____ , _____ , and the capability of achieving a _____ , thereby reducing _____ and _____ drag.

24. Composite structures can either be a _____ or a _____ construction.

25. A solid laminate is made by _____ together _____ of reinforcing fiber materials that have been impregnated with the resin matrix.

26. A sandwich assembly is made by taking a _____ or solid face and back plate and sandwiching a _____ between them.

27. The filler in a sandwich assembly can be honeycomb, which may be fabricated from _____ , _____ , _____ , _____ , or _____ .

28. The sandwich arrangement creates an improved structural performance and high _____ ratio.

29. In sandwich applications the core material is often constructed using _____ in order to produce additional strength, such as the inherent strength of a honeycomb design compared to a simple square pattern.

30. Fiberglass materials are manufactured in either _____ fiber (structural) or _____ fiber (electrical) forms for aircraft applications.

31. Carbon, Kevlar, boron, tungsten, quartz, and ceramics are collectively known as high-strength _____ .

32. Advanced composites are produced in the form of _____ , _____ , _____ , and fibers of various lengths.

33. The variations of fiber forms include: _____ , fibers of _____ , and _____ .

34. The most common of these are _____ fibers.

35. The performance of a fiber-matrix combination depends upon the fibers' _____ , _____ , _____ , and _____ .

36. The mechanical properties of a composite are directly proportional to the amount of fiber that is oriented by _____ in a _____ .

37. Continuous fibers can either be woven into fabrics that are _____ (woven at right angles to each other) or _____ (woven in a continuous straight line).

38. Filament winding consists of _____ continuous fibers wrapped on a mandrel simulating the shape of the part.

39. Short fibers are utilized in _____ and _____ parts.

40. The fibers are manufactured by first creating _____ filaments.

41. To create a fiber the filaments are assembled into _____ .

42. Tapes are processed _____ from the tow.

43. Fabric is created from the tow fibers that are _____ together in bundles to form _____ , and the yarns are then processed into fabrics.

44. The _____ yarn is the yarn woven _____ to the manufactured edge.

45. Fill yarn is woven so that it passes over and under warp yarns in a _____ pattern.

46. _____ is a closely woven pattern used to prevent the edges of the cloth from unravelling during handling.

47. To help the technician identify the warp yarn direction during the usage of the cloth, _____ , which are warp fibers of the same composition but dyed a different color, are woven into the fabric.

48. A plain-weave fabric pattern has an individual warp yarn woven _____ one individual fill yarn and _____ the next.

49. Satin weaves are manufactured when the warp yarns are woven over _____ fill yarns and then under _____ fill yarn.

50. When the warp yarns are woven over three fill yarns and under one fill yarn, it is known as a _____ pattern.

51. If the warp yarns are woven over _____ fill yarns and under _____ fill yarn, it is called a five-harness satin-weave pattern.

52. An eight-harness satin-weave pattern is identified by the warp yarns having been woven over _____ fill yarns first, then under _____ fill yarn.

53. Unidirectional fabrics are fabricated with all structural fibers laying in the _____ direction on the roll.

54. A composite matrix is the _____ medium that _____ the reinforcement fibers to protect them and help transmit the stress forces _____ the fibers.

55. Matrices can either be _____ or _____ in makeup.

56. A post cure requires additional time at elevated temperatures to ensure the _____ of the bonding process, to _____ , and to _____ .

57. The matrices can have metal flakes added to them during the manufacturing process, giving the part improved _____ and _____ conductivity.

58. The resin matrices are available in many forms, including a _____ , _____ , _____ , and _____ fibers.

59. The term *wet lay-up* is frequently used to describe the process of applying a _____ .

60. In a two-part liquid mixture, the proportions are measured in terms of _____ or _____ .

61. When the resin is in liquid form it is said to be in the _____ stage of the curing process.

62. The individual matrix components have a maximum storage life prior to use, called a

_____ .

63. After the matrix components have been thoroughly mixed, the combination then has a

_____ , which is the maximum time it can be applied prior to _____ .

64. Another form of matrix application, the sheet film-adhesive, has a maximum shelf life of

_____ .

65. When the material is in the sheet-film adhesive form, the resin is said to be in the _____ stage.

66. A sheet-film foaming adhesive is used when bonding together sections of _____ .

67. The foaming adhesive expands during the cure cycle to fill _____ that may occur due to

_____ of the core pieces.

68. A more accurate method of matrix application involves using fiber reinforcement materials that have been

_____ with matrix at the material manufacturer.

69. During this stage in the resin-curing process, the resin is blended with the reinforcement material and

_____ in the stage B condition.

70. Pre-preg materials must be kept at 0°F (−18°C) or below until ready for use. The maximum out time must be

controlled to assure ''freshness'' of the _____ .

71. When resin is fully cured it is said to be in the _____ stage.

72. Solid microspheres, or solid beads of plastic, are often added to matrices to _____ while
controlling costs.

73. When solid beads of plastic are introduced to the resin mixture, the mixture is often called

_____ .

74. Syntactic foams are _____ blown.

75. When hollow microspheres of glass are introduced to the resin mixture, the glass spheres have a tendency to

disperse throughout the part being manufactured, resulting in stronger _____ and

_____ .

76. Matrices with solid microspheres or hollow microspheres added are _____ , which means

that they have _____ .

77. Solid microspheres or hollow microspheres improve the resin's strength characteristics and overall

strength-to-weight ratio because the microspheres have _____ than the matrix.

78. Forming of complex configurations is accomplished by combining the fibers and matrix over a form, called a

_____ .

79. A _____ is a tool that conforms to the desired shape of the finished product.

80. _____ , often referred to as a bond form or lay-up tool, allow easy access to the composite
materials during the fabrication process.

81. _____ are designed in a matched male-female configuration.

82. An important consideration in the design of molds for close-tolerance composite parts is the

_____ of all the related materials.

83. If a mold is fabricated using materials with coefficients of expansion _____ than those of the composite materials, adaptations for the different expansion rates must be included in the mold design.

84. If the coefficient of thermal expansion of the mold material is different than that of the finished part, the dimensions of the mold and the finished part will be different at _____ .

85. The removal of the composite materials from the molds can result in damage to the part if the molds are not properly prepared with a _____ or _____ , which is used to _____ the bonding of the matrix to the mold itself.

86. In low-volume production processes and repairs, a _____ and a separate _____ may be used.

87. High-volume and critical composite structures are often heated using an _____ , which is an oven that heats the material while it is _____ .

88. The reinforcing fibers in a composite material will usually be designed to run _____ to the load.

89. It is important that the fabricator of the part understand the _____ of the fibers to the design of the part.

90. To establish directional relationships, the _____ is specified on part drawings.

91. The orientation of the warp fibers as the fabric is rolled off the bolt is defined as the _____ for the fabric.

92. Because the alignment indicator is not always in the same plane as the design loads, the engineer may specify a _____ in terms of degrees relative to the reference, or 0° plane.

93. Warp orientation relative to the 0° plane is frequently made in the form of a _____ , which is a circle divided into _____ quadrants.

94. Each quadrant of a warp clock has a plus and minus _____ , which reflects the _____ required of the warp fibers if they were to be positioned parallel to the alignment line.

95. On a typical warp clock, clockwise is usually _____ and counterclockwise is usually _____ .

96. If the warp fibers are positioned in such a manner that they lay in only one direction, they are said to be _____ , or _____ , in stress design.

97. Quasi-isotropic stress design refers to design capabilities that are capable of carrying loads in _____ but not in all directions.

98. If the warp fibers are laid perpendicular to each other—that is, at a 0° and a 90° point—they are said to be _____ because the stress design is in two intersecting directions; they are also considered quasi-isotropic.

99. If the warp fibers are placed in such a way that they fall at a point of 0° and 45° to the alignment point (0° on the lay-up tool), the lay-up is again said to be _____ .

100. When the warp fibers are assembled in a laminate with the fibers heading in the 0°, 45°, 90°, and −45° positions, the lay-up is said to be a _____ design.

101. Isotropic refers to the capability of a material to bear loads in _____ , so technically cross-ply applications are _____ isotropic.

102. Since composites are usually an assembly consisting of laminated layered materials, they are subject to _____ .

103. When drilling composites, the drill bit should be shaped in a _____ form or a _____ form.

104. When drilling carbon products it is best to use _____ combination with the drill motor.

105. Kevlar and fiberglass composite materials should be drilled with a _____ drill bit that causes the material to be _____ during the drilling process.

106. Honeycomb structures are best cut with a cutting wheel or a saw tipped with _____ or _____ materials, with the teeth of the saw shaped like a bread knife.

107. When routing out fiberglass or Nomex core, a _____ router bit should be used.

108. Acoustic emission, holography, ultrasonics, X and N rays, thermography, and ring tests are some of the _____ techniques currently in use for composite materials.

109. A ring test can be used to detect _____ and _____ between the layers.

110. If there is a void or delamination under the surface, the ring test tapping gives a _____ sound.

111. A _____ , or thin coating, of petroleum jelly, oil, or water is used between the sending unit and the material surface for a sound-transmission ultrasonic tester.

112. The couplant provides an _____ bond between the material being tested and the signal pickup device.

113. Radiology can be accomplished using X-ray and N-ray signals and can be used to locate _____ and _____ in honeycomb, delaminations, and separations of the core from the skin.

114. Acoustic emission monitoring is used to detect _____ and _____ of the adhesive bond.

115. Damage to one laminated skin surface with no damage to the core can be repaired by the installation of a _____ .

116. Cleaning and paint removal from composite materials should be accomplished using _____ .

117. The use of _____ for cleaning and paint removal on composite materials may lead to _____ of the composite structure.

118. The damaged area is either _____ or _____ using a small disk sander or a microstop setable air-powered grinder to remove each layer.

119. The damaged area is removed with ascending concentric circles of material in _____ increments.

120. If three layers of the fabric have to be cut back, then _____ patches are required.

121. The fourth patch is large enough to overlap the sanded area by _____ on all sides.

122. A thin coat of _____ is then applied over the cleaned and prepared area.

123. Each patch is _____ with adhesive.

124. Each layer patch is stacked sequentially, from _____ to _____ .

125. The warp fibers of the repair patches must _____ with the _____ of the parent material.

126. After the lay-up has been accomplished, the repair is sealed in a _____ bag with _____ attached to a temperature controller.

127. The temperature controller tells either the oven controller, the autoclave controller, or the heat blanket controller of the "hot bonder" how to control the temperature _____ , _____ , and _____ during the cure cycle.

128. The vacuum bag process can be used with either the _____ process or the _____ lay-up process.

129. After the repair patches have been put into place, a layer of _____ is placed directly over the patch.

130. This material is normally a _____ because excess resin needs to be _____ from the lay-up and the solvents and volatiles need to be vented.

131. If the repair surface is to be shiny and smooth, then this bagging layer is a smooth, _____ .

132. If the repair surface is to be painted, then a _____ , _____ , _____ material is the first bagging layer over the repair patch.

133. A _____ , such as felt, is placed on top of the release film.

134. The breather-bleeder material will provide a path for the _____ , _____ , and _____ to flow through during the curing process.

135. Once the release film and breather-bleeder are in position, a _____ is placed on one corner of the lay-up area with a piece of _____ material under it.

136. The patch area is then covered with a heavy piece of high-temperature _____ and sealed airtight.

137. The vacuum source should create a vacuum of at least _____ and the plastic over the patch should compress free of _____ .

138. If the repair uses a wet lay-up process, the excess resin matrix in the patch can now be worked out with a _____ .

139. All the air bubbles should be worked toward the edge of the patch and into the _____ .

140. If a pre-preg patch is used, the repair area is _____ using the available heating equipment _____ the vacuum has been applied.

141. Care should be taken to not apply too much heat _____ as the initial _____ of the matrix may cause _____ to appear in the patch.

142. Heat lamps and hand-held guns are not recommended because of the difficulty in maintaining a _____ on the patch for the required curing period.

143. If damage penetrates the skin surface and the core material, all the damaged material _____ .

144. If the damage is on a sloping surface, _____ must be used under the router to allow it to cut parallel with the undamaged surface.

145. If a syntactic foam is used to fill the core, the core material should be _____ beyond the edges of the surface opening to _____ the foam within the structure.

146. If the damage penetrates only one skin and is barely into the core, _____ foam can be used to fill the cavity if the damage is no more than 1 in in diameter.

147. If replacement of the core material is needed, the damaged area is prepared by _____ or _____ the outer skin and removing the damaged core with a _____ .

148. If a wet lay-up is to be used, the sides of the replacement core plug are coated, or "buttered," with liquid _____ and the core is pushed into place.

149. The replacement plies of the skin are impregnated with the liquid resin and stacked over the core in the same _____ as the parent material.

150. If pre-preg materials are used for the repair, then a _____ is used to install the core.

151. A layer of sheet adhesive (nonfoaming) is placed in the _____ on which the core sits.

152. If a pre-preg material is used for the skin, the properly identified material roll is removed from the freezer and allowed to thaw in the _____ storage bag in which the material is stored.

153. Using a sealed storage bag allows the material to come up to room temperature without having _____ form on the material surface.

154. The replacement plies are cut to shape after the material has thawed, then placed over the core in the _____ .

155. In a temporary or riveted repair for composite materials, the core material in the original structure is removed, a plug is inserted, and an _____ is _____ into place.

156. _____ and _____ are _____ to be used when installing solid rivets in composite structures because the pounding will delaminate more of the skin areas.

Chapter 11

APPLICATION QUESTIONS

1. You need to design a circular female mold to layup a plug that looks like a hat (see the accompanying figure). The material is to be cured at a temperature of 600°F. The composite material has a thermal coefficient of expansion of 0.00004 in/in/°F. The coefficient of expansion for the mold material is 0.00003 in/in/°F. To what dimensions should the diameters and depth of the mold be fabricated?

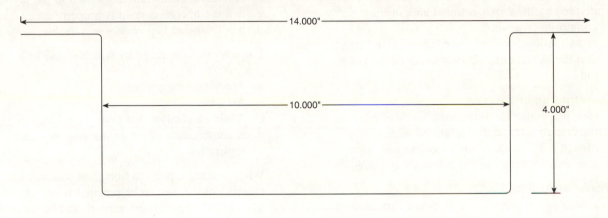

2. You are to repair a damaged area of a four-layer composite surface. The damage is 1 in in length but goes through only two layers of the composite material. To be sure you are removing all damaged material, you rout out three layers and use a cut-back type repair. The lowest layer (layer 4) plys run parallel to the 9 o'clock-3 o'clock plane.
   a. Describe the amount of material removed in each layer (use the recommended minimums).
   b. Describe the size of the materials cut for the repair.
   c. Describe the warp direction of each layer.

Chapter 11

MULTIPLE CHOICE QUESTIONS

1. The most critical properties of a composite are controlled by the
   a. direction of the reinforcement fibers.
   b. load-carrying capability of the matrix.
   c. cross-sectional area of the reinforcement fibers divided by the cross-sectional area of the composite as a whole.
   d. cross-sectional area of the reinforcement fibers divided by the cross-sectional area of the matrix only.

2. The warp yarn of a weave
   a. runs perpendicular to the manufactured edge.
   b. runs parallel to the manufactured edge.
   c. runs at a 30° angle to the manufactured edge.
   d. runs at a 45° angle to the manufactured edge.

3. Weaves are defined by
   a. a ratio of the diameter of the warp yarn divided by the diameter of the fill yarn.
   b. the over-under relationship of the warp and fill yarns.
   c. a ratio of the tensile strength of the warp yarn divided by the tensile strength of the fill yarn.
   d. the angles of the warp yarn related to the fill yarns.

4. Engineering drawings of composite components usually have an alignment reference called
   a. a travel indicator.
   b. an orientation segment.
   c. a post derivative.
   d. a warp clock.

5. The warp fibers in each layer of the repair material for a cut-back composite repair
   a. should be parallel to the direction of the warp fibers of the original material.
   b. should be perpendicular to the direction of the warp fibers of the original material.
   c. should be at a 30° angle to the direction of the warp fibers of the original material.
   d. should be at a 45° angle to the direction of the warp fibers of the original material.

6. How can stress concentrations be eliminated when making scarf repairs in composite structures?
   a. Use a core filter of higher density than the original material.
   b. Mix the resin catalyst in such proportions that the cured resin will be somewhat flexible.
   c. Avoid abrupt changes in cross-sectional areas.
   d. Use square or rectangular-shaped scarf patches.

7. When inspecting a fiberglass panel using the tapping test procedure, a dull thud from the tapping tool indicates
   a. a solid inner core of the laminated panel.
   b. separation of the laminates used in the lay-up.
   c. that the fiberglass resin is properly cured.
   d. that the panel is probably serviceable.

8. Polyester resin is cured by which of the following processes?
   a. Applying external heat
   b. Air cure
   c. Adding a catalyst that joins the molecules
   d. A combination of air drying and pressure application

9. When making repairs to fiberglass structures, cleaning of the area to be repaired is essential for a good bond. The final cleaning should be made using
   a. lacquer thinner.
   b. methyl-ethyl-ketone (MEK).
   c. soap, water, and a scrub brush.
   d. a thixotropic agent.

10. Fiberglass laminate damage not exceeding the first layer or ply can be repaired by
    a. filling with a putty consisting of a compatible resin and clean, short glass fibers.
    b. placing a sheet-metal plate over the damaged area and securing with self-tapping screws.
    c. sanding the damaged area until aerodynamic smoothness is obtained.
    d. trimming the rough edges and sealing with paint.

11. Fiberglass damage that extends completely through a laminated sandwich structure
    a. may be repaired.
    b. may not be repaired.
    c. must be filled with resin to eliminate dangerous stress concentrations.
    d. may be filled with putty that is compatible with resin.

12. Fiberglass laminate damage that extends completely through one facing and into the core
    a. cannot be repaired.
    b. requires the replacement of the damaged core and facing.
    c. can be repaired by using a typical metal facing patch.
    d. requires a plywood reinforcing plate installed with self-tapping screws over the damaged area.

13. Sandwich panels made of metal honeycomb construction are used in high-speed aircraft because this type of construction
    a. is lighter than single sheet skin of the same strength and is more corrosion-resistant.
    b. may be repaired by gluing replacement skin to the inner core material with thermoplastic resin.
    c. requires only self-tapping screws for the attachment of skin when repairing damaged areas.
    d. has a high strength-to-weight ratio and greater stiffness than a single sheet.

14. The simplest test in checking for a delaminated area in a honeycomb structure would be
    a. the metallic ring test.
    b. an X ray.
    c. an ultrasonic test.
    d. zyglo.

15. When repairing puncture-type damage of a metal-faced, laminated honeycomb panel, the edges of the doubles should be tapered to
    a. two times the thickness of the metal.
    b. five times the thickness of the metal.
    c. 100 times the thickness of the metal.
    d. whatever is desired for appearance.

16. What precaution, if any, should be taken to prevent corrosion inside a repaired metal honeycomb structure?
    a. Prime the repair with a corrosion inhibitor and seal it from the atmosphere.
    b. Paint the outside area with several coats of exterior paint.
    c. Coat mating surfaces and all fasteners with thin oil.
    d. None. Honeycomb is usually made from a man-made or fibrous material that is not susceptible to corrosion.

17. Which of the following are benefits of using microballoons when making repairs to laminated honeycomb panels?
    (1) Less filler shrinkage
    (2) Less density
    (3) Greater flexibility
    (4) Lower stress concentrations
    a. 1
    b. 1 and 2
    c. 1, 2, and 3
    d. 3 and 4

18. When inspecting a honeycomb structure using the metallic ring test, a clear metallic sound indicates
    a. core damage.
    b. facing and core sound.
    c. facing damage.
    d. facing and core separation.

19. Superficial scars, scratches, surface abrasion, or rain erosion on fiberglass laminates can generally be repaired by applying
    a. a piece of resin-impregnated glass fabric facing.
    b. a surface patch by means of epoxy resin cured for 1 h with an infrared heat lamp.
    c. one or more coats of suitable resin (room-temperature catalyzed) to the surface.
    d. a sheet of cellophane over the abraded surface and one or more coats of resin cured with infrared heat lamps.

20. A potted compound repair on honeycomb can usually be made on damages less than
    a. 4 in in diameter.
    b. 3 in in diameter.
    c. 2 in in diameter.
    d. 1 in in diameter.

Chapter 12

1. Although the assembly of different aircraft requires many varying procedures, basic guidelines to follow include:

   a. Always use the correct _____ and _____ of hardware.

   b. Insert bolts and clevis pins in the _____ , especially in the area of moving structures.

   c. Use only the correct type of hardware _____ .

   d. If no direction for bolts to be inserted is specified or indicated by component configuration, they should be installed with the bolt _____ or _____ .

   e. Never _____ components together _____ to determine why the force is necessary.

   f. Check the location and routing of all _____ , _____ , _____ , etc., before assembling components.

   g. Follow all recommended _____ when working with aircraft on jacks, hoists, and assembly supports.

2. If the aircraft had been disassembled for repair or shipment, it should be cleaned after disassembly and all the _____ checked for condition and replaced as necessary.

3. When the structure is disassembled, all the attaching hardware in airworthy condition should be _____ in the fittings on one of the separated structures to avoid the problem of trying to locate the correct bolt, washer, or screw from a pile of hardware removed from the aircraft.

4. An assortment of _____ is useful for lining up bolt holes.

5. During assembly operations, the technician must not _____ or _____ any part in order to make the bolt holes line up.

6. If parts will not fit together properly, the _____ of the misfit must be determined and corrected.

7. After the fuselage is assembled, it will usually be placed in a _____ or on a _____ for support while the other subassemblies are attached to it.

8. If the aircraft is to be lifted by a lifting strap placed around the fuselage, the strap should be _____ and placed at a _____ such as at a _____ or _____ .

9. Aircraft rigging involves two principal types of operations: the alignment of all _____ and the alignment of _____ and the controls that move the surfaces.

10. The fuselage is aligned at the time of manufacture in the assembly jigs to ensure that they are correctly positioned _____ they are riveted, bolted, or welded into a complete assembly.

11. When the major components are assembled, they are aligned with _____ .

12. Rigging of control surfaces require the adjustment of _____ , _____ , _____ , _____ , and various other parts.

13. When rigging an aircraft, it may be necessary to establish the aircraft in a _____ prior to checking and adjusting wings and control surfaces.

14. Once the aircraft is level longitudinally and laterally, the _____ can be rigged.

15. Leveling may be accomplished by placing a spirit level on a _____ structural member to establish the longitudinal level position and another level across specific structural members to establish the _____ level position.

16. Some aircraft make use of a _____ and a _____ to establish the aircraft level on both axes by suspending a plumb bob from a _____ and adjusting the aircraft until the plumb bob is _____ on the target.

17. A spirit level may be _____ attached to the aircraft for each of the two axes.

18. If an aircraft is not level, the aircraft may be leveled by the use of _____ under the aircraft, such as jacks or tail stands.

19. Regardless of the leveling means used, care must be taken _____ to place a support or jack at a _____ .

20. The fixed surfaces are checked for alignment with the fuselage and with each other to determine if the aircraft is properly rigged by checking the _____ both longitudinally and laterally and _____ adjustments.

21. _____ will normally be made after any major structural repairs or after the airplane has been subjected to severe conditions.

22. Aircraft symmetry is determined by first _____ the aircraft and then _____ the distances from reference points on the aircraft central axis to reference points on the adjustable components.

23. The _____ of an aircraft is checked in a like manner.

24. Reference points can be laid out on the floor of a hangar; a plumb bob is then suspended from the _____ and the position is marked with chalk.

25. As adjustments are made, a plumb bob suspended from the reference point immediately indicates the _____ of adjustment.

26. One of the first steps in preparing to mount a structure in a jig is to establish an undamaged _____ or points on the structure that can be used as a _____ for locating the structure accurately and in proper alignment.

27. During the process of replacing damaged parts such as skins, formers, and stringers, the structure should be checked from time to time for _____ .

28. A properly rigged and trimmed airplane will fly _____ , "hands off," at its normal cruising speed.

29. If the aircraft is out of rig, meaning that components are not properly aligned, then the total drag of the aircraft will be _____ or the amount of control movement available will not provide the correct response.

30. Stability around the longitudinal axis is provided by rigging the _____ and _____ correctly.

31. The wings on a monoplane are rigged for _____ , _____ , and _____ or _____ .

32. _____ is the angle between the lateral plane of a wing and the horizontal plane.

33. Dihedral produces stability around the _____ axis because of the difference in vertical wing lift when the aircraft rolls slightly off of level flight.

34. The _____ of a wing is the angle formed by the intersection of the wing chord line and the horizontal axis of the aircraft.

35. _____ is an increase in the angle of incidence of the wing from the root to the tip.

36. If a wing has an angle of incidence of 2° at the root and an angle of incidence of 3° at the outer end, it has a _____ of _____ .

37. _____ is a decreasing angle of incidence from the root to the tip of a wing.

38. Washin and washout are employed to give the wings on each side of an aircraft a slightly different amount of lift in order to aid in _____ the effect of engine and propeller torque.

39. Washing out a wing _____ the lift a wing produces.

40. Washing in a wing _____ the lift the wing produces.

41. If an airplane flies hands off, with the right wing low, the right wing can be _____ and the left wing can be _____ to correct this condition.

42. The information the technician must have for rigging the biplane includes _____ , _____ , _____ , and _____ .

43. _____ is the longitudinal difference in the positions of the leading edges of the wings of a biplane.

44. If the leading edge of the upper wing is ahead of the leading edge of the lower wing, the stagger is _____ .

45. _____ is the difference between the angles of incidence of the upper and lower wings.

46. If the upper wing has a greater angle of incidence than the lower wing, the decalage is said to be _____ .

47. The first step in rigging a biplane is to level the fuselage, which should be supported in a _____ or _____ .

48. If the fuselage is supported by means of the landing gear, the flexibility of the shock struts and tires will permit _____ , which is _____ desirable.

49. The three primary controls for an airplane are the _____ , _____ , and _____ .

50. The primary flight controls are responsible for maneuvering the aircraft about its _____ axes.

51. Ailerons are primary flight-control surfaces utilized to provide _____ of aircraft; that is, they control aircraft movement about the _____ axis.

52. Aileron control systems operated by the pilot through mechanical connections require the use of _____ so that the pilot can overcome the air loads imposed on the ailerons during flight.

53. Balancing ailerons can be achieved through _____ by extending part of the aileron structure ahead of the hinge line and shaping this area so the airstream strikes the extension and helps to move the surface, or by using _____ to place a weight ahead of the hinge line to counteract flight loads.

54. Transport category aircraft use _____ operated ailerons and may not employ these forms of balancing.

55. In many aircraft, the operation of ailerons causes the aircraft to _____ against the direction of the control movement.

56. _____ is caused when the aileron that moves downward creates lift and drag and the aileron that moves upward reduces lift and creates much less drag.

57. The rudder is the flight control surface that controls the aircraft movement about its _____ .

58. Rudders are usually balanced both statically and aerodynamically to provide for greater ease of operation and to eliminate the possibility of _____ .

59. Elevators are the control surfaces that govern the movement of the aircraft around the _____ axis.

60. The construction of an elevator is similar to that of other control surfaces, and the design of the elevator may be _____ or _____ aerodynamically and/or statically.

61. A _____ combines the function of a horizontal stabilizer and an elevator.

62. _____ are flight-control surfaces that serve the functions of the rudder and elevators.

63. When serving as elevators, the surfaces on each side of the ruddervator move in the _____ direction.

64. When serving as a rudder, the surfaces of a ruddervator move in _____ directions.

65. _____ are surfaces that combine the operation of flaps and ailerons.

66. The flaperon allows the area of the wing normally reserved for the aileron to be lowered and creates a _____ .

67. Tabs are small secondary flight-control surfaces set into the trailing edges of the _____ to _____; these reduce the work load required of the pilot to hold the aircraft in some constant attitude by ''loading'' the control surface in a position to maintain the desired attitude.

68. A fixed trim tab is normally a piece of sheet metal attached to the trailing edge of a control surface. This tab is adjusted on the ground by _____ it in the appropriate direction to eliminate cabin flight-control forces for a specific flight condition. The fixed tab is normally adjusted for _____ forces while in cruising flight.

69. Fixed tabs are normally found on light aircraft and are used to adjust _____ and _____ .

70. Controllable trim tabs are found on most aircraft with at least the _____ tab being controlled.

71. Controllable trim tabs are normally operated _____ by a cable and chain system, _____ by a screwjack mechanism or a motor to drive the cable and chain system, or _____ through actuators.

72. Servo tabs are used to aid the pilot in the operation of _____ .

73. When the pilot moves a primary flight control, a servo tab _____ in the proper direction to aid the pilot in moving the control surface.

74. An antiservo tab is used to aid the pilot in _____ to the neutral position and prevent it from moving to a full deflection position due to aerodynamic forces.

75. The antiservo tab often also serves as the _____ tab by allowing the pilot to adjust the _____ position.

76. A control tab is used on some transport aircraft as a manual backup to flight controls that are normally operated _____ .

77. The purpose of wing flaps is to change the _____ of the wing and in some cases to increase the area of the wing, thus permitting the aircraft to operate at lower flight speeds for landing and takeoff.

78. The _____ acts as if the trailing edge of the wing were deflected downward to change the camber of the wing, thus increasing both lift and drag.

79. The _____ , when retracted, forms the lower surface of the wing trailing edge; when extended, it provides an effect similar to that of the plain flap.

80. The _____ and others with similar operation are designed to increase substantially the wing area as the flap is extended.

81. A _____ is similar to a plain flap except that as the flap is extended, a gap develops between the wing and the flap.

82. The leading edge of the slotted flap is designed so that air entering this gap flows smoothly through the

_____ and aids in holding the airflow on the surface, increasing the lift of the wing with the

flap _____ .

83. The _____ , when retracted, forms the leading edge of the wing.

84. When extended, the leading-edge flap moves _____ and _____ to

_____ the camber of the wing and provide greater lift at low flight speeds.

85. Leading-edge fixed slots allow airflow to be directed over the top of the wing at _____ .

86. Leading-edge fixed slots _____ the stalling speed of the wing and

_____ aileron control when flying at high angles of attack.

87. The use of _____ on the leading edge of high-performance wings is a common method of reducing stalling speed and increasing lift at comparatively slow speeds.

88. The slat forms the leading edge of the wing when not extended and creates a _____ at the leading edge when extended.

89. _____ , also called lift dumpers, are control surfaces used to reduce, or ''spoil,'' the lift on a wing.

90. _____ are used in flight to reduce the amount of lift that the wing is generating to allow controlled descents without gaining excessive air speed.

91. _____ are only used when the aircraft is on the ground and are used along with the flight spoilers to greatly reduce the wing's lift upon landing.

92. Ground spoilers also increase the aerodynamic drag of the aircraft after landing to aid in

_____ the aircraft.

93. Speed brakes, also called divebreaks, are large _____ used to control the speed of aircraft.

94. If located on the wings, speed brakes are deployed _____ from the top and the bottom of the wing surface to control the speed of the aircraft as well as to act as spoilers to decrease the lift of the wings.

95. Components utilized in assembling a simple control system include: _____ ,

_____ , _____ , _____ ,

_____ , _____ , _____ ,

_____ , and _____ .

96. Aircraft control cables are generally fabricated from _____ or _____ wire and may consist of either flexible or nonflexible construction.

97. _____ are used in aircraft-control systems to change the direction of a cable.

98. _____ are commonly used for adjusting the tension of the control cables.

99. The _____ is used between bell cranks and from bell cranks to

_____ (''horns'') to transmit the force and motion from one to the other.

100. A _____ is used to transmit force and permit a change in the direction of the force.

101. A _____ serves the same purpose as a wheel; however, the quadrant moves through a relatively small arc, perhaps as much as 100°.

102. A _____ tube is a hollow shaft by which the linear motion of a cable or push-pull tube is changed to rotary motion.

103. _____ or _____ are installed in the flanges of pulley brackets.

104. A _____ serves as a guide to prevent wear and vibration of a cable.

105. In no case should a fairlead be permitted to deflect a cable more than _____ .

106. In a pressurized turbine aircraft, cables leading from a pressurized section of the airplane to a nonpressurized

section must have _____ installed where the cable passes through the bulkhead.

107. The basic guidelines for the installation and rigging of control surfaces for small aircraft include:

   a. _____ and place the airplane on _____ during the rigging and adjustment of controls.

   b. Remove turnbuckle barrels from cable ends _____ withdrawing cables through the structure.

   c. Tie a cord to the cable end before drawing the cable through the structures to facilitate the

   _____ of the cable.

   d. _____ all cable ends, etc., before disconnecting.

   e. When turnbuckles have been set to correct cable tension, no more than _____ should be exposed from either end of the turnbuckle barrel.

   f. Cable tension should be taken with the appropriate surface control in its _____ position.

   g. When the control system includes a bellcrank, pins are placed through the holes of the bellcrank to prevent it

   from moving, and the mechanism is then rigged to achieve a _____ control surface

   setting and a _____ cabin control position.

108. Among the objectives to be accomplished during the control surface rigging procedure are correct

_____ , balance or _____ between dual controls, synchronization of

the cockpit control with the _____ to which it is linked, and setting the

_____ of control surface movement.

109. The sequence of events for rigging a light aircraft is typically:

   a. Lock the cockpit controls in the _____ .

   b. _____ the cables and _____ cable _____ by means of the turnbuckle adjustment so that the bellcrank assemblies are in the neutral position.

   c. _____ and _____ the control surface travel range.

   d. _____ all turnbuckles.

   e. Remove neutral _____ .

110. Change in control cable tension will likely produce a change in control surface _____ .

111. Cable tension is measured by means of a _____ or cable-tension indicator.

112. Control surface travel may be measured by means of a _____ or a

_____ .

113. No cable splice or fitting can come within _____ of a fairlead, pulley, guide, cable guard, or other unit that could cause the control to jam.

114. After the airplane undergoes overhaul, painting, or repair of the control surfaces, the _____ may be altered to the extent that _____ will occur in flight.

115. During an inspection of a light aircraft's flight-control systems, examine all cables for _____ and/or _____ .

116. During an inspection of a light aircraft's flight-control systems, examine all pulleys for

_____ , _____ , and _____ .

117. During an inspection of a light aircraft's flight-control systems, where cables pass through fairleads or guides, the _____ of the cable should be noted.

118. During an inspection of a light aircraft's flight-control systems, wear of _____ ,

_____ , _____ , _____ , and all other moving parts should be checked.

119. During an inspection of a light aircraft's flight-control systems, control surface travel should be checked to verify that it corresponds to the _____ .

120. Upon completion of inspection, adjustment, and service, the control system should be given an

_____ .

121. The helicopter flight controls consist of the _____ , _____ , and

_____ .

122. The _____ operates the main rotor system swash plate, which tilts and causes the rotor blades to increase or decrease their blade angle at appropriate positions in the rotor plane of rotation. This causes the rotor to tilt and increase the rotor lift on one portion of the rotor disk and decrease the lift on the opposite portion of the disk.

123. The rotor tilts and causes the helicopter to move in the appropriate direction, left or right

_____ or forward or back _____ .

124. The tail rotor thrust is controlled by the pilot's foot pedal, called the _____ or

_____ .

125. As the pilot changes the power being delivered to the main rotor system or the amount of pitch in the main rotor blades, the _____ of the tail rotor blades is altered to maintain the

_____ .

126. The collective control lever controls the amount of lift being generated by the main rotor system. This causes all the blades to _____ their blade angle and lift when the control is pulled up and

_____ their blade angle and lift when it is moved down.

127. The three basic designs for the main rotor system are _____ , _____ , and _____ .

128. The fully articulated rotor system normally has three or more rotor blades and each blade can move by three different motions, _____ of the other blades in the system.

129. One motion of a blade in a fully articulated rotor system is called _____ ; it is allowed through the rotor blade flap hinge, located near the rotor hub, and causes the blade to rise and fall as it rotates around the hub.

130. The _____ motion of a blade in a fully articulated rotor system is through the drag hinge, which allows the blade to move ahead of (lead) or fall behind (lag) the normal axis of the hub extension.

131. In a fully articulated rotor system each blade is also free to rotate about its central axis, called _____ .

132. A _____ rotor system uses only two rotor blades.

133. The blades in a semirigid rotor system are rigidly attached to the _____ .

134. In a semirigid rotor system, a _____ hinge is used to connect the hub to the rotor shaft so that the blades can flap, one up and one down, and feather, one increasing pitch and one decreasing pitch, as a unit.

135. In a _____ rotor system the blades are not allowed to flap or drag, only _____ .

136. If the blades are not in track—that is, if each blade does not _____ , then a _____ vibration will exist during flight.

137. The conventional tail rotor counteracts _____ movement resulting from the torque effect of the engine-transmission–main rotor system.

138. During cruising flight and hovering changes in altitude, the tail rotor corrects for _____ or changes the _____ of the helicopter when it is in a hover.

139. The _____ control changes pitch on all blades of the main rotor simultaneously and controls the vertical flight of a helicopter.

140. The _____ system is employed to change the pitch or angle of the _____ through which the main rotor blades rotate.

141. The rotor disk is caused to tilt because the cyclic control changes the blades' pitch angles to _____ as the blades rotate through their paths of travel around the disk.

142. An upward force caused by increase of pitch on a blade at a point _____ the blade has passed the forward point of the helicopter will cause the rotor disk to tilt forward due to _____ .

143. When the cyclic control stick is moved forward, the up force on the rotor is applied at one side, and the rear of the disk _____ .

144. The direction in which a helicopter is pointed is controlled by the _____ .

145. The control system for the tail rotor changes the pitch of the rotor blades, thus changing the _____ exerted by the rotor.

146. _____ vibrations are less than one vibration cycle per revolution of the main rotor.

147. The extremely low vibration is controlled, primarily, by the design and _____ of the transmission.

148. _____ vibrations, 1/rev or 2/rev, are associated with the _____ and are of two basic types, _____ or _____ .

149. In a vertical vibration, the entire helicopter tends to move _____ , and in a lateral vibration one side of the helicopter moves _____ while the opposite side moves _____ , the movements occurring alternately in time with the vibration frequency.

150. Lateral vibrations due to an unbalance in the rotor are of two types: _____ and _____ .

151. Spanwise unbalance is caused by one blade and hub being _____ than the other.

152. A chordwise unbalance occurs when there is more weight toward the _____ of one blade than the other.

153. _____ frequencies of 4/rev or 6/rev are inherent vibrations associated with most rotors.

154. _____ vibrations can be caused by anything in the helicopter that vibrates or rotates at a speed equal to or greater than that of the tail rotor.

155. Tracking of a helicopter rotor simply means determining if one blade _____ the _____ or track of the other blade or blades as they rotate during operation.

156. The items required for analyzing the operation of a main rotor using a strobosopic light tracking technique are a _____ on the fixed swashplate, _____ on the rotating swashplate, _____ on the rotor blade tips, _____ on the airframe, a Strobex light, and the _____ , which includes the _____ .

157. The magnetic pickup consists of a _____ wound on a permanent magnet.

158. Electrical pulses from the magnetic pickup are used to trigger the _____ each time an _____ passes to provide light for viewing tip targets and observing the track and lead or lag of the blades.

159. The pulses also provide an _____ reference for the Phazor section of the balancer against which the accelerometer signal is measured to determine _____ .

160. An accelerometer generates an electrical signal representative of the _____ of the point to which it is attached, resulting in variances in the _____ (from plus to minus as the point vibrates back and forth) and the _____ of the signal, which is proportional to the amplitude of the vibration.

161. _____ material is self-adhesive tape with a coating that reflects light back to its source.

162. The _____ is the electronic circuitry that receives the signals from the _____ and _____ and then converts these inputs to readings that are transferred to the charts from which corrective information regarding the location and amount of weight required is obtained.

163. In the _____ method, a flag is positioned so that the main rotor blade tips, which are colored with grease pencils, will touch the flag, giving an indication of their _____ position.

164. There should be only _____ mark for each main rotor blade.

165. Colored tracking marks will be left on the flag for an indication of any out-of-track condition, which may be corrected by adjusting the _____ .

Chapter 12

Name _____

Date _____

MULTIPLE CHOICE QUESTIONS

1. The main load bearing member of a wing is (are) the
   a. rib.
   b. spar.
   c. strut.
   d. drag wires.

2. If there are no leveling points on an aircraft, leveling may be established by placing a level on
   a. the cabin overhead structure.
   b. a vertical structural member.
   c. any straight portion of the longeron.
   d. the longitudinal and lateral braces.

3. The angle of incidence may be measured by
   a. dropping a plumb bob from the leading edge of the wing and measuring back to the leading edge of the horizontal stabilizer.
   b. using a straightedge and a bubble protractor.
   c. using a steel tape.
   d. measuring the angle adjoining the wing fittings.

4. To rig the center section of a biplane the sequence is to check
   a. stagger, incidence, and symmetry.
   b. symmetry, stagger, and incidence.
   c. cable tension, angle of attachment, and symmetry.
   d. symmetry, stagger, and angle of attachment.

5. If an aircraft with fixed tabs flies right-wing heavy, the
   a. tab of the right wing should be bent down.
   b. tab of the left wing should be bent down.
   c. tab of the right wing should be bent up.
   d. right wing should be washed out.

6. An aircraft should be rigged to fly hands off at
   a. cruise speed.
   b. top speed.
   c. near stalling speed.
   d. slightly below cruise speed.

7. If the angle of incidence of one wing of a plane is altered, the aircraft will tend to
   a. yaw.
   b. pitch.
   c. buffet.
   d. spin flat.

8. The stabilizer may be checked for alignment by measuring from the
   a. front spar to the rear spar.
   b. center section.
   c. trailing edge.
   d. leading edge.

9. If the rudder pedals are set in an even position, the rudder is rigged
   a. to the neutral position.
   b. with both pedals moved slightly forward.
   c. slightly to the left to compensate for engine torque.
   d. slightly to the right to compensate for engine torque.

10. Washin and washout are accomplished by changing the
    a. angle of incidence.
    b. angle of dihedral.
    c. angle of stagger.
    d. angle of decalage.

11. The difference between a movable trim tab and a fixed balance tab is
    a. the balance tab is used on the rudder only to correct directional instability.
    b. the balance tab is used for correcting instabilities due to changes in flight conditions.
    c. a balance tab is attached rigid to any control surface and the trim tab is hinged at the trailing edge of any control surface.
    d. they have an opposite reaction on the control surface movement.

12. Control cable tension is checked by
    a. measuring the vibration cycles.
    b. measuring turnbuckle length.
    c. using a tensiometer.
    d. measuring the flutter frequency.

13. Medium-frequency helicopter vibration is caused by
    a. ground resonance.
    b. ground cushion.
    c. lateral beat of the main rotor.
    d. tail rotor rotation.

14. In flying a helicopter, horizontal flight and airspeed are controlled
    a. by throttle coordination only.
    b. by cyclic pitch and throttle.
    c. by collective pitch.
    d. by the continual use of the collective pitch and cyclic control.

15. The purpose of a flap is to
    a. increase drag and decrease airspeed in flight.
    b. increase drag and increase airspeed in flight.
    c. change the camber of the wing.
    d. rotate the aircraft around its lateral axis.

16. Slats on the leading edge of a wing
    a. increase the stall speed.
    b. decrease the stall speed.
    c. counteract aileron-induced yaw.
    d. counteract rudder-induced yaw.

17. A bellcrank is designed to
    a. change rotary motion to linear motion.
    b. multiply torque.
    c. permit a change in the direction of a force.
    d. automatically change an aircraft's pitchbell limits.

18. Fairleads must
    a. deflect control cables away from nongrounded components.
    b. improve the aerodynamic flow for antidrag wires.
    c. automatically increase the tension on drag wire.
    d. may not deflect a cable more than 3°.

19. All control surface travels must conform to
    a. the requirements of AC 43.13-1A & 2A.
    b. the aircraft's Type Certificate Data Sheet.
    c. FAR Part 147.
    d. All of the above.

20. When pins are properly located in their alignment hole, the control surfaces are typically rigged to
    a. their uppermost limit.
    b. their neutral position.
    c. their lowermost limit.
    d. halfway between the neutral position and the uppermost travel limit.

Chapter 13

STUDY QUESTIONS

1. Hydraulic and pneumatic systems in aircraft provide a means for the _____ of large aircraft _____ .

2. The majority of aircraft that have pneumatic systems use them only as _____ systems for the operation of hydraulic components when the hydraulic system has failed.

3. Among the uses of hydraulic systems in aerospace-vehicle systems are the operation of _____ and _____ , _____ , _____ , and a wide variety of other devices requiring _____ , _____ , and/or _____ .

4. _____ is the measurement of a surface.

5. _____ is the amount of push, pull, or twist on an object.

6. The force per unit area is called _____ and is measured in _____ or _____ .

7. _____ is a measurement of distance expressed in inches or centimeters, and it represents the distance a piston moves in a cylinder.

8. Volume, also called _____ , is a measure of quantity, expressed in cubic inches or liters.

9. A liquid is a fluid whose particles form a _____ volume.

10. _____ is used as the common name for the fluid used in aircraft hydraulic systems and devices.

11. In general, fluids _____ when they are heated and contract when they are _____ .

12. If a fluid is confined so that it cannot escape when it is heated, pressure on the walls of the confining vessel will _____ .

13. _____ equals pressure times area.

14. _____ equals force divided by area.

15. _____ equals force divided by pressure.

16. Liquids are regarded as being _____ , so the volume of a given quantity of a liquid will remain constant even though it is subjected to high pressure.

17. The _____ of the cylinder through which the piston moves is equal to the _____ of the piston head multiplied by the _____ of the cylinder.

18. A given output volume from a hydraulic pump will provide an _____ volume of fluid at the operating unit.

19. A basic principle of hydraulics is expressed in Pascal's law, which states that a confined hydraulic fluid exerts _____ pressure at _____ point and in _____ direction in the fluid.

20. One of the principal factors in liquid motion is the _____ that exists between the molecules of the liquid and between the liquid and the pipe through which it is flowing.

21. The rate of _____ can be determined by measuring the pressure differential on opposite sides of a given restrictor.

22. Fluid-flow gauges typically operate using _____ as liquid velocity through a _____ increases or decreases.

23. Friction in a moving liquid produces heat, and this heat represents a _____ in a hydraulic system.

24. Energy converted to heat must be _____ from the total energy of the moving liquid.

25. Through the use of hydraulics, force can be _____ to almost any degree by the proper application of hydraulic pressure.

26. The force developed by one piston driving another is _____ to the squares of the diameters.

27. Since energy cannot be created or destroyed, the multiplication of force is accomplished at the expense of _____ .

28. A _____ or _____ is necessary between the pump and the valve in order to relieve the pressure when the cylinder reaches the end of its travel.

29. There are three principal types of hydraulic fluids: _____ , _____ , and _____ .

30. Vegetable-base fluids are usually mixtures containing castor oil and alcohol and are colored _____ or _____ or are almost _____ .

31. Mineral-base fluids consist of a high-quality petroleum oil and are usually colored _____ and comply with MIL-0-_____ .

32. Mineral-base fluids are _____ and less damaging to certain parts than other types of fluid.

33. A mineral-base, synthetic hydrocarbon fluid called Braco 882 is used extensively by the military services in place of MIL-0-5606; it is _____ in color and meets the specifications of MIL-0-_____ .

34. Hydraulic fluids complying with MIL-O-83282 have the advantage of increased _____ and can be used in systems having the same types of seals, gaskets, hoses, etc., that are used with petroleum base MIL-0-5606.

35. The seals required for mineral-base fluid may be _____ , _____ , or _____ composition.

36. Phosphate ester–base fluids utilized in most transport category aircraft are _____ fire resistant but are _____ fireproof.

37. Typical examples of current Type _____ fluids are Skydrol LD-4 and Skydrol 500B-4.

38. Two distinct classes of Type IV hydraulic fluid exist. The class definition is according to the airframe manufacturer's hydraulic fluid specification: Class 1 is _____ and Class 2 is _____ .

39. Seals, gaskets, and hoses used with the phosphate ester–base fluids are made of _____ rubber or Teflon fluorocarbon resin.

40. When fire-resistant hydraulic fluid is spilled, it should immediately be removed and the area washed, because fire-resistant hydraulic fluid will _____ or _____ many types of paints, lacquers, and enamels.

41. In addition to any other instructions given in the airplane manufacturer's manual, the following should be observed in the use of hydraulic fluids.

   a. The filler cap or filler valve should be _____ with the _____

   _____ , so that it is immediately apparent to a technician what type of fluid should be added to the system.

   b. _____ , under any circumstances, service an airplane system with a type of fluid different from that shown on the instruction plate.

   c. Make certain that hydraulic fluids and fluid containers are protected from contamination of any kind. If there is any question regarding the cleanliness of the fluid, _____ .

   d. Never allow hydraulic fluids of different types to _____ .

   e. Do not expose fluids to high _____ or open _____ .

   f. Avoid contact with the fluids.

      (i) If skin contact occurs, wash the fluid off with _____ and

      _____ .

      (ii) For eye contact, flush well with _____ and, if a phosphate ester fluid is involved,

      apply an _____ eye solution.

      (iii) Reaction to _____ vapors (coughing and sneezing) stops after the vapor or mist is eliminated.

      (iv) For all cases of _____ contact and _____ of hydraulic fluids, consult a physician.

   g. Wear protective _____ and a _____ whenever handling phosphate

   ester fluids and whenever working around any hydraulic _____ .

42. A _____ is a tank or container designed to store sufficient hydraulic fluid for all conditions of operation.

43. When accumulators, actuating cylinders, and other units do not contain their maximum quantities of fluid, the

   unused fluid must be stored in the _____ .

44. Reservoirs in hydraulic systems that require a reserve of fluid for the emergency operation of landing gear, flaps,

   etc., are equipped with _____ .

45. During normal operation, fluid is drawn through the _____ . When system fluid is lost,

   emergency fluid is drawn from _____ .

46. Reservoirs can be broken down into two basic types, _____ and

   _____ , and these can be further classified as _____ and

   _____ .

47. Reservoirs are _____ designed to be completely filled; they must provide for an

   _____ above the fluid level to allow for _____ when it is heated during system operation.

48. The hydraulic fluid quantity-indicating method may be a _____ on the filler cap or a

   _____ to display the quantity on the aircraft flight deck.

49. In-line reservoirs are those that are _____ in the hydraulic system.

50. Unpressurized reservoirs are normally used in aircraft flying at _____ or in aircraft whose

   hydraulic systems are limited to use in _____ , such as brakes.

51. The most basic rule of hydraulics states that fluid cannot be _____; it can only be

_____ .

52. At higher altitudes, atmospheric pressure decreases, which allows the hydraulic fluid to

_____ and causes _____ to form in the low part of the system.

53. Aircraft that fly at higher altitudes can provide a continuous supply of fluid to the pumps because the hydraulic

reservoir is _____ .

54. Along with providing a _____ to the hydraulic pumps, a pressurized reservoir reduces or

eliminates the _____ of the fluid when it returns to the reservoir.

55. The reservoir may be pressurized by _____ , _____ , or

_____ .

56. The desired pressure to be maintained ranges from approximately _____ psi to

_____ psi.

57. When air pressure is used to pressurize a reservoir, _____ air or a

_____ are the typical sources of pressurized air.

58. When more than one source of air or hydraulic pressure is used to support a single system, a

_____ is used.

59. A _____ , usually located below the relief-and-bleed valve in the upper portion of the
diaphragm-guide cylinder above the main portion of the reservoir, provides an indication of excessive accumulation
of air in the reservoir.

60. The _____ valve relieves excessive reservoir pressure and bleeds off excessive accumulated
system air.

61. An _____ allows the upper, ambient air section of the reservoir to breathe air in and out as
the reservoir diaphragm lowers and raises with pressurization of the hydraulic system and operation of the various
subsystem actuators.

62. A filter screen removes _____ from the air that enter the upper portion of the reservoir.

63. Internally, the reservoir is equipped with a piston and diaphragm assembly that utilizes system pressure from the

small pressure-line port to maintain a _____ on the supply fluid.

64. Integral reservoirs are _____ with the hydraulic pump.

65. A _____ opens to allow fluid to bypass the filter element and flow directly from the return
portion of the hydraulic fluid tank to the supply portion.

66. Hydraulic filters are required to filter out any _____ that may enter the hydraulic fluid.

67. Particles may enter the hydraulic fluid system when it is being serviced or during _____ .

68. Filters in a hydraulic system are normally found at the _____ and

_____ of the _____ and the _____ .

69. A _____ contains a treated paper element to trap particles in the fluid as the fluid flows
through the element.

70. _____ are composed of metal particles joined together by a sintering process.

71. Most hydraulic filter assemblies are located in the _____ and _____
lines.

72. A _____ in the filter prevents the system from becoming inoperative should the filter become
clogged.

73. Many filters incorporate a "pop-out" differential pressure indicator to allow ready identification of a

_____ .

74. The typical filter bowl assembly is mounted on the bottom of the head assembly and is sealed with an

_____ .

75. When filters are serviced, all _____ should be removed from the hydraulic system.

76. The old element can be opened to check for _____ .

77. If the contamination indicator pin has popped out, then the fluid and filters _____ from the filter must be checked for contamination and the system flushed if required.

78. A _____ cools the heated hydraulic fluid.

79. The heat exchanger is equipped with a temperature-operated bypass valve to increase the fluid flow through the

cooling element as the fluid _____ .

80. Heat exchangers are often installed in the _____ to cool the hydraulic fluid before it enters the reservoir.

81. The heat exchangers for some aircraft are installed in fuel cells and cool the hydraulic fluid by

_____ the heat of the fluid to the fuel.

82. Hydraulic fluids may also be cooled with _____ in flight and _____ when the airplane is on the ground.

83. The temperature-operated bypass valve in the hydraulic cooler fluid inlet controls the _____ of return fluid circulating through the fluid cooler.

84. As fluid temperatures rise, the bypass valve starts to close, porting return fluid through the

_____ .

85. _____ are designed to provide fluid flow.

86. When the handle of a single-acting hand pump is moved, the piston movement creates a low-pressure condition and

draws fluid from the _____ through the _____ and into the

_____ .

87. The check valves allow the fluid in a single-acting hand pump to flow only in _____ .

88. Another type of hand pump is the double-acting _____ hand pump.

89. A _____ pump will deliver a _____ volume of fluid, provided the pump is not worn and no leakage occurs.

90. One of the two gears of a _____ pump is driven by the power source, which could be an engine drive or an electric-motor drive.

91. The _____ pump is classed as a _____ pump because of its positive action in moving fluid.

92. Since the rotor of a vane-type pump is eccentric with respect to the casing, the vanes form chambers that increase

and decrease in _____ as the rotor turns.

93. A _____ consists of a housing containing an eccentric-shaped stationary liner, an internal gear rotor having five wide teeth of short height, a spur driving gear having four narrow teeth, and a pump cover that contains two crescent-shaped openings.

94. One of the most widely used hydraulic pumps for modern aircraft is the _____ pump.

95. In an axial multiple-piston pump, the axis of rotation for the cylinder block is _____ to the axis of rotation of the drive shaft; therefore, the pistons are caused to move in and out of the cylinders as rotation occurs.

96. The valve plate of an axial multiple-piston pump is made with two slots such that one slot is bearing against the _____ on which the pistons are moving away from the valving surface; the other slot is bearing against the side on which the pistons are moving _____ the valving surface.

97. In the axial multiple-piston pump valve plate, the slots in the valving surface are connected to _____ and _____ chambers to provide fluid feed to the pistons on the inlet side and an outlet for the pressure fluid on the other side.

98. _____ means that the pump will normally deliver a fixed amount of fluid at a given number of revolutions per minute.

99. A variable-delivery pump is designed so the alignment of the rotational axis of the cylinder block can be changed as desired to vary the _____ of fluid being delivered at a given rpm.

100. By changing the angle of the rotational axis on a variable-delivery pump, the stroke of the pistons is decreased or increased; therefore, the volume of fluid pumped during each _____ of the pistons is reduced or increased.

101. A _____ pump operates on the principle of the multiple-piston pumps described except that the drive shaft axis is _____ to the pistons.

102. In a _____ pump, the movement of the pistons necessary to create a pumping action is caused by a cam or _____ .

103. The output of a variable-displacement pump is determined by the _____ of a cam plate, which rotates to produce a reciprocating action of the pump pistons.

104. The cam-plate angle of a _____ pump is changed by varying the position of the _____ upon which it is mounted.

105. To protect the engine-driven pump and hydraulic system, pumps are provided with a shear section on the drive shaft so that if the pump seizes or is prevented from rotating, the shaft will _____ and _____ .

106. A method used on many turbine transport-category aircraft in the event of engine and electrical system failure is the utilization of a _____ to power a pump.

107. A ram air turbine installation typically consists of an air turbine, a _____-governing device, and a _____ .

108. Numerous devices have been designed to control pressure in hydraulic systems; among these are _____ , _____ , _____ , and _____ .

109. Electrically operated pressure switches are used in hydraulic systems with electrically driven pumps to maintain _____ pressure within _____ .

110. The Bourdon-tube type pressure switch is frequently used to control _____ within a hydraulic system.

111. A pressure regulator is designed to maintain a certain _____ of pressures within a hydraulic system.

112. Some pressure regulators are also called _____ , because they unload the pump when hydraulic pressure is not required for operation of landing gear, flaps, or other subsystems.

113. The function of a _____ is to limit the maximum pressure that can be developed in a hydraulic system.

114. During operation, the relief valve remains closed unless the system pressure _____ that for which the valve is adjusted.

115. When a relief valve opens, it allows the fluid to flow through a _____ to the _____ .

116. When several relief valves are incorporated in a hydraulic system, the _____ valves should be adjusted first, the others in the order of _____ pressure values.

117. A _____ valve is similar to a regular system relief valve but is installed where fluid may be _____ and may need to be relieved because of the increased pressure caused by _____ .

118. Thermal relief valves are adjusted to pressures that are _____ those required for the operation of the systems.

119. A _____ valve is a _____ valve used in an aircraft brake system to reduce system pressure; in addition to reducing pressure it will provide for a _____ volume of fluid flow to the brakes for rapid application of braking forces.

120. To determine the value of a _____ produced by pressure that acts on a given area, multiply the _____ by the _____ of the _____ to the pressure.

121. To find the volume of fluid delivered per stroke required to move a piston within a cylinder or the amount of fluid exhausted, the _____ of the piston is multiplied by the _____ or the distance through which the piston _____ as it discharges fluid.

122. A debooster valve operates by the _____ of two pistons.

123. In a debooster valve, if a small-area piston is connected by a rod to a large-area piston, the two pistons will be capable of developing pressure in _____ to their areas.

124. An _____ is basically a chamber for storing hydraulic fluid under pressure.

125. An accumulator can _____ pressure surges caused by the operation of an actuator, _____ the system pump when several units are operating at the same time when the demand is beyond the pump's capacity, _____ for limited operation of a component if the pump is not operating, and _____ fluid under pressure to make up for small system leaks that would cause the system to cycle continuously between high and low pressure.

126. Accumulators are divided into _____ types according to the means used to _____ the air and fluid chambers.

127. The three types of accumulators are _____ , _____ and _____ .

128. In a diaphragm-type accumulator, _____ or an _____ is used to provide sustained pressure on the fluid for energy storage.

129. In the typical accumulator a volume of compressed air is applied to a volume of fluid so the fluid will be _____ .

130. During operation of the accumulator, the air chamber is _____ , or _____ , with air pressure.

131. The charge of an accumulator is typically _____ maximum system pressure.

132. As soon as a _____ amount of fluid is forced into the fluid side of the accumulator, the system _____ will show the pressure in the _____ .

133. Some aircraft hydraulic systems monitor the hydraulic pressure by indicating the pressure on the _____ of the accumulator.

134. If the aircraft's hydraulic systems monitor the hydraulic pressure by indicating the pressure on the air side of the accumulator, then when the system has no hydraulic pressure, the gauge for the system indicates the _____ .

135. If the aircraft's hydraulic systems monitor the hydraulic pressure by indicating the pressure on the air side of the accumulator, as soon as the hydraulic pressure is greater than the air charge, the air is compressed to the value of the _____ .

136. The _____ usually consists of a metal sphere in which a bladder is installed to separate the _____ and the _____ .

137. The bladder serves as the _____ , and the space _____ the bladder contains the hydraulic fluid.

138. When fluid is forced into a charged bladder-type accumulator, the bladder _____ to the extent necessary to make space for the fluid, depending upon the fluid pressure.

139. Many modern hydraulic systems employ piston-type accumulators because they require _____ than an equivalent spherical accumulator.

140. If the accumulator must be charged, system _____ is _____ from the system _____ the accumulator is charged.

141. _____ is a commonly used gas to charge accumulators, but _____ may also be used in some cases.

142. _____ an accumulator or any other unit is removed, the technician must make certain that _____ the pressure in the system has been _____ .

143. If hydraulic fluid is found in the air chamber of an accumulator, there is a _____ between the two chambers.

144. _____ are used to direct the flow of hydraulic fluid to or from a component and achieve the desired operation.

145. Selector valves fall into one of four general types: _____ , _____ , _____ or _____ , and _____ selector valves.

146. The selector valves may be positioned by the pilot _____ , by an _____ , by _____ , or by _____ .

147. When a rotary valve is rotated 90°, the fluid to and from the actuating cylinder will be in the _____ direction.

148. Individual _____ are used to open and close the ports to change the direction of fluid flow.

149. The _____ valve directs hydraulic fluid under pressure to one end of an actuating cylinder and simultaneously directs fluid from the opposite end of the actuating cylinder to the return line.

150. The advantage of an open-center selector valve is that the valve _____ returns to neutral when the actuating cylinder reaches the end of its stroke.

151. In an open-center selector valve, the fluid output of the power pump is directed through this valve to the _____ when the valve is in neutral position.

152. An _____ valve is one that is designed to operate without being positioned or activated by any force outside of the hydraulic fluid pressure or flow.

153. Automatic-operating control valves are located in line with the system flow and function to perform operations such as _____ or _____ flow in a line, allow flow at the proper time, and change control of components between independent pressure systems.

154. An _____ is merely an opening, passage, or hole.

155. A _____ can be described as an orifice or similar to an orifice.

156. A _____ is an orifice that can be changed in size so its effect can be altered.

157. The purpose of an orifice, or a variable restrictor, is to limit the _____ of the fluid in a hydraulic line.

158. In limiting the rate of flow, the orifice causes the mechanism being operated by the system to move _____ .

159. A _____ is often necessary to prevent hydraulic fluid flow in one direction while permitting free flow in the opposite direction.

160. During the installation of a check valve, the technician must observe the _____ indicated on the body of the valve.

161. Usually there is an _____ on the body or case of the valve to show the direction of the free fluid flow.

162. An _____ is designed to provide free flow of hydraulic fluid in one direction and restricted flow in the opposite direction.

163. A _____ , or one-way restrictor, serves the same purpose as an orifice check valve.

164. The metering check valve is _____ , whereas an orifice check valve is _____ .

165. The hydraulic fuse permits normal flow in a line; but if the flow increases above an established level, the valve in the fuse closes the line and _____ .

166. A _____ is sometimes called a _____ because it times certain hydraulic operations in proper sequence.

167. A shuttle valve in hydraulic systems provides an _____ or _____ source of power with which to operate critical parts in the system.

168. A _____ is a sequence valve that is operated by hydraulic pressure rather than by a mechanical means and gives one component priority over another component in _____ operations.

169. The hydraulic _____ is a unit that hydraulically synchronizes the movement of two actuating cylinders.

170. The flow equalizer divides a single stream of fluid from the selector valve into _____ streams, causing each cylinder to receive the same rate of flow, and both to move in unison.

171. The flow equalizer also combines two streams of fluid at an equal rate; therefore, it synchronizes the actuating cylinders in _____ .

172. Since the flow equalizer unit equally divides the combined flow, it is said to be _____ .

173. The flow equalizer is actually two _____ valves joined together with check-valve features to provide for _____ .

174. Hydraulic actuators are devices for converting hydraulic pressure to _____ .

175. The most commonly utilized actuator is the _____ ; however, servo actuators and hydraulic motors are also employed for special applications where modified motion is required.

176. Actuating cylinders are used for _____ and _____ movement such as retracting and extending landing gear and the extension and retraction of wing flaps, spoilers, and slats.

177. Servo actuators are used when accurately controlled _____ of units are required.

178. The servo unit _____ position information to the pilot's control, thus making it possible for the pilot to select any control position required.

179. Servo units are also used to aid the pilot in the operation of _____ and _____ pitch controls in a helicopter.

180. The single-acting cylinder has pressure applied to one side of the piston to provide force in _____ only.

181. When hydraulic pressure is removed from the piston in a single-acting cylinder, a _____ moves the piston to its start position.

182. A _____ actuating cylinder is designed so hydraulic pressure can be applied to both sides of the piston.

183. The _____ actuator allows the hydraulically operated mechanism to be locked in one of the extreme positions without the use of an external locking device.

184. Servo actuators usually include _____ , _____ , _____ , and _____ valves together with connecting linkages.

185. The rpm of the hydraulic motor depends upon hydraulic fluid _____ and the _____ on the motor.

186. A hydraulic motor has the advantage over an electric motor of being able to operate through a wide range of speeds from 0 rpm to the maximum for the particular motor _____ loss of efficiency as speed decreases.

187. The purpose of hydraulic packing rings and seals is to _____ of the hydraulic fluid.

188. Seals used in hydraulic and pneumatic systems and components are of two general classes, _____ and _____ .

189. Packing rings are used to provide a seal _____ of a unit that move in relation to each other.

190. The gasket is used as a seal between _____ .

191. Typical shapes for hydraulic packing rings, seals, and gaskets include the standard _____ , _____ , _____ , and _____ .

192. The O-ring seal is probably the most common type used for sealing pistons and rods because it is effective in _____ .

193. O-rings have either a series of _____ arranged clockwise or a _____ around the outer circumference.

194. The first dot or the stripe used in O-ring coding (reading in a clockwise direction) indicates the _____ in which the O-ring is used. Red indicates use in the _____ . Blue indicates use in _____ and _____ systems. Yellow indicates use in _____ . A _____ dot appearing first indicates a nonstandard seal and the second dot then indicates the system.

195. A white dash with a yellow dot 90° from the dash indicates a system using _____ .

196. Always install _____ O-rings with each disassembly.

197. Do _____ use old O-rings that have been in service.

198. The O-ring must be the _____ and _____ defects such as cuts, nicks, or other flaws.

199. The seal and O-ring groove must be lubricated freely with the _____ of hydraulic fluid that is used in the system unless otherwise specified in the repair manual.

200. Care must be exercised when installing O-rings to prevent scratching or cutting the seal on _____ or _____ .

201. Make certain that the O-ring is not installed in a _____ .

202. The O-ring seal should not be _____ in a system where the pressure is greater than _____ .

203. When the O-ring is used in higher-pressure systems, _____ are installed.

204. If pressure is exerted on the O-ring seal in one direction only, the backup ring should be placed on the side _____ .

205. If V-shaped or U-shaped seals are used and pressure is alternately applied, first in one direction and then in the other, _____ are required because this type of seal works effectively in only one direction.

206. The general procedure to follow in installing V-shaped or U-shaped seals is as follows:

   a. Install _____ .

   b. Use _____ to protect the packing rings if the packing crosses sharp edges or threads; after the packing is installed, the shim stock is removed.

   c. If the unit in which the packing is being installed does not have an _____ , insert metal shims of graduated thickness behind the adapters to hold the packing securely in place.

   d. If the unit in which the packing is being installed has an adjustable packing gland, adjust the gland nut until the V-ring stack is held together _____ ; then _____ the gland nut to the first lock point.

   e. Whenever possible, the technician should check the unit _____ for free operation after installation before the hydraulic pressure is applied.

   f. In all cases, the technician should consult _____ regarding the installation of seals.

207. The _____ of an aircraft's hydraulic system provides for fluid _____ , regulates and _____ , and _____ to the various selector valves in the system.

208. The _____ or subsystems of an aircraft hydraulic system are the sections containing the various _____ .

209. The power section of an aircraft hydraulic system may either be an _____ or _____ system using an engine-driven pump or a pump driven by an electric motor.

210. Pressure developed by the pump in an open system is controlled by one of the following three valves; an _____ , a _____ , or a _____ .

211. All three types of open system valves are automatically shifted by hydraulic pressure to the _____ after the units have been actuated.

212. All three valves employ _____ or _____ features to prevent them from shifting to "bypass" too soon, which would result in a loss of fluid flow and pressure to the units before the hydraulic cycle has been completed.

213. When the power valve, pump-control valve, or the open-center valve is in the _____ position, the pump is said to be idling under no load and with little power-input requirement.

214. In a closed system the pressure developed by the engine-driven or electric motor–driven power pump may be regulated by a _____, by a _____, or by a _____.

215. The closed system will always have fluid stored _____ whenever the power pump is operating.

216. In a closed system, after the hydraulic pressure is built up to a predetermined value, the load is automatically _____ from the pump by an unloading valve called the _____ or the _____ of the pump; the pump is then allowed to _____ when no units are in operation and until there is further demand upon the system.

217. An _____ is one having fluid flow but no appreciable pressure in the system whenever the actuating mechanisms are idle.

218. A _____ valve or a _____ valve is placed in a line that goes directly from the pump to the reservoir. When closed, these valves _____ the flow to the reservoir and _____ the flow to a two-position valve and then to the actuating unit(s) requiring the pressure.

219. Open systems develop no pressure except when a mechanism is being _____ ; a _____ limits the maximum pressure of the system.

220. A disadvantage of the open-center system is that the operation of _____ at a time is possible without interference from other systems.

221. A _____ is one that directs fluid flow to the main system manifold and builds up pressure in that portion of the system that leads to all the selector valves.

222. There are two basic types of closed systems: one has a _____ pump and a pressure regulator to control the pressure at a working range and to "unload" the pump when there is no flow requirement and pressure builds up in the system manifold; the second closed system utilizes a _____ and directs the flow to the system manifold, similar to the constant volume system.

223. System pressure is always maintained between the kick-out and kick-in settings of the regulator when the actuating mechanisms are _____ .

224. Multiple power pumps may supply the same system by combining their volume output into a common pressure _____ .

225. The _____ assembly is a modular unit that includes the reservoir, relief valve, hand pump, landing-gear selector valve, wing-flap selector valve, filters, and numerous other small parts essential to the operation.

226. The advantage of high-pressure hydraulic power systems (as in the Boeing 727) is that they can deliver _____ for a given weight of fluid and system components than can the lower-pressure systems.

227. The Boeing 727 incorporates _____ and independent hydraulic power systems.

228. In a Boeing 727 a _____ is used in each of the systems to combine a number of the smaller system components in one case to simplify maintenance.

229. The Boeing 727 has one heat exchanger installed in each engine-driven pump-case drain _____ .

230. The L-1011 hydraulics are arranged in four _____ , _____ , _____ operating systems; each are independent for maximum flight-control safety and performance.

231. The L-1011 has _____ hydraulic pumps in the hydraulic system, including _____ , _____ , _____ , _____ , and _____ .

232. In the L-1011, _____ hydraulic system(s) is (are) sufficient to operate all flight controls.

233. The hydraulic power systems on the Bell 214ST helicopter consist of _____ separate and independent systems: _____ flight-control hydraulic systems, and one _____ hydraulic system.

234. On the Bell 214ST helicopter, the two flight-control systems operate in _____ so that if either system should fail, the remaining system will provide full control capabilities.

235. The Bell 214ST helicopter pneumatic systems are primarily used as an emergency source of _____ for many of the hydraulically actuated subsystems.

236. The principle of operation for a pneumatic power system is the same as that of a hydraulic power system, except that the air in a pneumatic system is _____ and can reduce _____ from the maximum system pressure to zero pressure.

237. The entire pneumatic system, including the air-storage bottles, can act to _____ air pressure.

238. The air in a pneumatic system is kept clean from moisture and oil droplets or vapor by means of _____ , _____ , and/or _____ incorporated in the systems.

239. _____ in a pneumatic system may freeze in the low temperatures encountered at high altitudes, resulting in serious system malfunctions.

240. Another important feature of a pneumatic system is that there is no need for _____ .

241. Air for the pneumatic operation of controls can be provided by an _____ or _____ .

242. Air-storage bottles are used for _____ operations when hydraulic or pneumatic pressure sources have been lost.

243. The bottles are normally pressurized with _____ , but some aircraft require the use of _____ .

244. Aircraft that use the pneumatic system only for emergency purposes have the storage bottles equipped with a _____ valve for ground servicing and a _____ to release pressure into the system being controlled.

245. When servicing a hydraulic reservoir, the technician must make certain to use the _____ .

246. Hydraulic fluid type can be identified by _____ and _____ .

247. Fluid containers should always be _____ except when fluid is being removed.

248. Funnels and containers employed in filling the hydraulic reservoir must be _____ and free of dust and lint.

249. When a system has lost a substantial amount of fluid and air has entered the system, it is necessary to _____ , _____ , and then add fluid to the _____ mark on the reservoir.

250. _____ in a system causes a variety of sounds including banging, squealing, and chattering.

251. When inspection of hydraulic filters indicates that the fluid is contaminated, _____ the system is necessary.

252. Tubing must not be nicked, cut, dented, collapsed, or twisted beyond _____ .

253. The identification markings or lines on flexible hose will show whether the hose has been _____ .

254. All connections and fittings associated with moving units should be examined for _____ evidencing wear.

255. Accumulators should be checked for _____ , air or gas _____ , and _____ .

256. Lack of pressure in a system can be caused by a _____ , _____ , _____ or _____ stuck in the "kicked out" position, _____ _____ , _____ , or any condition that permits free flow back to the reservoir or overboard.

257. If a system fails to _____ in the pressure section, the likely cause is the pressure regulator or unloading valve, a leaking relief valve, or a leaking check valve.

258. If the pump fails to keep pressure up during operation of the subsystem, the pump may be _____ , or one of the pressure-control units may be _____ .

259. High pressure in a system may be caused by a defective or improperly adjusted _____ or _____ or by an _____ in a line or control unit.

260. During the process of removing and reinstalling flexible hose sections, the technician should make no effort to _____ or _____ the shape of the hose.

261. When it is necessary to replace metal tubing, the old section of tubing can be used as a _____ or pattern for forming the new part.

262. During maintenance, all openings in hydraulic and pneumatic systems should be _____ or _____ to prevent contamination of the system.

263. Too much torque applied to nuts and fittings will damage metal and _____ , and too little torque will result in _____ and _____ .

Chapter 13

Name _____

Date _____

APPLICATION QUESTIONS

1. A hydraulic pump is regulated to produce 60 psi. The hydraulic line from the pump to a flap actuator has a 1/2-in inside diameter and is 20 ft long to the actuator. The flap actuator has a piston of 2 in². Assume the piston in the cylinder moves 2 in:

   a. How much fluid is required for the actuator to travel its full stroke?

   b. What force would be exerted on the flap?

2. A hydraulic jack is used to raise a 5000-lb aircraft 6 in off the ground (ignore strut oleo extension). The hand pump on the jack has a diameter of 2 in with a stroke of 2 in and the jack piston is 12 in in diameter and has the capability of a 10-in stroke. Once the pump is primed, how many strokes must the technican apply to the hand pump and with what force?

3. An aircraft equipped with a simple hydraulic braking system (similar to that shown in Fig. 13–8 of the text) has a master cylinder with a 1-in-diameter piston and two double-action brake cylinders (one for each wheel) with 1.5-in-diameter pistons. If the pilot exerts 30 lb of pressure to the master cylinder, what force is exerted to the brakes?

Chapter 13

Name _____

Date _____

1. The ability of a hydraulic fluid to multiply force is based upon
   a. Newton's law.
   b. Pascal's law.
   c. the first law of thermodynamics.
   d. Hooke's law.

2. MIL-O-5606 is a
   a. vegetable-based hydraulic fluid.
   b. mineral-based hydraulic fluid.
   c. phosphate ester–based hydraulic fluid.
   d. polycarbon-based hydraulic fluid.

3. Check valves
   a. are used to ensure that the correct type of fluid is being added to the hydraulic system.
   b. multiply the system pressure once a minimum pressure is attained.
   c. allow the fluid to flow in one direction only.
   d. reverse the fluid flow if the system pressure begins to drop.

4. Hydraulic pressure is expressed in terms of
   a. feet per minute.
   b. foot-pounds.
   c. pounds per square inch.
   d. multiple pounds per square inch.

5. The two primary variables related to the operation of a hydraulic system are
   a. pressure and volume.
   b. temperature and pressure.
   c. cavitation and pressure.
   d. pressure and temperature.

6. The primary function of a pressure regulator is to
   a. increase the pressure to a minimum valve.
   b. maintain the system pressure with a specified range of pressures.
   c. increase the hydraulic multiple from 3 to more than 10.
   d. activate system components in a given sequence.

7. The unloading function often performed by a pressure regulator
   a. automatically lowers the cabin and cargo compartment doors when the electrical signal is given from the cockpit (and verified by ground personnel).

   b. removes all fluids from the hydraulic lines associated with the portions of the system not in active use.
   c. redirects the hydraulic fluid no longer required to perform work directly to the hydraulic reservoir, relieving back pressure on the pump(s).
   d. decreases the hydraulic multiple from a boosted level back to a factor of one.

8. Relief valves
   a. direct unused force from inactivated portions of the hydraulic system to portions of the system doing work (provides work relief).
   b. automatically cycles the pump duties of multiple pump systems from one pump to another, providing the pump relief from its normal duties.
   c. acts to limit the maximum pressure in the hydraulic system.
   d. boosts pressures applied manually to assist the flight crews in activating a component operation system (relieving the flight crew from having to generate all the operating pressure).

9. Pressure-reducing valves
   a. drop the system pressure of all secondary control systems to zero in the case of an emergency.
   b. may operate by redirecting some hydraulic force back to the reservoir or by reversing the hydraulic multiplier principles.
   c. lower the density of the hydraulic fluid being used with a corresponding reduction in pressure.
   d. restrict the flow of a hydraulic line, thereby reducing the hydraulic pressure in the line.

10. Accumulators
    a. store hydraulic fluid under pressure.
    b. remove the natural contaminants in a hydraulic fluid and accumulate and store them in a single location.
    c. receive all the accumulated unused pressure in the hydraulic system.
    d. direct the accumulated pressure of the system to a pressure reservoir.

11. All accumulators, regardless of their type, store energy by
    a. heating the fluids to a predetermined temperature.
    b. compressing gases.
    c. compressing fluids.
    d. increasing the capacity of the hydraulic system.

12. Selector valves are positioned in such a manner as to
    a. limit the travel of manual components so that they do not interfere with the operation of hydraulic components.
    b. require that the pilot select only one hydraulic pump to provide system power.
    c. ensure the most efficient operation of a hydraulic system by measuring the effect of components and directing flow to the most efficient of those available.
    d. direct the flow to or from a component.

13. Ensuring that the hydraulically operated landing-gear doors open before a hydraulically operated landing gear extends is a function of
    a. a sequencing valve.
    b. a hydraulic fuse.
    c. an orifice.
    d. an actuator.

14. To ensure that one operation is totally completed before another operation is started, you would install a
    a. deviation diverter.
    b. bellcrank actuator.
    c. variable orifice.
    d. priority valve

15. To maintain flight stability the flaps must be extended and retracted symmetrically (the configuration at any time between the left and right wings must be the same). In a hydraulically operated flap system, this is ensured by the installation of
    a. a sequencing valve.
    b. an equalizer valve.
    c. internal-locking actuators.
    d. servos.

16. If a hydraulic subsystem is designed to both extend and retract a particular component, to save weight a design engineer would first consider the use of a
    a. servo actuator.
    b. variable-displacement actuator.
    c. single-acting actuator.
    d. double-acting actuator.

17. Hydraulic seals are generally classified into two groupings:
    a. pressure-activated seals that expand when pressure is applied and pressure-activating seals that generate additional pressure in the system.
    b. pressure-activating seals that expand when pressure is applied and pressure-activated seals that generate additional pressure in the system.
    c. packings that are used when the sealed parts move in direct relation to one another and gaskets that seal stationary parts.
    d. gaskets that are used when the sealed parts move in direct relation to one another and packings that seal stationary parts.

18. If seals are used in a double-acting actuator of a high-pressure system, the seal must have
    a. a backup ring on the extension cycle side of the O-ring.
    b. a backup ring on the retraction cycle side of the O-ring.
    c. backup rings on both sides of the O-ring.
    d. multidirectional O-rings installed on the extension side of the piston only.

19. The primary difference between a hydraulic system and a pneumatic system is the
    a. weight of the entire system.
    b. necessity for a tight system design.
    c. medium through which force is transferred.
    d. All pneumatic systems must be closed systems and all hydraulic systems must be open systems.

20. When removing an accumulator from a hydraulic system
    (1) the system hydraulic system pressure should be relieved.
    (2) the accumulator's preload should be discharged.
    (3) when discharging an accumulator's preload, if hydraulic fluid is present the accumulator is faulty.
    (4) all hydraulic fluid must be replaced to avoid certain contamination.
    Regarding the above statements,
    a. All the statements are true.
    b. Only statement 2 is false.
    c. Only statement 3 is false.
    d. Only statement 4 is false.

Chapter 14

1. The majority of aircraft are equipped with landing gear that can be classified as either _____ or _____ .

2. Tricycle landing gear is characterized by having a _____ assembly and two _____ assemblies.

3. _____ aircraft have two main wheel assemblies, one on each side of the aircraft, and a tail wheel.

4. The landing gear supports the airplane during ground operations, _____ when the airplane is being taxied or towed, and _____ .

5. The main landing gear provides the _____ support of the airplane on land or water.

6. The auxiliary landing gear consists of _____ or _____ landing-wheel installations, skids, and outboard pontoons.

7. Nonabsorbing landing gear includes those types of landing gear that do not _____ the energy of the aircraft contacting the ground during landing but only temporarily store the energy and quickly return it to the aircraft. These types of gear include rigid landing gear, shock-cord landing gear, and spring-type gear.

8. A _____ is commonly found on helicopters and sailplanes and is mounted to the aircraft with no specific component to cushion the ground contact other than through the flexing of the landing gear or airframe structure.

9. When rubber _____ is used, the landing-gear struts are usually made of steel tubing mounted in such a manner that a stretching action is applied to tightly wound rubber cord. When landing shock occurs, the cord is stretched, thus storing the impact energy of landing.

10. The landing-gear struts for some aircraft consist of single, tapered strips or tubes of strong _____ or _____ .

11. Both the spring-oleo strut and the air-oleo strut use fluid _____ as their energy absorbing medium during landing, but on the ground the spring-oleo strut's spring supports the aircraft weight on the ground and during taxiing, whereas an air-oleo strut supports the aircraft with the air in the landing-gear struts.

12. Nonretractable (fixed) landing gear is generally attached to _____ of the airplane with _____ .

13. The retraction of landing gear is normally accomplished with _____ or _____ power.

14. _____ airplanes have _____ or a _____ for operating on water and retractable wheels for land operation.

15. On a conventional ski landing-gear system, skis replace the _____ on the axle.

16. The ski is designed to mount on the aircraft _____ the tire.

17. Retractable wheel-ski arrangements have the ski mounted on a _____ axle with the wheel.

18. The _____ is the portion of the landing-gear assembly attached to the airframe.

19. The _____ is the vertical member of the landing-gear assembly that contains the shock-absorbing mechanism.

20. The strut is also called the _____ .

21. The _____ is the moving portion of the air-oleo shock absorber.

22. The _____ releases when the weight is off the landing-gear strut to allow the strut to extend.

23. The _____ restricts the flow of fluid from the lower part of the cylinder to the upper part when the cylinder is being compressed during landing or taxiing.

24. The _____ prevents dirt or other foreign material from being drawn into the cylinder as the piston moves into the cylinder during compression.

25. The shock strut is serviced with _____ or _____ through the air valve to the specified shock-strut extension provided on a servicing chart.

26. During the strut-extension stroke, the fluid is forced to return through the metering orifice to prevent the strut from extending too rapidly on takeoff or during a bad landing; this is often referred to as a _____ action.

27. Keeping the nose gear straight ahead when the gear is retracted and when landing is accomplished by means of external, mechanical centering devices or by _____ inside the strut.

28. The _____ restrict the extension of the piston during gear retraction and hold the wheels and axle in a correctly aligned position in relation to the strut.

29. The _____ is located on the bottom of the strut piston and has the axles attached to it.

30. The _____ is designed to stabilize the landing-gear assembly longitudinally.

31. The _____ is designed to stabilize the landing-gear assembly laterally.

32. An _____ is used to apply pressure to the center pivot joint in a drag or side brace link, preventing the link from pivoting at this joint except when the gear is retracted.

33. The overcenter link is also called a _____ or a _____ .

34. A _____ is a flexible joint with internal passages that route hydraulic fluid to the wheel brakes and the bungee cylinder of a landing gear.

35. The _____ is a hydraulic snubbing unit that reduces the tendency of the nose wheel to oscillate from side to side.

36. A _____ is a hydraulic cylinder containing a piston rod and piston and filled with hydraulic fluid.

37. _____ are designed with a set of moving vanes and a set of stationary vanes.

38. Mechanical steering systems are found on _____ where the pilot can press on the rudder pedal and cause the nose wheel or tail wheel to turn without any form of powered assistance.

39. For tail-wheel aircraft, the rudder-control cables are connected to the tail-wheel _____ through springs so that when the rudder is deflected, one spring is stretched and the aircraft begins to turn as it rolls forward.

40. An _____ landing-gear system is often used on light aircraft, where the weight of the landing gear is not so great as to require large operating motors or complex hydraulic systems.

41. The four methods used to extend the landing gear if hydraulic power is lost are an _____ to ''blow'' the gear down; a _____ , where the operation of a hand crank or ratchet performs the extension operation; a _____ powered by a hand pump to extend the gear; and the use of a mechanical system to _____ , allowing the gear to free-fall into the down-and-locked position.

42. The purpose of the _____ system is to provide air or gas pressure to lower the gear in the event of hydraulic power failure.

43. An important landing-gear safety mechanism consists of an electric circuit, which includes switches, sometimes called _____ , operated by the extension and compression of the landing-gear struts. This prevents _____ while the airplane is on the ground.

44. If the landing gear is in the retracted position and the throttle is retarded to a _____ setting, a _____ sounds an alarm advising the pilot that the landing gear is not in the down position.

45. An electrically controlled _____ in transport aircraft provides a locked-wheel protection feature and affords maximum efficiency to the brake system.

46. The _____ mechanism provides a mechanical means of establishing a ground or flight mode, with the functions of various systems differing as the mode changes.

47. One concern with skid gear construction in helicopter landing gear is the possibility the gear may impart a _____ into the airframe.

48. _____ is caused when the helicopter is on the ground and the vibrations (frequencies) combine in an additive nature to a destructive level that can cause the aircraft to bounce or roll over and be destroyed.

49. Some helicopters are equipped with _____ on the rear ends of the skid gear to dampen vibrations of the gear in order to reduce the tendency toward ground resonance.

50. Fixed landing gear should be examined regularly for _____ , _____ , _____ , _____ , and other factors that may cause failure or unsatisfactory operation.

51. When landing gear that employs rubber shock (bungee) cord for shock absorption is inspected, the shock cord should be checked for _____ , _____ , _____ , and _____ at points of contact with the structure.

52. If the age of the shock cord is near 5 years or more, it is _____ to replace it with new cord, regardless of other factors.

53. The cord is _____ to indicate when it was manufactured, thus giving the technician the information needed to determine the life of the cord.

54. According to MIL-C-5651A, with shock cord the color code used for the year of manufacture is repeated in cycles of _____ .

55. Shock struts of the spring-oleo type should be examined for _____ , _____ , looseness between _____ , and _____ at the attaching points.

56. The extension of the shock struts should be checked to make sure that the _____ are not worn or broken.

57. Before an air-oil strut is removed or disassembled, the air valve should be opened to make sure that _____ .

58. During the operational testing of a retractable landing-gear system _____ , effectiveness of up-and-down _____ , operation of the _____ , operation of _____ , clearance of tires _____ , and operation of _____ should be checked.

59. Wheel alignment is generally checked for _____ and _____ .

60. Camber is the amount wheels are tilted from the _____ .

61. If the top of the wheel tilts outward, the camber is _____ .

62. Toe is the amount wheels are angled from the _____ .

63. The wheels of an aircraft are _____ if lines drawn through the center of the wheels, perpendicular to the axles, cross ahead of the wheels.

64. As the airplane moves forward, toe-in causes the wheels to try to move _____ .

65. Wheel alignment of oleo-equipped landing gear is adjusted by means of _____ installed between the torque links at the joint between the upper and lower links.

66. For spring steel landing gear, alignment is adjusted by the use of _____ between the gear leg and the axle mount.

67. When checking wheel alignment in a light airplane, if a square contacts the rear side of the brake disk, leaving a gap between it and the front flange, the wheel is _____ .

68. To rectify the toe-in and toe-out conditions, remove the bolt connecting the upper and lower _____ and remove or add _____ to move the wheel in the desired direction.

69. Floats should be carefully inspected for _____ damage at periodic intervals, especially if the airplane is flown from salt water.

70. Small blisters on the paint, either inside or outside the float, should be _____ and the area _____ .

71. Underinflating or overloading a tire will increase _____ and cause separations in the _____ and _____ of the tires, rapidly decreasing the life of the tire.

72. _____ is an index of tire strength and specifies its maximum recommended load.

73. The higher the ply rating, the _____ the load a tire will carry.

74. The aircraft tire's ply rating _____ necessarily represent the actual number of nylon fabric _____ .

75. _____ are placed on tires in the form of a red dot on the side of the tire at the lightest point.

76. Tires classified as Types III, VII, and VIII are manufactured under the provisions of _____ and are approved under _____ .

77. Tires classified as Types III, VII, and VIII are required to be permanently marked with the _____ ; the _____ , _____ , and _____ ; the _____ and _____ when the test speed is greater than 160 mph [257.6 km/h] and the word "_____" if applicable; and the applicable _____ .

78. Type III tires and those specified as low-speed tires are approved for ground speeds of less than _____ .

79. All new sizes are designated by a _____-part size designation and a _____ .

80. The prefix of a new tire indicates a relationship between the _____ of the tire section divided by its _____ and the angle at the _____ of the bead.

81. Following the prefix of a new tire is the nominal _____ diameter of the tire.

82. The nominal outside diameter of the tire is followed by × and then the _____ of the tire.

83. In the tire designation for a radial tire the × is replaced by an _____ .

84. _____ serve as the foundation for the attachment of the fabric plies and provide firm mounting surfaces on the wheel.

85. The _____ are diagonal layers of rubber-coated nylon cord fabric, laid in alternating directions, that provide the strength of the tire and wrap around the wire beads.

86. The _____ and _____ prevent the bead from abrading the plies.

87. _____ are used to protect the tire during mounting and demounting, to insulate the carcass from brake heat, and to provide a good seal between the tire and wheel.

88. An inner layer of rubber is used to form an _____ on tubeless tires and to prevent tube _____ on tube-type tires.

89. _____ and the tread-reinforcing plies are used to increase the structural strength on some tires.

90. All the parts of the tire except the _____ make up the tire carcass.

91. The beads, which are made of steel wires embedded in rubber, anchor the plies and provide firm _____ on the wheel.

92. The _____ is the outer bead edge, which fits against the wheel flange.

93. The _____ is the inner bead edge closest to the tire center line.

94. The _____ is the rubber compound on the surface of the tire, which is designed for runway contact.

95. A _____ may be molded as an integral part of the sidewall to deflect runway water away from rear-mounted engines.

96. Exposure to _____ can cause the rubber to age rapidly.

97. Tires should be stored _____ in racks.

98. If tires must be stacked on their sides the stacks should be no more than _____ .

99. Ribs on the tube are designed to provide _____ between the tire liner and the tube so that the tire will not rotate in relation to the tube, causing abrasion damage.

100. The tires are protected against blowouts resulting from excessive pressure created by heat by three _____ equally spaced around the wheel.

101. Aircraft wheels are commonly made in _____ to facilitate the changing of tires.

102. Before a wheel is removed from the airplane, the tire should be _____ .

103. With the wheel lying flat, the tire beads are broken away from the rims by applying pressure in _____ increments around the entire sidewall as close to the _____ as possible.

104. The O-ring air seal or packing found in tubeless tire installations should be carefully removed and placed in a _____ where it will not be damaged or contaminated with dirt.

105. Before placing the tube in the tire, the tube should be lightly dusted with _____ to prevent the tube from sticking to the inside of the tire.

106. To obtain the proper balance of the tire and tube, the inner tube should be placed in the tire so that the _____ (the heavy spot) on the tube is located adjacent to the _____ (the light spot) on the tire.

107. Before the tube is placed in the tire, the tube should be inflated sufficiently to _____ but not so much that the rubber is stretched.

108. The air-seal mating surface of the wheel should be cleaned with _____ .

109. The wheel air seal (O-ring) should be lubricated with a _____ .

110. When the bolts of a split-wheel construction are installed, they are brought down flush with the wheel using an

_____ .

111. When the bolts of a split-wheel construction are tightened, the bolts are first torqued to about

_____ of final torque, and then torque is brought up to the final installation torque in

_____ , using an _____ .

112. The tire should be placed in an _____ before being inflated.

113. Tires should be allowed to set, fully inflated, for _____ before being installed on an aircraft.

114. The use of a soap solution to make the bead of the tire slip more easily over the rim _____
be done with airplane tires.

115. If the tread is worn in the center of the tire, but not on the edges, this indicates that the tire is

_____ and the operational air pressure should be _____ .

116. If the tire is worn on the edges, but not in the center, this indicates _____ .

117. Any damage that does not penetrate through the tread and into the carcass plies is _____
acceptable.

118. If the tread damage involves _____ , _____ , or

_____ that could lead to peeling or throwing, the tire should be

_____ .

119. _____ and _____ indicate a separation within the tread or between ply
layers and the tire should be removed from service.

120. Flat spots indicate excessive use of brakes for _____ and when

_____ .

121. If plies are showing, if insufficient tread remains, or if the tire is out of balance, then the tire should be

_____ .

122. Damage to the sidewalls that is acceptable includes cuts, small cracks, and weather checking (a random pattern of

shallow cracks), provided that _____ .

123. Tires can be recapped as often as _____ times.

124. Tires that are recapped must be _____ to provide required information.

125. Each retreaded tire must display the letter R followed by a number such as 1, 2, or 3 to signify the

_____ number of recaps that have been applied.

126. A marking must be applied to display the speed category increase if the tire is qualified for increased speed in

accordance with the requirements of _____ .

127. The _____ and _____ of recapping must be shown, together with the

_____ of the person or agency that applied the recap.

128. Each repaired or recapped tire should not exceed the _____ limits as set forth in TSO-C62.

129. Tubes should be inspected for _____ , _____ , and

_____ .

130. To thoroughly inspect a wheel, the wheel must first be _____ and then cleaned of all

_____ , _____ , _____ , and

_____ .

131. The valve stem should be checked for _____ where it attaches to the tube.

132. Inspection of large cast or forged wheel parts is accomplished with _____ ,

_____ , _____ , and _____ .

133. Split-type wheels must be examined to determine the amount of wear in the _____ .

134. Wheel bearings rollers should show no signs of _____ , _____ , or

_____ and should _____ in their cages.

135. In the absence of specific instructions, the wheel-retaining nut is tightened until _____ is felt

and then backed off about _____ (castellation) or one-sixth turn before bending up the tab on
the tab-lock washer or installing the cotter pin.

136. Internal expanding-shoe brakes are either the _____ or _____ type.

137. Servo action in a brake of this type means that the rotation of the brake drum _____ braking
energy to the brake shoes and makes them operate more effectively and with less effort by the pilot.

138. In single-servo brakes, the servo action is effective for _____ of the wheel only, as
contrasted with a dual-servo or reversible type, which operates to give servo action in

_____ .

139. Each expander-tube brake consists of four main parts: _____ ,

_____ , _____ , and _____ .

140. When the brake pedal is pressed, the fluid is forced into the _____ in such a manner that the

pressure of the fluid in the tube forces the _____ radially outward against the brake drum.

141. In single-disk brakes, braking is accomplished by applying hydraulic pressure to the _____ ,

which then force the _____ to rub against the _____ .

142. In multidisk brakes, the braking action is produced by hydraulic pressure forcing the _____

against the _____ , which, in turn, forces the disk stack together and creates friction between

the _____ and _____ disks.

143. _____ are rods that are an extension of the return pins; as the brake linings wear, the wear
indicator moves into the assembly.

144. The braking action of segmented rotor-disk brakes results from several sets of stationary,

_____ making contact with rotating (rotor) segments.

145. Because of the _____ between the rotor segments and the space between the

_____ , segmented rotor-disk brakes have more brake cooling than can be achieved with the
multiple-disk brake, allowing more braking action to be achieved before a limiting temperature is reached.

146. The life and heat limitations of steel disks have been improved through the use of _____
disks.

147. The factors determining the amount of energy absorbed by the brakes in a given situation are the

_____ in knots at the time the brakes are applied, the _____ of the

airplane, and the _____ at the airport where the braking occurs.

148. If an airplane is equipped with _____ , the energy absorbed by the brakes is

_____ .

149. An independent brake system is _____ and _____ of the aircraft's main hydraulic system.

150. The reservoir of an independent braking system is vented to the _____ to provide for feeding the fluid to the master cylinders under the force of gravity.

151. If the reservoir of an independent braking system is not kept at the correct level, _____ will enter the system and reduce its effectiveness.

152. The master cylinder in each main landing-gear wheel is the _____ ; it is a

_____ , _____ reciprocating pump, the purpose of which is to build up hydraulic fluid pressure in the brake system.

153. _____ are required to transmit the energy of the foot to the master cylinder.

154. The brake pedals may be _____ or _____ brakes mounted on the rudder pedals.

155. When brakes of an independent braking system are pressed, it is necessary for pilots to

_____ the force on one pedal with _____ on the other pedal unless they wish to turn the airplane.

156. Power boost braking systems receive pressure from the _____ through a check valve, which prevents loss of fluid and pressure if the main hydraulic system should fail.

157. When the brake pedals of a power brake system are depressed, an inward movement is imparted to the metering

valve rod through the mechanical linkage and cables; the return port is _____ , and the

pressure port is _____ to direct hydraulic fluid pressure to the brakes.

158. A _____ is used in systems where the high pressure of the hydraulic system is used to operate brakes that are designed for use with lower pressure.

159. _____ prevent the loss of airplane control on the ground caused by skidding of the wheels.

160. Antiskid protection is accomplished through the control of _____ at the point of

_____ , just before an impending skid.

161. The three elements to the antiskid system are the frequency-modulated _____ transducers,

which sense speed change, the _____ circuitry, which works on the basis of speed-change

information, and the _____ , which meter the appropriate brake pressure to prevent stoppage of wheel rotation.

162. The sensing of _____ of wheel speed, rather than _____ itself, creates an anticipatory feature that provides the high response necessary for wheel-torque control.

163. The pilot's function in an antiskid system is to _____ and _____ a steady brake pressure high enough to skid a tire under normal conditions; the antiskid system's function is to

_____ the pressure selected by the pilot to give the _____ stopping performance under existing airplane and runway conditions.

164. The _____ circuit achieves its mean level by integrating the amplitude and duration of the control signal.

165. A _____ measures a voltage for all other wheels; should this voltage drop while any other

wheel is rolling and delivering a voltage, an overdriving signal would be sent to the _____ , effecting full pressure release at the locked wheel.

166. The variable-reluctance, sine-wave-generating antiskid-system _____ are used to detect a skid condition in each of the four main-gear wheels; they are installed in the _____ of each main-gear wheel and are coupled to the wheel hubcap.

167. When wheel speed decreases to approximately 15 mph [24 km/h], the voltage produced by the transducers will be at a level to _____ the antiskid system and revert the braking system to _____ operation.

168. If brake linings are not _____ by the manufacturer, the curing operation must be completed by accelerating the aircraft to a moderate speed and then applying moderate-to-heavy braking force to heat up the linings.

169. The brake disks should be inspected for _____ and _____ .

170. With single-disk-type brakes, if the disk is _____ or the _____ , the brake disk will not stay in the correct position and brake failure will result.

171. Wear of multiple-disk brakes is determined by noting the extension of the _____ .

172. Brake systems may be serviced with different types of fluid, and the technician must be sure to use the _____ .

173. Flexible hoses used in the brake system must be examined for _____ , _____ , _____ , and _____ of the outer covering.

174. _____ can be caused by air in the brake hydraulic system, broken-down or weak return springs, sticking return pins, or defective valves.

175. _____ are usually caused by oil or some other foreign matter on the disks and linings, or worn disks and drums can cause grabbing.

176. _____ are usually caused by the condition of the lining.

177. Excessive brake pedal travel can be caused by _____ , _____ _____ , _____ , and _____ _____ .

178. A leaking _____ in a brake master cylinder will cause the pedal to slowly creep down while pedal pressure is applied.

179. When a brake line has been disconnected for any reason, or after overhaul or replacement of any part of the brake hydraulic system, it is usually necessary to _____ the system to remove _____ from lines, valves, and cylinders.

180. Air in the brake hydraulic system causes _____ and may cause the brakes to _____ .

181. Aircraft brake systems usually incorporate _____ for the attachment of bleeder hoses.

182. In gravity brake bleeding, the brakes are _____ to pump fluid through the lines, valves, and cylinders until no air bubbles are seen passing through the line.

183. During the pressure-bleeding process, brake fluid is forced through the system by means of a pressurized reservoir connected to the system brake-bleed fitting, and fluid is _____ through the system, _____ , until no bubbles appear in the fluid outflow.

Chapter 14

Name _____

Date _____

1. Oleos are shock-absorbing components that
   a. regulate the rate of absorption by use of an orifice.
   b. turn the energy absorbed into useful electrical energy.
   c. turn the energy absorbed into useful hydraulic energy for braking.
   d. have color-coded shock cords that indicate the age of the cord assembly.

2. The trunnion portion of a landing-gear system
   a. diverts the landing loads to the tires.
   b. is the portion of the landing gear where all tires are placed in tandem.
   c. allows the gear to pivot during extension and retraction.
   d. is what makes the hull of an amphibious aircraft buoyant.

3. A landing gear strut
   a. is also referred to as a side brace and absorbs the torsion force upon landing.
   b. is also referred to as the outer cylinder of landing gear's oleo shock absorber.
   c. keeps the wheels of the landing gear in alignment.
   d. locks the landing gear in the down position when extended and the up position when retracted.

4. Snubbing
   a. regulates the maximum rate of turn (turning radius).
   b. dampens the wheel shimmy typically experienced on landing.
   c. controls the maximum rate of landing-gear extension.
   d. stops the tires from rotating after the landing gear is retracted.

5. Landing-gear wheel and axle alignment is maintained by the landing gear's
   a. torque link(s).
   b. drag link(s).
   c. antidrag link(s).
   d. side brace link(s).

6. Maintaining the longitudinal alignment of a landing-gear system is the function of the
   a. torque link(s).
   b. drag link(s).
   c. antidrag link(s).
   d. side brace link(s).

7. Shimmy dampers are usually employed in the
   a. nose gear.
   b. outboard main gear tires.
   c. inboard main gear tires.
   d. retractable tail wheels.

8. The age of a shock cord may be ascertained from the
   a. color code painted on the cord.
   b. color code of the rubber cords.
   c. color code woven into the cord sheath.
   d. the date stamped on the outermost metallic protective shield.

9. Ply ratings indicate the
   a. number of actual cord plies used in the manufacture of the tire.
   b. strength of the tire.
   c. type of cord used in the tire (nylon, steel, etc.)
   d. weight of the tire as it differs from original equipment and is supplied for weight and balance calculations.

10. A red dot on the side of an aircraft tire indicates
    a. that the tire may not be recapped.
    b. the tire is certified for landing speeds in excess of 150 mph.
    c. landing speeds in excess of 120 mph are not permissible.
    d. the lightest point of the tire.

11. The prefix number of a modern tire designation code identifies
    a. the ply rating of the tire.
    b. the width of the tire and the number of actual plies.
    c. a combination of section width, rim width, and bead ledge angle.
    d. the nominal outside diameter and the nominal section width combination.

12. To prevent rubbing between a tube and its tire
    a. tubes are fabricated with ribs.
    b. tires are fabricated with internal ribbing.
    c. tires and tubes are paired (matched) at the factory (and therefore may not be interchanged.)
    d. the valve stem must be positioned as close to vertical as possible during the tire/tube assembly.

13. Aircraft wheels are most commonly fabricated
    a. in two halves and must be welded together using a heliarc welding process.
    b. in two halves and must be inflated in a gauge.
    c. in four equal quadrants and are held together by bolts.
    d. in eight equal bilateral quadrants and are held together by bolts.

14. The yellow strip on a tube indicates the
    a. heavy spot on the tube and must be located adjacent to the heaviest spot on the tire.
    b. heavy spot on the tube and must be located adjacent to the lightest spot on the tire.
    c. light spot on the tube and must be located adjacent to the heaviest spot on the tire.
    d. light spot on the tube and must be located adjacent to the lightest spot on the tire.

15. Recapping of an aircraft tire is
    a. not permissible.
    b. limited to three occurrences in general aviation application.
    c. limited only by the condition of the tire carcass in airline application.
    d. not done for tiers designed for nose-wheel applications.

16. The amount of air in the brake hydraulic system should be
    a. 10 percent air by weight.
    b. 15 percent air by volume.
    c. 20 percent air by pressure.
    d. There should be no air in a hydraulic braking system.

17. Power-boost braking systems
    a. supplement the brake hydraulic system with pneumatic pressure.
    b. supplement the brake hydraulic system with the aircraft's basic hydraulic system pressure.
    c. use a supplemental electrically powered pump.
    d. employ only dual-servo-designed braking systems.

18. The purpose of antiskid generators is to
    a. eliminate brake drag.
    b. monitor hydraulic pressure applied to brakes.
    c. indicate when a tire skid occurs.
    d. measure wheel rotational speed and speed changes.

19. What safety device is actuated by the compression and extension of a landing-gear strut?
    a. Ground lockpins
    b. Up-lock switch
    c. Down-lock switch
    d. Ground safety switch

20. In brake service work, bleeding brakes is the process of
    a. withdrawing only air from the system.
    b. withdrawing fluid from the system for the purpose of removing air that has entered the system.
    c. replacing lines that tend to leak small amounts of fluid.
    d. eliminating excessive pedal travel by lengthening actuator rods and attendant linkages.

Chapter 15

1. The purpose of a fuel system is to deliver a _____ of clean fuel under _____ to the carburetor or other fuel-control unit.

2. Each fuel system must be constructed and arranged to ensure a flow of fuel at a _____ and _____ established for proper engine and auxiliary power-unit functioning under each likely operating condition.

3. Each fuel system must be arranged so that any air that may be introduced into the system as a result of fuel depletion in a tank will not result in _____ for more than 20 s for a reciprocating engine and will not cause the flameout of a turbine engine.

4. Each fuel system must meet engine-operation requirements by allowing the supply of fuel to each engine through a system that is _____ of parts of another system supplying fuel to any other engine.

5. If a single fuel tank or a series of tanks interconnected to function as a single tank is used on a multiengined airplane, there may be a separate tank outlet _____ , and each outlet may be equipped with a _____ .

6. The tank or series of tanks shall have at least _____ arranged to minimize the probability of both vents becoming obstructed simultaneously.

7. Filler caps must be designed to minimize the probability of _____ or _____ of the caps in flight.

8. Some fuel caps incorporate vents that keep the fuel tank at _____ .

9. The filler cap or the area immediately next to the cap should be placarded with the word _____ and the proper _____ and the _____ of fuel approved for use in the aircraft.

10. The fuel system must be designed and arranged to prevent the _____ of fuel vapor within the system by direct or swept lightning strikes to areas where these are likely to occur, and the design must be such that fuel vapor cannot be ignited at _____ .

11. The fuel flow for a _____ system must be at least 150 percent of the takeoff fuel consumption of the engine.

12. For pressure pump systems, the fuel flow for each reciprocating engine must be at least _____ of takeoff fuel flow.

13. For transport-category airplanes, each fuel system must provide at least _____ of the fuel flow required under each intended operating condition and maneuver.

14. If an engine can be supplied with fuel from more than one tank, the fuel system for each reciprocating engine must supply the full fuel pressure to that engine not more than _____ after switching to any other tank containing usable fuel.

15. In the case of a turbine engine that can be supplied from more than one tank, in addition to having appropriate manual switching capability, the system must provide an _____ switching capability.

16. If fuel can be pumped from one fuel tank to another in flight, the fuel tank vents and the fuel-transfer system must be designed so that no structural damage to the tanks can occur because of _____ .

17. It must be impossible, in a gravity-feed system with _____ , for enough fuel to flow between the tanks to cause an overflow from any tank vent under any condition of intended operation or flight maneuver.

18. Systems must be free of _____ when operating with fuel at 110°F [43°C] under critical conditions.

19. Vapor lock is a condition of _____ that can occur in a reciprocating engine fuel system in which the fuel in the fuel line is heated enough to cause it to vaporize, forming a _____ of fuel vapor in the line and blocking fuel from flowing to the engine.

20. Indicators, either gauges or warning lights, must be provided at pressure fueling stations to indicate failure of the _____ means to stop fuel flow at the desired level.

21. If a fuel-flowmeter system is installed in a fuel system, each metering component (fuel-flow transmitter) must have a means of _____ the fuel flow if malfunction of the metering component severely restricts fuel flow.

22. Each _____ , including each fuel jettisoning and fluid-shutoff control, must be colored red.

23. Fuel tanks for aircraft may be constructed of _____ , _____ , _____ , or _____ .

24. Metal fuel tanks generally are required to withstand an internal test pressure of _____ psi [24.13 kPa].

25. Fuel tanks must be equipped with _____ to collect sediment and water.

26. The filler connection must be marked with the word _____ , the _____ of fuel, and the _____ of the tank.

27. Fuel-quantity indicators must be calibrated to show _____ gallons when the usable fuel supply is exhausted.

28. Fuel-tank outlets must be provided with _____ .

29. If a fuel booster pump is installed in the tank, the pump _____ must be provided with a screen.

30. An _____ is a tank that is part of the basic structure of the aircraft.

31. _____ are frequently installed inside fuel tanks. The primary purpose of the baffle is to _____ of the fuel.

32. When an integral type of tank is used in a wing, the aircraft is said to have a _____ .

33. A _____ fuel tank is one that is installed in a compartment designed to hold the tank.

34. A _____ cell or tank is essentially a reinforced rubberized bag placed in a non-fuel-tight compartment designed to structurally carry the weight of the fuel.

35. Surge tanks, which are normally _____ , are designed to contain fuel _____ and prevent _____ , particularly when fueling the aircraft.

36. Fuel-measuring dipsticks are usually used only as an _____ means of measuring fuel quantity.

37. _____ are used to move fuel from the tanks to the engines, from tanks to other tanks, and from the engine back to the tanks when _____ is insufficient.

38. Fuel pumps are often classified according to the purpose of the pump such as _____ , _____ , or _____ .

39. In vane-type fuel pumps, fuel enters the inlet port and is forced by _____ vanes through the outlet port.

40. A variable-volume vane-type pump delivers _____ amounts of fuel under _____ pressure to the carburetor.

41. Bypass valves provide a means for the boost pump to force fuel _____ the vanes and rotor of the main pump for _____ or for _____ if the main pump fails.

42. When relief valves are designed to compensate for atmospheric-pressure variations, they are known as _____ .

43. To compensate for lowered fuel-pump inlet pressure as an airplane climbs to higher altitudes, the relief valve _____ is vented to the atmosphere or to the fuel tanks.

44. To adjust the pressure setting on a fuel pump, the adjusting-screw locknut is _____ and the adjusting screw is turned in the appropriate direction.

45. The centrifugal pump pressurizes the fuel by drawing fuel into the _____ of a centrifugal impeller and expelling it at the outer edge of the _____ .

46. Centrifugal pumps may be designed for the entire pump and motor to be located inside the fuel tank, in which case it is referred to as a _____ .

47. An _____ is normally used to scavenge fuel from remote areas of fuel tanks and to provide fuel under pressure to an operating engine fuel-control unit.

48. An ejector pump has no moving parts but relies on the flow of _____ fuel from the engine-driven pump to pump fuel.

49. The ejector pump works on the _____ principle.

50. As the motive flow fuel exits the ejector nozzle in the venturi area, a _____ is created and fuel from the inlet screen is _____ into the low-pressure area.

51. Since ejector pumps require a motive flow for operation, they do not begin operating until _____ .

52. Fuel is usually strained at three points in the system: first, through a _____ or boostpump strainer in the bottom of the fuel tank; second, through a _____ , which is usually located at the lowest point in the fuel system; and third, through a strainer in the _____ or near the _____ .

53. A fuel strainer or filter is required between the _____ outlet and the inlet of either the _____ (carburetor or other fuel-control unit) or an _____ pump, whichever is nearer the fuel-tank outlet.

54. The main strainer, located at the _____ point in the system, collects foreign matter from the line between the tank and the strainer and also serves as a _____ .

55. The filter, or screen, in the carburetor, fuel-injection unit, or near the fuel control in a turbine-engine system removes the _____ particles that may interfere with the operation of the sensitive valves and other operating mechanisms.

56. Fuel filters for turbine-engine systems include _____ that allow fuel to flow even though the filter becomes clogged.

57. _____ system switches are included in many filter assemblies to provide a signal to the cockpit notifying the pilot or other crew member that a particular filter is bypassing fuel or is nearing a condition where it will bypass fuel.

58. Fuel sump drain valves are used for draining _____ from fuel tanks and for draining trapped fuel remaining after defueling.

59. Fuel-selector valves provide a means of shutting off _____ , selecting _____ from which to draw fuel in a multiple-tank installation, _____ from one tank to another, and directing the fuel to _____ engines in a multiengined airplane.

60. Fuel-shutoff valves for large aircraft are interconnected with _____ systems so fuel may be _____ off automatically if there is an overheat or fire situation in any engine nacelle.

61. _____ are used with fuel systems for turbine engines to prevent ice crystals in the fuel from clogging system filters.

62. The fuel heater is a heat exchanger that uses _____ , _____ , or, if the hydraulic system generates enough heat, hydraulic fluid to heat the fuel above freezing and melt ice crystals.

63. The installation of the fuel lines must be such that there are _____ —that is, bends with a radius of less than _____ fuel-line diameters.

64. Fuel lines must be routed so that there are no _____ where water or vapor can collect.

65. Parts of the fuel system attached to the engine and to the primary structure of the airplane must be connected by means of _____ .

66. Metal fuel lines should be _____ to prevent radio interference.

67. A gravity-feed fuel system uses _____ to cause fuel to flow to the engine fuel-control mechanism.

68. For the gravity-feed system to work, the bottom of the fuel tank must be _____ to assure a proper fuel-pressure head at the inlet to the fuel-control component on the engine.

69. A pressure-feed fuel system uses a _____ to move fuel from the fuel tank to the engine fuel-control component.

70. Engine-driven fuel pumps are positioned in _____ with the electric pump so that the fuel can be moved by either pump without the need for a bypass valve.

71. The _____ pump supplies fuel for starting the engine, and the engine-driven pump supplies the fuel pressure necessary for normal operation.

72. The _____ usually draws fuel from the carburetor inlet bowl or fuel strainer and directs it to a distributor valve, which, in turn, distributes the fuel to the various cylinders.

73. _____ systems are designed to prevent the buildup of pressure in the fuel tanks and allow proper flow of fuel from the tanks.

74. The fuel vent system maintains the fuel tanks at near _____ pressure under all operating conditions.

75. If fuel-tank pressure exceeds the predetermined value, a tank vent valve opens and vents the tank to a special vent compartment called a _____ , _____ , or _____ .

76. The vent compartment allows fuel to vent from the tanks, thus preventing _____ as well as fuel _____ .

77. A vent scoop is an aerodynamically designed duct that will maintain _____ within the tank under all operating conditions.

78. The _____ is a passive device, comprising a stainless steel honeycomb core that acts as a heat sink to cool a flame below the ignition point; it also prevents an external flame from spreading into the surge tank.

79. A pressure fueling system uses pressure from the _____ or _____ to force fuel into the aircraft tanks.

80. The _____ allows the operator to monitor the fuel quantity in each tank and control the fuel valves for each tank.

81. On most multiengine aircraft, the fuel manifolds are connected is such a manner that may supply fuel to

_____ .

82. The _____ system is used to dump fuel overboard during an in-flight emergency in order to reduce the weight of the airplane to allowable landing weight or to dump all the fuel except the reserve quantity required for landing.

83. The _____ permits dumping of fuel from the opposite wing should the nozzle valve on one side fail to operate.

84. After _____ the engine is immediately shut down with the dilution valve open so that the fuel will remain in the oil.

85. In a large turbine aircraft, the _____ is the attachment for the pressure fueling hose.

86. A restricting orifice is a _____ device to prevent excessive fuel flow during pressure fueling.

87. Manually operated shutoff valves are provided at the pressure fueling station to permit a

_____ of fuel lines.

88. The _____ automatically closes the fueling line to a tank when that tank is filled to its maximum level.

89. The _____ closes when the full fuel level is reached causing pressure to be applied to the fueling-level-control shutoff valve, thus causing it to close.

90. _____ are slide valves operated by electric motors used for fuel control throughout the system.

91. The fuel-flow transmitter is an electrically operated unit that senses the rate of fuel flow

_____ .

92. During engine run-up, the fuel pressure and the proper operation of booster pumps _____ .

93. Fuel tanks should be checked for _____ , _____ , and

_____ .

94. Fuel tank caps should be examined for proper _____ .

95. Fuel tank vents and vent lines should be checked for _____ .

96. The _____ of the vent tubing should be examined to assure that it conforms to the requirements for fuel lines.

97. Fuel-shutoff valves and tank-selector valves should be checked for _____ and

_____ of valve handle position.

98. Fuel-pressure, fuel-quantity, and fuel-temperature gauges should be given an _____ .

99. During a test of the fuel-quantity gauge, the airplane should be in a _____ .

100. Fuel-pressure and fuel-temperature warning systems are checked by _____ the conditions in the systems that should produce the appropriate alarm.

101. Fuel leaks are classified as a _____ , a _____ , a _____ , and a _____ .

102. The general rule for these leaks is that any leak _____ is considered a fire hazard and the aircraft should not be flown.

103. Stains, seeps, and heavy seeps are not flight hazards when on the _____ of the aircraft and _____ ignition sources.

104. A running leak on the outside of the aircraft is considered a _____ .

105. _____ leaks should be considered a fire hazard until evaluated, and each situation should be evaluated based on the aircraft manufacturer's recommendations.

106. The interior surfaces and especially the bottoms of fuel tanks should be examined for the _____ .

107. After the microbial growths are removed, the metal surfaces of the fuel tank should be _____ .

108. _____ apply heat to a tank when it is installed in an airplane.

109. The purging of fuel tanks with an inert gas is an acceptable procedure and may be accomplished by first filling the tank with water, then introducing CO_2, nitrogen, or some other inert gas into the tank _____ .

110. Fuel tanks constructed of commercially pure aluminum 3003S, 5052SO, or similar metals may be repaired by _____ .

111. Heat-treated aluminum alloy fuel tanks are generally put together by _____ .

112. When it is necessary to repair a riveted fuel tank with a riveted patch, a _____ that is insoluble in gasoline should be used to seal the patch.

113. After a soldering repair is made, the fuel tank must be flushed with warm water to remove all traces of the _____ and any _____ that may have fallen into it.

114. Another often-used method for correcting minor seepage in a metal fuel tank is _____ the inside of the tank with an approved compound.

115. Dripping or running leaks in a riveted fuel tank must be repaired by _____ .

116. It is good practice to dip the new rivets in a _____ before installation in a riveted fuel tank.

117. When metal fuel tanks are reinstalled, the felt padding should be examined for _____ .

118. If new felt is installed, it should be treated to make it _____ .

119. Rawhide leather, which contains free alkalies, is unsuitable for padding an aluminum tank because _____ will take place where the pad comes in contact with the metal.

120. The area in which the synthetic-rubber fuel cell is installed must be inspected to make sure that there are no _____ or _____ to cause wear or other damage to the cells.

Chapter 15

Name _____

Date _____

MULTIPLE CHOICE QUESTIONS

1. If an aircraft has multifuel systems,
   a. each fuel system must be able to supply the fuel needs for its respective engines.
   b. each fuel system must be able to supply the fuel needs for each engine on the same side of the aircraft.
   c. each fuel system must be able to supply the fuel needs for any two engines simultaneously.
   d. each fuel system must be able to supply the fuel needs for each engine simultaneously.

2. Fuel ports, the area where fuel is supplied to the aircraft, must be clearly labeled with
   a. the word FUEL.
   b. the type of fuel used by the aircraft.
   c. the minimum grade of fuel used by the aircraft.
   d. All the above.

3. Vapor lock
   a. is a system that returns all fuel vapor to the fuel tanks, i.e., locks the vapor within the fuel system.
   b. is a condition that starves the aircraft powerplants of fuel by forming a gas (vapor) bubble in the fuel lines and blocking fuel flow.
   c. secures (locks) the aircraft's ignition systems in the off position if fuel vapors are detected in the engine area during engine starting.
   d. is a required integral fuel system function that interlocks the fuel venting system of each tank to a system surge tank and prohibits fuel vapors from being released into the atmosphere.

4. By regulation, each fuel flowmeter must be
   a. grounded directly to the aircraft battery's negative terminal.
   b. grounded directly to the aircraft battery's positive terminal.
   c. able to be disengaged in flight.
   d. equipped with a bypass system.

5. Fuel-tank baffles are used to
   a. create tank subcompartments in order to better control fuel usage.
   b. provide a rigid structure for the installation of fuel pumps.
   c. prevent or reduce fuel sloshing.
   d. provide a visual reference for individual tank quantity readings.

6. Integral fuel tanks
   a. are not removable because they are part of the aircraft structure.
   b. must fit into their designed location with no more than 1/2-in clearance between the tank and the aircraft structure.
   c. collapse as fuel is removed from them.
   d. are considered semirigid in construction.

7. The purpose of a surge tank is to
   a. provide extra fuel to the engines when g forces exceed 1.5 g.
   b. provide extra fuel pressure for takeoffs and landings.
   c. provide a ''leveling'' tank when transferring fuel from one tank to another.
   d. contain fuel overflows and prevent fuel spillage.

8. Fuel pumps for multiengine aircraft must
   a. deliver a pressure equal to that obtained through gravity feed.
   b. be independently operable.
   c. not increase fuel pressure greater than twice the force that would be provided by an equivalent gravity-feed system.
   d. be installed inside the aircraft's fuel tanks.

9. When a relief valve is designed to compensate for atmospheric pressure variations, it is properly referred to as
   a. a balanced relief valve.
   b. a variance compensator relief valve.
   c. an atmopress relief valve.
   d. bypass relief valve.

10. When the entire fuel pump, including its motor, is located inside a fuel tank it is referred to as a
    a. wet pump.
    b. dry pump.
    c. submerged pump.
    d. salvage pump.

11. An ejector-type fuel pump
    a. has no moving parts.
    b. is designed to dump fuel overboard in an emergency.
    c. separates water from fuel, ejecting the water overboard.
    d. motor is always electrically operated.

12. The major difference between a fuel strainer and a fuel filter is
    a. the location of each in the fuel system.
    b. the size of the foreign matter separated from the fuel.
    c. that strainers are fabricated from brass and filters are made of aluminum.
    d. strainers have left-hand threads and filters have right-hand threads.

13. The purpose of a fuel sump is to
    a. provide a location for water to separate from the fuel and be collected for later removal.
    b. provide a location for fuel reserve.
    c. allow fuel to be jettisoned in case of an emergency.
    d. provide a consistent location for fuel supply to auxiliary systems such as heaters and auxiliary power units.

14. Fuel heaters are installed for turbine-powered aircraft to
    a. improve fuel vaporization.
    b. boil off water vapors that may be present in the fuel.
    c. improve fuel utilization.
    d. prevent the formation of ice crystals in the fuel at fuel filters.

15. Bends in fuel-system lines may not have a radius of less than
    a. two times the fuel-line diameter.
    b. three times the fuel-line diameter.
    c. four times the fuel-line diameter.
    d. five times the fuel-line diameter.

16. A fuel-system primer
    a. places raw fuel into cylinders.
    b. places a 50-50 fuel-air mixture into cylinders.
    c. stops fuel from eating through painted surfaces near fuel tank vents.
    d. stops fuel from attacking the sealant materials used in integral fuel-tank systems.

17. The purpose of a fuel-system venting system is to
    a. maintain tank integral pressures near ambient pressure.
    b. ensure that there is always head pressure in the system.
    c. provide a restricted path for fuel overflow.
    d. allow water vapors to escape the fuel system.

18. A fuel jettison system is required for transport-category aircraft if
    a. the aircraft carries more than 30 passengers, excluding the crew.
    b. the aircraft's gross takeoff weight exceeds 100 000 lb.
    c. the capacity of the fuel system exceeds 100 000 lb.
    d. the maximum takeoff weight of the aircraft is 105 percent greater than the certified landing weight.

19. Oil dilution
    a. thins the aircraft's oil with fuel for ease of engine starts in cold weather.
    b. mixes oil with the aircraft's fuel to lubricate the system's moving parts.
    c. mixes oil in the aircraft's fuel to drive water from the fuel system by displacing it, since oil is heavier than water and the two do not mix.
    d. is used to reduce the flashpoint of the fuel in high-temperature areas, particularly around the engines.

20. When testing fuel-quantity systems,
    a. the aircraft's tanks should all be half full.
    b. every other tank should be half full and the remaining tanks near empty.
    c. the aircraft must be at maximum takeoff weight.
    d. the aircraft should be in its normal flight attitude.

Chapter 16

1. The simplest type of heating system, often employed on light aircraft, consists of a _____ around the engine exhaust stacks, an _____ to draw ram air into the heater muff, _____ to carry the heated air into the cabin, and a _____ to control the flow of heated air.

2. A heat exchanger is any device by which _____ is _____ from one independent system to another independent system.

3. A heat exchanger may be used to reduce or _____ the level of heat in a system or to _____ heat from one system where it is a by-product into another system that requires the additional heat to function.

4. Exhaust heating systems must be given regular inspections to assure that exhaust fumes _____ enter the _____ of the airplane.

5. One method of checking for cracks is to pressurize the exhaust pipes with _____ and apply soapy water to all areas where cracks may possibly occur.

6. _____ , also referred to as _____ , are often employed to supply the heat needed for the cabin by burning _____ in a combustion chamber or tube to develop the required heat.

7. In a South Wind heater, the heater fuel pump and all external fittings on the heater are enclosed in metal housings that are _____ and _____ as a precaution against fire in the event of leaky fittings.

8. Combustion air for a Janitrol heater enters the combustion chamber tangent to the inner surface, which imparts a _____ to the air, in turn producing a whirling flame that is _____ and sustains combustion under the most adverse conditions.

9. Typical inspections of a combustion heater system include a visual inspection of the _____ and _____ for obstructions and conditions; inspection of the igniter plug for _____ , _____ , and _____ ; a check for any leakage in the _____ or _____ ; an operational check of _____ system components; and an operational check of the _____ system.

10. The auxiliary electric heat system draws air from the _____ the aircraft cabin by the use of a recirculation fan; the air then passes over electrically heated coils and flows back into the cabin through the aircraft heat supply ducting.

11. When a turbine engine compresses air prior to directing it to the engine combustion chamber, the air temperature of this air is increased by several hundred degrees Fahrenheit by the compressing action; some of this hot compressed air, called _____ , can be diverted to a cabin-heating system.

12. The cabin-heating system of a turbine engine aircraft consists of ducting to contain the flow of air, a chamber where the bleed air is _____ with _____ or _____ , valves to control the flow of air in the system, and temperature sensors to prevent excessive heat from entering the cabin.

13. The vapor-cycle machine is a _____ system using the evaporation and condensation of _____ to remove heat from the cabin interior.

14. The air-cycle machine uses the _____ and _____ of air to _____ the temperature of the cabin air.

15. When a liquid changes to a gas (vaporizes), it absorbs heat, called the _____ heat of vaporization.

16. As a given quantity of gas is condensed to a liquid, it _____ heat in the _____ that it absorbs when being changed from a liquid to a gas.

17. When a gas is compressed, its temperature _____ , and when the pressure on a gas is decreased, its temperature _____ .

18. Heat transfers only from a material having a given temperature to a material having a _____ temperature.

19. A vapor-cycle cooling system takes advantage of the laws of nature and with the use of _____ heat exchangers controls the temperature of the cockpit and cabin.

20. One heat exchanger of a vapor-cycle cooling system works by taking heat from the closed system and is called an _____ .

21. The other heat exchanger of a vapor-cycle cooling system draws heat from the air and adds it to the closed system; it is called a _____ .

22. The refrigerant of a vapor cycle cooling system, usually freon, takes two forms during the process, _____ and _____ .

23. The function of the compressor of a vapor-cycle cooling system is to _____ the refrigerant, _____ , through the entire system.

24. As the gas enters the condenser of a vapor-cycle cooling system , heat is drawn from the _____ and passes it to the _____ .

25. The cooling of the refrigerant causes it to condense into a _____ .

26. In a vapor-cycle cooling system, the pressurized liquid is metered into tiny droplets by an _____ , but because of the compressor, the liquid is still under pressure.

27. The droplets of freon in a vapor-cycle cooling system then enter the evaporator, where they draw _____ from the air and change into a _____ .

28. As a result of heat being drawn from the air by the freon droplets, the temperature of the ambient air passing through the condenser is _____ ; this cooler air is introduced to the cabin for cooling.

29. A vapor-cycle cooling system for aircraft usually employs _____ as the refrigerant.

30. The gas leaving the compressor is at a high _____ and _____ .

31. The _____ is essentially a reservoir containing a filter and a desiccant.

32. A _____ is usually located on top of the receiver to allow observation of the fluid flow through the unit.

33. If bubbles are seen in the fluid through the sight glass, the system refrigerant is known to be _____ .

34. Refrigerant liquid flowing from the receiver-dryer-filter is under _____ pressure and has been cooled by the _____ .

35. If the liquid is _____ below the condensing temperature, this condition assures that there will
be no _____ before the liquid reaches the expansion valve.

36. When liquid refrigerant appears between the _____ and the compressor, the condition is
called _____ .

37. The _____ consists of a _____ orifice through which the
high-pressure liquid is forced.

38. Low pressure exits at the _____ side of the expansion valve, through the evaporator, and to
the _____ of the compressor.

39. The cabin air to be cooled is carried by ducting into one side of the _____ and out the other
side to the cabin.

40. The thermal expansion valve orifice is adjusted automatically by the pressure from a thermal sensor, which senses
the temperature of the gas _____ .

41. The _____ provides the cooling for cabin air, and the _____
dissipates the heat developed when the gas is compressed.

42. The vapor-cycle refrigeration system has a high-pressure section from the _____ to the
_____ and a low-pressure section from the _____ to the
_____ .

43. The high-pressure section is commonly referred to as the _____ , and the low-pressure
section is referred to as the _____ .

44. An operational check involves running the engine of the aircraft, turning on the refrigeration system, and checking
the _____ at the evaporator; the _____ should be checked for bubbles
or foam.

45. If a refrigeration system operates satisfactorily for a few minutes and then stops cooling, it is an indication of
_____ in the system.

46. Servicing of a vapor-cycle refrigeration system requires the use of a _____ , which makes it
possible to ''plug in'' to the system as required to _____ , _____ ,
and _____ , _____ , and _____ the system.

47. When it becomes necessary to change a unit in a vapor-cycle refrigeration system, the refrigerant must be released
by connecting the manifold port to a _____ , which is connected to a
_____ .

48. The escaping gas should be monitored for escaping _____ , which indicates that the system
is being purged too quickly.

49. When one or more units are removed from the system, all fittings should be _____ to
prevent the entrance of any detrimental material.

50. Before the system is evacuated, the drying agent in the _____ must be replaced.

51. The reason for evacuation of the system is that all _____ and _____
must be removed from the system.

52. As pressure drops below atmospheric because of the vacuum, the _____ of water decreases.
Thus, all water in the air is vaporized.

53. The R-12 refrigerant is _____ and _____ at normal temperatures, but
it _____ air and therefore may remove the availability of breathing air from the area.

54. R-12 refrigerant converts to a _____ gas at _____ .

55. In case of leakage during the evacuation system, purging the system should be accomplished in an

_____ where there is adequate ventilation and no chance of exposure to high temperatures.

56. Refrigerant in a liquid state can cause _____ due to the low temperature created as the refrigerant evaporates.

57. When recharging the system, the aircraft's maintenance manual or system manufacturer's service manual should

specify the _____ and _____ of refrigerant for the most efficient operation of the system.

58. The refrigerant container should be held in an _____ position to assure that only gas flows into the system.

59. After the prescribed amount of refrigerant has been placed in the system, the service manifold should be removed

and the _____ capped.

60. The air-cycle machine has the ability to provide cabin _____ as well as heated and pressurized air.

61. When a gas is compressed, it becomes _____ , and when the pressure is reduced, the gas

becomes _____ .

62. In an air-cycle system, the air is continuously compressed and then cooled by means of

_____ through which _____ is passed; then the pressure is reduced by

passing the air through an _____ .

63. The cooled air is directed through ducting with control valves to regulate the amount of

_____ needed to produce the desired cabin temperature.

64. The turbine-compressor unit by which air is cooled is called an _____ .

65. Hot compressed air from the compressor of one of the turbine engines flows through the

_____ that is exposed to ram air, which removes heat from the air.

66. The cooled but still compressed air is then ducted to the _____ of the ACM; there the air is further compressed, which causes it to increase in temperature.

67. This air is directed to the _____ , which, being exposed to ram air, removes heat from the compressed air.

68. The compressed air is then directed to the _____ , which absorbs energy from the air and utilizes the heat energy and pressure to drive the compressor.

69. As the air exits the expansion turbine, it enters a large chamber, which allows the air to expand and causes a

further reduction in the _____ .

70. Thus the air leaving the turbine is cooled by the loss of _____ and by the

_____ that takes place.

71. The great reduction in temperature causes the moisture in the air to condense, and this moisture is removed by

means of a _____ .

72. The _____ is then routed to ducting to be utilized as required to provide the desired temperature in the cabin.

73. A bypass duct with the cabin-temperature-control valve will bypass air around the cooling system when cooling is

_____ .

74. In order to make the cabin environment comfortable for the aircraft occupants, the cabin must normally be pressurized to maintain the cabin air pressure at the level reached at no higher than _____ .

75. By being able to control the cabin rate of climb and descent pressure independent of the aircraft climb and descent pressure, the aircraft occupants are spared any discomfort from _____ .

76. The normal limiting factor as to how high the aircraft can operate is often the maximum allowed _____ .

77. Cabin differential pressure is the difference in pressure between the _____ air pressure and the pressure _____ the aircraft.

78. The source of pressure for an aircraft varies, depending on the _____ being used and the design requirements of the aircraft manufacturer.

79. A _____ is an engine-driven air pump, mechanically driven from the engine drive train, which compresses air for use by the engine in the combustion process.

80. A _____ is used in a similar manner as a supercharger except that the turbocharger is driven by exhaust gases from the engine, which drives an air compressor to supply an air charge to the engine.

81. Aircraft using turbine engines usually make use of engine _____ to pressurize the cabin.

82. If the air leaving the compressor is cooled _____ , the air temperature is increased by using a heat source to bring the air back up to the desired value.

83. The amount of heated air mixed with the cooled air may be automatically or manually controlled by a _____ .

84. The _____ is used as the primary means of controlling the cabin pressure.

85. The outflow valve controls the amount of air allowed to _____ from the cabin.

86. Outflow valves may be operated directly by _____ , or their operation may be by _____ whose operation is controlled by pneumatic pressure.

87. The _____ , also called a _____ , opens automatically and starts releasing cabin pressurization when its preset value is reached.

88. The preset value of the _____ is about 0.5 psi [3.4 kPa] _____ than the maximum setting of the _____ .

89. The safety valve prevents the cabin from being _____ , which could result in aircraft structural failure.

90. The safety valve and the outflow valve are often identical in design, with the only differences being the _____ and the pneumatic connections for operation.

91. The negative pressure-relief valve prevents the cabin from being at a _____ than the ambient air.

92. The operation of the negative pressure-relief valve is _____ .

93. It opens to equalize the cabin and ambient pressure if the ambient pressure exceeds cabin pressure by more than about _____ .

94. A _____ is used to release all cabin pressurization when the aircraft lands.

95. The dump valve is commonly controlled by a _____ .

96. When the landing-gear oleo is compressed, the squat switch causes the dump valve to _____ ; this _____ the cabin and ambient atmospheric pressures.

97. The safety valve is designed to _____ above a preset value and _____ require the use of a separate controller.

98. When considering the operation of a safety valve, if cabin pressure exceeds the combined force of atmospheric pressure and the _____ , the metering valve is lifted off its seat.

99. The controller that operates the outflow valve is located on the flight deck and is used by the pilot to select the desired _____ of cabin _____ and the _____ .

100. The individual air-distribution system, also called the _____ , routes only the cold air from the air-conditioning packs to individually regulated outlets in the control and passenger cabins.

101. The pressure in the cabin of an airplane is usually designated as _____ rather than in terms of pounds per square inch gauge or kilopascals.

102. The _____ system in the controller maintains a constant cabin altitude until the altitude of the aircraft produces a differential pressure above that which is safe for the aircraft.

103. A lack of oxygen causes a person to experience a condition called _____ .

104. Oxygen systems, classified according to source of oxygen supply, may be described as _____ , _____ or _____ , and _____ (LOX) systems.

105. High-pressure cylinders are designed to contain oxygen at a pressure of approximately _____ .

106. High-pressure cylinders can be identified by their _____ and by the words ''Aviators' Breathing Oxygen'' on the side of the cylinder.

107. Low-pressure cylinders are painted _____ to distinguish them from the high-pressure cylinders.

108. Oxygen cylinders are often fitted with _____ , which rupture if the pressure in the cylinder becomes too great.

109. Regulators typically _____ in the oxygen system to the range of 40 to 75 psig [279 to 517 kPa], so it is suitable for individual use.

110. Oxygen masks vary considerably in size, shape, and design; however, each is designed for either a _____ system or a _____ system.

111. An oxygen mask for a demand system must fit the face closely, enclosing both the mouth and nose, and must form an _____ with the face.

112. _____ by the user will then cause a low pressure in the demand regulator, which results in opening of an oxygen valve and a _____ to the mask.

113. An oxygen mask for a constant-flow system is designed so that some _____ is mixed with the oxygen.

114. When the oxygen is turned on to a _____ , it fills the reservoir through a valve, and as the user inhales, he or she draws oxygen directly from the reservoir bag. When the oxygen in the reservoir bag is depleted, the user breathes _____ .

115. When the user of a constant-flow mask _____ , the reservoir bag refills with oxygen.

116. When oxygen is turned on to the _____ mask, it enters the bottom of the reservoir bag and causes it to inflate. When inhaling, the user draws oxygen from the reservoir bag until it is _____ and then begins to breathe cabin air plus a small amount of oxygen flowing through the reservoir.

117. The _____ burns a mixture of sodium chlorate ($NaClO_3$) and iron (Fe) to produce pure oxygen suitable for human use.

118. The fuel unit of a chemical oxygen generator is sometimes called a _____ , as it burns somewhat like a candle, starting at the ignited end and burning slowly from one end to the other.

119. Use extreme caution to assure that every port in the oxygen system is kept thoroughly clean and free of

_____ , _____ , _____ , and

_____ .

120. Thin _____ conforming to MIL-T-27730 may be used to aid in sealing tapered pipe threads.

121. _____ compounds shall be used on _____ .

122. No compound is used on the _____ or on the _____ .

123. Sealant tape is not applied to the _____ of a coupling.

124. Tools used for the installation of oxygen lines and fittings must be _____ and free of all dirt, grease, or oil.

125. Each cylinder must have a Department of Transportation (DOT) _____ .

126. Standard-weight cylinders are marked _____ or _____ and have no total life limitations and may be used until they fail _____ at five-thirds of their operating pressure.

127. The hydrostatic test must be made every _____ .

128. Lightweight cylinders are designated _____ and must be hydrostatically tested every

_____ to five-thirds of their operating pressure.

129. Lightweight cylinders must be retired from service after _____ or

_____ , whichever occurs first.

130. _____ must conform to DOT-E-8162 and are rated for 1850 psi [12 746.5 kPa].

131. Composite cylinders have a life of _____ or _____ , whichever occurs first.

132. Each filling of an oxygen cylinder requires _____ .

133. DOT numbers, serial numbers, and dates of hydrostatic testing are _____ on the

_____ or _____ of each cylinder.

134. Whenever a component of a high-pressure oxygen system has been removed and replaced or whenever the system has been disassembled in any way, the system must be _____ and

_____ .

135. Leak testing is accomplished by applying an approved _____ conforming to MIL-L-25567A, Type 1, to all fittings as instructed.

136. _____ the oxygen system involves fully charging the system in accordance with service instructions, then releasing oxygen from the system.

137. When recharging an oxygen system, only _____ oxygen conforming to

_____ can be used.

138. Do _____ that because a cylinder is colored green it contains breathing oxygen, because cylinders containing other gases are sometimes colored green.

Chapter 16

MULTIPLE CHOICE QUESTIONS

Name _____

Date _____

1. An exhaust heating system
   a. is illegal.
   b. is a simple form of a heat exchanger.
   c. requires little care.
   d. is required on all aircraft certified to a cruise altitude equal to or greater than 8000 feet.

2. Aircraft combustion heaters
   a. require a separate fuel storage system.
   b. usually require ignition prior to fuel flow.
   c. do not require any type of heat exchanger.
   d. vent cooled exhaust gas into the cabin for heating.

3. Bleed air heat
   a. may not be used in single-engine applications.
   b. is mixed (blended) with combustion exhaust heat before entering the cabin.
   c. is the heat lost as wheel braking systems are bled.
   d. comes from the compression of gases (air).

4. In a vapor-cycle aircraft-cooling system, the compressor
   a. turns the entering freon gas into a liquid under high pressure.
   b. turns the entering freon gas into a liquid under low pressure.
   c. increases the pressure and temperature of the input freon gas.
   d. decreases the pressure and temperature of the input freon gas.

5. The function of the condenser in a vapor-cycle cooling system is to
   a. change the high-pressure incoming gases to a high pressure liquid.
   b. change the high-pressure incoming gases to a higher pressure gas.
   c. change the low-pressure incoming liquid to a high pressure gas.
   d. change the low-pressure incoming gases to a high pressure liquid.

6. The receiver-dryer in the vapor-cycle cooling system
   a. acts as a small reservoir for freon liquid.
   b. removes condensation (water) from the freon.
   c. often provides a visual verification of sufficient system freon.
   d. All the above.

7. The high-pressure liquid leaving the receiver-dryer (or subcooler) passes through a
   a. deviation bar, which diverts the gases present in the liquid and sends (diverts) them back to the receiver-dryer.
   b. thermal diverter valve, which diverts the hot gases present in the liquid and sends (diverts) them directly to the compressor.
   c. thermal expansion valve, which converts the liquid freon into droplet form and sends the droplets to an evaporator.
   d. heat dissipater, which adds more liquid, supplied by the receiver-dryer reservoir, to the flow as needed.

8. The evaporator in a vapor-cycle air-conditioning system
   a. cools the freon gases to a level sufficient to mix with ambient air and then introduces them into the cabin.
   b. draws heat from the ambient air and turns the liquid droplets into a low-pressure gas.
   c. draws heat from the ambient air and turns the liquid droplets into a low-pressure liquid.
   d. increases the pressure of the liquid droplets before they are sent to the compressor for cooling.

9. Freon gas should be used with care because
   a. it can displace the ambient air, leaving no oxygen to breathe, and because it is toxic at elevated temperatures.
   b. it is toxic at standard temperatures and combines with oxygen to form a chlorine gas.
   c. it is explosive as it changes from a gas to a liquid.
   d. it is explosive as it changes from a liquid to a gas.

10. When a vapor-cycle system is purged all freon is removed and
    a. a vacuum is created to lower the boiling point of any water that might be in the system.
    b. a slight vacuum is created to suck any water out of the system.
    c. a slight positive pressure is used to push water from the system, because a vacuum would collapse the tubing.
    d. a slight positive pressure is used to lower the boiling point of any water that might be in the system and push water vapor from the system.

11. The air used in air-cycle cooling is
    a. compressed and then cooled by heat exchange, then subcooled by a second heat exchange, and then cooled further by using some of its heat energy to drive a turbine.
    b. cooled by heat exchange, compressed and cooled by another heat exchange, and then cooled further by using some of its heat energy to drive a turbine.
    c. mixed with pure oxygen before being compressed.
    d. stored under pressure in the APU auxiliary tank.

12. In aircraft pressurization, the degree of pressurization is normally controlled by
    a. an outflow valve that regulates the rate of escaping air.
    b. a mixing valve that blends the incoming pressurized air on a demand basis.
    c. a pressure regulating valve at the engine bleed valve.
    d. the powerplant throttle position.

13. The maximum pressure altitude attainable
    a. is limited by the maximum pressure differential the cabin will withstand.
    b. may be found on the aircraft's Type Certificate Data Sheet.
    c. is stamped on the outflow valve.
    d. is stamped on the safety valve.

14. The component of an aircraft pressurization system that prevents the pressure inside the cabin from being less than the ambient pressure is the
    a. outflow valve.
    b. safety valve.
    c. negative pressure-relief valve.
    d. This question does not make sense because the pressure inside the cabin is always less than that outside.

15. A lack of oxygen
    a. first causes hypoxia, and if permanent damage is done, anoxia.
    b. first causes anoxia, and if permanent damage is done, hypoxia.
    c. first causes anemia, and if permanent damage is done, anoxia.
    d. None of the above statements are true.

16. Which type of oxygen-regulating system should be used if the aircraft is flown at extremely high altitudes?
    a. Continuous-flow regulators
    b. Demand regulators
    c. Diluter demand regulators
    d. Pressure-demand regulators

17. If the pressure in an oxygen bottle becomes too great, a safety device will release the pressure in the bottle. This may be detected by
    a. the presence of a red flag on the oxygen-pressure gauge.
    b. a rupturing of the safety (blowout) disk.
    c. the same color change of the oxygen bottle that usually occurs when the bottle is used under normal conditions.
    d. a color change on the carbon monoxide indicator.

18. High-pressure oxygen bottles are
    a. red in color.
    b. blue in color.
    c. green in color.
    d. yellow in color.

19. Oxygen bottles must be
    a. hydrostatically checked to DOT specifications.
    b. rinsed with a weak acid once a year to remove oxides.
    c. rinsed with a weak base once a year to remove any acid build up.
    d. None of the above statements are true.

20. If a chemical oxygen generator is spent
    a. it will change color to red.
    b. it will indicate zero pressure on the gauge.
    c. its heat-sensitive paint mark will be black.
    d. a ''spent'' pin will extend from the generator.

Chapter 17

1. _____ are used to monitor many aircraft flight situations, such as

   _____ , as well as the condition of systems such as hydraulic pressure and

   _____ .

2. Instruments that measure pressures in relatively high-pressure fluid systems are usually operated through a

   mechanism known as a _____ .

3. When pressure enters the bourdon tube, the tube tends to _____ ; as it does so, it moves the

   mechanical linkage connected to the _____ gear.

4. Pressure gauges designed to provide readings of comparatively low pressures are usually of the

   _____ or _____ .

5. The diaphragm consists of two disks of thin metal _____ and _____

   together at the edges to form a cavity or capsule.

6. Changes in the pressure of the air outside the diaphragm cause it to expand or contract, thus producing a movement

   that is _____ to a dial reading through the instrument mechanism.

7. The bellows is made of thin metal with corrugated sides and formed into a _____ .

8. Pressure instruments may be designed to indicate pressure as a value referenced to the _____

   air pressure [pounds per square inch gauge (psig)], to _____ [pounds per square inch

   absolute (psia)], or to some other reference value _____ .

9. If a value on a pressure gauge is identified as indicating pressure in psig, then the pressure indicated is a gauge

   pressure—that is, the pressure _____ .

10. If the face of the gauge does not show that a pressure differential is indicated and if the gauge reads zero when the

    system is inactive, the instrument is indicating _____ .

11. Instruments such as manifold pressure gauges are referenced to _____ and indicate the

    _____ in the engine intake manifold.

12. The absolute pressure thus indicated is valued _____ .

13. Other instruments such as the engine-pressure-ratio indicator for a turbine engine compare the

    _____ at the inlet of the engine to the ram air pressure of the exhaust gases at the engine

    outlet to give a _____ .

14. The gyroscope is a device consisting of a wheel having much of its mass _____ , mounted
    on a spinning axis.

15. The principle of rigidity in space is based on the fact that a spinning mass tends to stabilize with

    _____ fixed in space and will continue to spin in the _____ unless
    outside forces are applied to it.

16. The rigidity of a gyro is increased as the mass at the rim of the gyro wheel is _____ and/or

    as the _____ is increased.

17. In order to allow the necessary freedom of movement, a gyroscope is mounted in _____ so that the mounting can be rotated in any direction without disturbing the gyro; this is called a

_____ .

18. The rings in which the gyro is mounted and that permit it to move are called _____ .

19. _____ can be described briefly as the tendency of a gyro to react to an applied force 90° in the direction of rotation from the point the force is applied.

20. Gyroscope rotors are designed to be operated either _____ .

21. _____ electrical resistance systems use variable resistors to indicate position or quantity.

22. A _____ circuit is a type often used to monitor operating temperatures that do not exceed 300° F [149°C].

23. _____ are used where the variations in electrical voltage in the aircraft electrical system cause the bridge circuit to give inaccurate readings beyond acceptable limits.

24. The _____ is used to indicate the height of the aircraft above sea level.

25. As altitude increases, the density of the air _____ , resulting in a decrease in

_____ .

26. The _____ is rarely used in aircraft because of the very compressed altitude scale.

27. The pressure element of the sensitive altimeter consists of two or three diaphragm capsules

_____ , and there may be either two or three dial pointers.

28. An altimeter must be _____ for atmospheric pressure changes if it is to give true indications under all conditions.

29. An accurate altimeter must be corrected for _____ or _____ .

30. Position error applies to a _____ airplane.

31. The sensitive altimeter must have automatic compensation for _____ .

32. _____ are required on aircraft that fly in controlled airspace above 12 500 ft [3810 m] altitude, aircraft that are equipped with Category II and Category III landing systems, and aircraft operating in Group I and Group II Terminal Controlled Areas.

33. The purpose of the airspeed indicator is to show the speed of the aircraft _____ .

34. The mechanism of an airspeed consists of an airtight diaphragm enclosed in an airtight case, with linkages and gears designed to multiply the _____ and provide an indication on the dial of the instrument.

35. Airspeed indicators actually measure _____ between the inside of the diaphragm and the inside of the instrument case.

36. In level flight, as the speed of the airplane increases, the _____ becomes greater but the static pressure remains the same; this causes the diaphragm to _____ more and more as the pressure increases inside.

37. _____ is the airspeed indicated on the instrument.

38. _____ is indicated airspeed corrected for instrument and sensor position error.

39. The true airspeed scale is a movable scale that is positioned by the pilot to compensate for variations in

_____ and _____ by aligning the ambient temperature and the

pressure altitude; it is read through a _____ that is provided in the standard airspeed scale.

40. The dial or cover glass of an airspeed indicator is required to be marked with color arcs and radial lines to indicate

_____ .

41. A _____ is applied at the never-exceed speed (V_{ne}).

42. A _____ is applied through the caution range of speeds.

43. A green arc is placed to indicate the _____ of speeds, with the lower limit at the stalling speed with maximum weight and with landing gear and wing flaps retracted (V_{sl}), and the upper limit at the maximum structural cruising speed (V_{no}).

44. A white arc is used for the _____ with the lower limit at the stalling speed at maximum weight with the landing gear and flaps fully extended (V_{so}) and the upper limit at the flaps' extended speed (V_{fe}).

45. For multiengine aircraft, a blue radial line is used for the one-engine-inoperative _____ speed (V_{yse}) and a red radial line indicates the one-engine-inoperative minimum control speed (V_{mc}).

46. These markings are normally placed on the _____ of the instrument.

47. Where the required markings are placed on the instrument cover glass, an indicator line must be painted or otherwise applied from the glass to the case so that any _____ of the glass is apparent.

48. An _____ indicator indicates airspeed, the maximum allowable indicated airspeed, and angle of attack.

49. Angle-of-attack information is obtained by reading the indicated airspeed pointer against a _____ about the periphery of the instrument's dial.

50. The maximum allowable pointer of an airspeed-angle-of-attack indicator shows "maximum allowable" and/or "never exceed" _____ .

51. Since the speed of sound varies according to _____ and _____ , it is obvious that an airspeed indicator will not give the pilot an accurate indication of the airplane speed relative to the speed of sound.

52. An instrument that gives the airplane speed in proportion to the speed of sound under the atmospheric conditions in which the airplane is flying is the _____ , or Mach indicator.

53. A Machmeter, or Mach indicator, measures the ratio of _____ to the _____ .

54. The Machmeter is similar in construction to an airspeed indicator; however, it includes an additional expanding diaphragm that modifies the magnifying ratio of the mechanism in proportion to _____ .

55. Also referred to as a rate-of-climb indicator, a vertical-speed indicator is valuable during instrument flight because it indicates the _____ at which the airplane is _____ .

56. The climb indicator is a differential-pressure instrument measuring the differential between _____ and the pressure of a chamber that is vented to the _____ through a small, calibrated capillary restriction.

57. It is characteristic of the rate-of-climb indicator to _____ in its readings.

58. Temperature changes have a tendency to cause variations in the flow of air through the _____ in the rate-of-climb instrument.

59. Variometers and total-energy variometers are _____ usually associated with gliders and sailplane operations.

60. A total-energy variometer can be an electronic or mechanical device and is designed to indicate the change in aircraft _____ by indicating a rate of climb or descent.

61. The _____ is frequently used on new airplanes during test flights to measure the _____ on the aircraft structure; it serves as a basis for stress analysis because it gives an accurate indication of stresses imposed on the airplane during flight.

62. The accelerometer's function is to measure in _____ units the accelerations of gravity being exerted on the airplane.

63. The magnetic compass is an _____ instrument described as mechanical because it requires no power from any aircraft source.

64. The magnetic compass is a comparatively simple device designed to indicate the _____ in which an aircraft is headed.

65. The compass provides an indication of _____ direction rather than _____ direction.

66. Since the magnetic poles of the earth are _____ located at the geographical poles, the magnetic compass reading is subject to _____ , depending upon its location on the earth's surface.

67. Magnetic compasses are subject to _____ , which is an inaccuracy caused by magnetic influences in the _____ .

68. Small compensating magnets mounted in the case are adjustable to correct for _____ deviation and east-west _____ .

69. The process of compass compensating is done by _____ the compass on a _____ . This is a circle on which are marked magnetic directions in degrees, the 0° mark showing the magnetic north direction.

70. Before attempting to compensate the compass, every effort should be made to place the aircraft in _____ . Check to see that the _____ , _____ , _____ , and _____ . All _____ , _____ , and _____ should be on.

71. The sequence of events in swinging a compass are:

    a. Set adjustment screws of compensator on _____ .

    b. Head the aircraft in a _____ direction and _____ the N-S adjustment screw until the compass reads exactly north (0°).

    c. Head the aircraft in a _____ direction and adjust the E-W screw until the compass reads exactly _____ .

    d. Head the aircraft in a magnetic south direction, note the resulting south error, and adjust the N-S screw until _____ has been removed.

    e. Head the aircraft in a magnetic west direction and adjust the E-W screw to remove _____ .

    f. Head the aircraft in _____ and _____ on the appropriate _____ .

72. Deviations must not exceed _____ on any heading.

73. The compass on an airplane should be checked (swung) whenever there is an installation or removal of any _____ or any _____ that could have an effect on the compass.

74. The compass and correction card should be checked for deviation at least once a year _____ .

75. The mounting location is chosen so that the compass is as far away as possible from items that might affect its operation, such as the _____ and _____ , but still in easy view of the pilot.

76. The _____ indicator is actually a direct-reading magnetic compass; instead of the direction's being read from the swinging compass card, however, the reading is taken from a vertical dial.

77. The reference index on the vertical dial can be set at any desired heading by turning the knob at the bottom of the dial, and it is necessary only to match the indicator needle with the reference pointer to hold a

   _____ .

78. The _____ compass system is one type of remote-indicating earth-inductor compass system; it consists of a flux gate (flux valve) transmitter, master direction indicator, amplifier, junction box, caging switch, and one or more compass repeaters.

79. The flux gate is a special three-section transformer, which develops a signal whose characteristics are determined by the position of the unit with respect to the _____ .

80. The _____ is a gyro-operated directional reference instrument designed to eliminate some of the problems associated with the magnetic compass.

81. The directional gyro does not seek the north pole; however, it will continue to tell the pilot of an aircraft whether the aircraft is holding a _____ .

82. Since the spin axis is horizontal and the instrument case can be considered aligned with the directional axis of the aircraft, the angle presented on the dial is also the angle between the _____ and the direction of the _____ .

83. Any change in the heading of the aircraft is indicated on the dial, since the position of the gyro is

   _____ in space and is not affected by the _____ .

84. A _____ is a refined version of the directional gyro. Its principles of operation are the same as for the directional gyro, but the display presentation is a compass card.

85. Gyro instruments must necessarily be limited in the degree of movement through which the

   _____ can travel.

86. If the degree of permitted movement is exceeded because of violent maneuvers of the airplane, the gyro rotor will be moved out of its normal position of rigidity, and it is then said to be _____ .

87. In order to restore the gyro to its correct alignment, a _____ mechanism is installed.

88. When a gyro is air-driven, the _____ that spin the rotor are used to keep it level.

89. A _____ , or HSI, is an instrument that combines the information supplied by a heading indicator with radio navigation information.

90. Information from the glideslope radio receiver is displayed on the left side of the HSI unit, and

   _____ , such as NAV, HDG, and GS, are displayed whenever that function is inoperative.

91. The gyro horizon indicator, also called the _____ , _____ , or

   _____ , is designed to provide a visual reference horizon for an airplane that is flying "blind."

92. A white bar across the face of the gyro horizon indicator represents the _____ , and a small figure of an airplane in the center of the dial represents the _____ .

93. On a gyro horizon indicator, the position of the airplane symbol relative to the horizon bar indicates the

   _____ of the aircraft with respect to the _____ .

94. A gyro erection mechanism is incorporated into the design of an artificial horizon to correct for any force such as precession, which might cause the gyroscope to tilt out of its _____ .

95. The _____ indicator, sometimes called the "needle and ball," actually consists of two instruments.

96. The "needle" part of the instrument is a gyro instrument that indicates to the pilot the _____ at which the aircraft is turning.

97. The "ball" part of the instrument is an _____ , which denotes the quality of the turn by indicating whether or not the turn is _____ .

98. The turn-indicating section of the turn-and-bank indicator is actually a _____ , and it produces an indication in _____ to the rate of turn.

99. The face of the instrument normally includes marks, or "_____ ," on each side of the centered needle position.

100. When the needle is pointing at one of these marks, the aircraft is in a _____ of _____ .

101. Some rate indicators are designed to indicate a turn at _____ of standard rate when the needle points at the "doghouse." These instruments can be identified by the words "4 MINUTE TURN" at the bottom of the instrument, meaning that a 360° change in direction will take _____ rather than 2 min.

102. A _____ is similar to a turn-and-bank indicator in that the pilot uses it to determine the rate of turn.

103. Suction or vacuum gauges indicate the amount of vacuum being created by the _____ or venturi tube and assist in the proper setting of the relief valve in the vacuum system.

104. The purpose of a _____ is to provide the pressures necessary to operate such instruments as the altimeter, airspeed indicator, and vertical-speed indicator.

105. _____ is also required for such control units as air data transducers and automatic pilots.

106. The purpose of the head used in a pitot-static system is to pick up indications of _____ and _____ to be transmitted through tubing to the instruments requiring these pressures for operation.

107. The static pressure is supplied through the _____ mounted flush with the fuselage skin toward the rear of the airplane.

108. An important feature of the pitot pressure system is its provision for removing _____ before it can reach the instruments.

109. If there is a leak in the static line inside a pressurized airplane, pressure from the cabin will leak into the static line, and the instruments will _____ .

110. Many of the electrically powered instruments have the word *electric* on the face, and all electrically operated instruments should have a _____ that is _____ when electrical power is _____ to the instrument.

111. Regardless of the type of pump used, the air inlet to gyro instruments should be _____ to keep contaminants out of the instruments and out of the pump.

112. A _____ generates a vacuum by moving air through a _____ passage.

113. As the air accelerates through the restricted passage of a venturi, the _____ is _____ , and air can be drawn into the venturi core through a hole placed on the side of the tube at the restriction.

114. Vacuum pumps can be either the _____ or _____ design.

115. A wet pump relies on _____ oil to lubricate the operating mechanism.

116. A dry pump relies on the proper selection of construction materials to provide lubrication. The materials selected for the vanes are normally carbon-based, which means they provide _____ and _____ against the metal case walls.

117. An air data computer is used on most turbine-powered airplanes to power indication and control systems needing information about the _____ and _____ .

118. _____ are used to measure engine rpm.

119. For turbine engines, the engine rpm is indicated in _____ .

120. Tachometers may be _____ or _____ operated.

121. A mechanically operated oil pressure gauge uses an oil-pressure line from the engine to the instrument to operate a _____ and _____ to position the indicator needle.

122. Oil temperature indicators can be _____ or _____ .

123. Exhaust-gas-temperature systems are operated by placing _____ in the stream of _____ exiting the engine; they are used to monitor the performance of the engines and make flight and maintenance adjustments.

124. The thermocouples generate a _____ , which drives the indicator.

125. The amount of current is usually very low and is _____ or _____ in order to drive the indicator display.

126. _____ is used to indicate the amount of _____ being generated by a turbine engine. EPR is determined by measuring the total pressure at the engine inlet and comparing it to the total pressure of the engine exhaust.

127. The _____ gauge measures the sidewall pressure in a reciprocating-engine intake manifold downstream of the carburetor throttle.

128. A _____ temperature gauge uses a thermocouple under a spark plug or mounted on the side of the cylinder head to determine if the engine is operating at the proper temperature.

129. The _____ is used on aircraft equipped with the gasoline tank located in the upper wing.

130. The _____ gauge is a round drum-shaped device that has a revolving disk inside that is attached long arm with a float on the end.

131. The _____ gauge has the float arm directly connected to the pointer by a link arm.

132. The _____ basically identical to the water-level gauge on a water tank and can be used only when the fuel tank is approximately at the same level as the cockpit.

133. _____ gauges use a metal or cork float on an arm to operate a gear segment.

134. A _____ fuel-quantity indicator uses a float on an arm attached to a tank mount. The float arm moves a wiper across a resistance wire winding, varying the resistance in the circuit.

135. A _____-quantity-indicating system is also referred to as an electronic quantity indicating system and measures the _____ of fuel in the tanks rather than the volume.

136. Fuel has a different _____ than air, so the capacitance value of the probe changes as the tank is filled or drained of fuel and the fuel is replaced with air.

137. Any fuel system utilizing an engine-driven or electric fuel pump must have a _____ to ensure that the system is working properly.

138. A _____ line will be placed at each end of the pressure-range band to indicate that the engine must not be operated outside the specified range.

139. If an engine is equipped with either a direct-fuel-injection system or a continuous-flow fuel-injection system, the fuel pressure is a _____ of _____ .

140. The face of the fuel-pressure gauge used in a direct-fuel-injection system is color-coded _____ to show the normal cruise range during which the engine can be operated in _____ and _____ to show the range during which the _____ mixture setting should be used.

141. Fuel-pressure gauges are constructed similar to other pressure gauges used for relatively low pressures; the actuating mechanism is either a _____ or a _____ .

142. Some fuel-pressure gauges on light aircraft are marked as if they were _____ .

143. If a cylinder line is bent or blocked, the pressure in the system would _____ , indicating a _____ fuel flow, when the actual situation is a reduced fuel flow.

144. All standard instruments panels are equipped with at least one _____ clock.

145. Variance on properly shock-mounted and properly calibrated clocks does not exceed _____ .

146. Under _____ should a technician open an aircraft clock for inspection or adjustment.

147. Two metals commonly used in bimetallic thermometers are _____ and _____ .

148. As the temperature rises, both brass and iron expand; but the length of the brass strip increases faster than the length of the iron strip, which causes the bimetallic combination to _____ .

149. Electronic display instruments are basically color television displays that are presented according to signals generated by _____ .

150. The computer is commonly referred to as a _____ , designed to accept information about the condition of the aircraft and convert the information into a set of signals to drive a video display.

151. The video displays are usually divided into three basic types: _____ _____ , _____ , and electronic systems _____ .

152. The _____ is a primary flight instrument used to supply attitude information.

153. The _____ is used to display lateral guidance information along with the location of ground facilities and weather in relation to the aircraft, depending on the sophistication of the system being used.

154. Two of the common types of system monitoring displays include the _____ _____ and the _____ .

155. Instrument mounting can be achieved by the use of two or more _____ , _____ , or _____ , depending on the instrument design.

156. _____ , usually 440 size brass screws, are used to attach the instrument to the panel.

157. If a separate fastener is required, _____ nuts or special instrument _____ can be used.

158. When handling instruments, treat them as delicate mechanisms; avoid hitting or dropping the instrument, and avoid sudden movements of the instrument as this may cause internal components to contact _____ with some force.

159. Never apply _____ , _____ , or _____ to instruments unless directed to by the manufacturer's instructions or other competent references.

160. When installing the instruments, never _____ them into position.

161. When instruments are removed from an aircraft, all lines and openings should be _____ with _____ or _____ and all electrical connections should be properly _____ .

162. If the instrument is not going to be immediately reinstalled, it should be _____ with appropriate information as to time in service, when removed, and reason for removal.

163. The instrument should then be placed in a plastic bag sealed against _____ and _____ in a safe place.

164. Operational ranges and limitations can be obtained from the _____ , _____ , and _____ .

165. Minimum and maximum operational limitations are indicated by a _____ on the instrument.

166. A green arc is used to indicate a _____ .

167. A _____ on the instrument indicates a caution range.

168. A tachometer may incorporate a red arc to indicate a _____ .

169. When marking instructions by placing markings on the cover glass of an instrument, a _____ should be placed on the glass and onto the case next to the glass.

170. Airspeed indicators are tested by applying _____ pressure to the pressure port of the instrument.

171. An altimeter is tested by _____ the altitude reading on the instrument with the actual altitude at the point of testing when the local barometric pressure is adjusted into the instrument.

172. Positive pressure _____ to an altimeter except in the small amount that may be specified by the manufacturer.

173. _____ to altimeters should be recorded in the _____ .

174. Pitot-static systems on aircraft should be tested on a _____ in accordance with the manufacturer's instructions.

175. The static system should be tested in accordance with _____ and flight regulations for aircraft flying under _____ .

176. During the testing of pitot-static systems, care must be taken to see that positive pressure is not applied to the altimeter or _____ applied to the _____ .

177. Positive pressure should not be applied to the _____ .

178. Negative pressure should not be applied to the pitot system when instruments _____ .

179. Pressure in the pitot system must always be equal or greater than that in the _____ .

180. System inspection, instrument replacement, and required repairs are completed _____ the leak tests are made.

181. Instruments should be checked for proper operation, condition of the _____ , condition and placement of _____ , condition of _____ , cleanliness of _____ , security of _____ , and tightness of tube and electrical _____ .

182. The shock mounts by which panels or instruments are attached should be checked for

_____ .

183. Gyro instruments should be checked for _____ time and unusual

_____ during operation.

184. If the run-down time in gyro instruments is shorter than normal, _____

_____ , or _____ has accumulated inside the instrument.

185. Instrument systems should be checked for condition of _____ ,

_____ , _____ , and _____ .

186. A vacuum system may be checked for operation by running the engine that drives the vacuum pump at a medium

speed and verifying that the suction gauge indicates the correct _____ , about 5 ±0.1 in Hg
[16.93 kPa].

187. Before blowing air through a pitot or static system, all instruments connected to the system must be

_____ .

188. In a pitot or static system, air is blown from the _____ of the lines outward toward the

_____ .

Chapter 17

Name _____

Date _____

MULTIPLE CHOICE QUESTIONS

1. The operating mechanism of most hydraulic pressure gauges is
   a. a Bourdon tube.
   b. an airtight bellows.
   c. an airtight diaphragm.
   d. an evacuated bellows filled with inert gas to which suitable arms, levers, and gears are attached.

2. The basic principle upon which gyroscopic instruments are based is
   a. precession.
   b. rigidity in space.
   c. centripetal force.
   d. centrifugal force.

3. In order to be a free gyro, a gyro must be
   a. operating in a vacuum.
   b. securely attached to the instrument case.
   c. free of all gravitational forces.
   d. mounted on rings constructed from a gimbal.

4. Precession is described as the
   a. tendency of one gyro to follow the path of an adjacent gyro.
   b. loss of gyroscopic tendencies due to bearing friction.
   c. tendency of a gyro to react to a force 90° in the direction of rotation.
   d. tendency of a gyro to increase speed when the aircraft is in a dive.

5. A common type of electrically operated oil-temperature gauge utilizes
   a. either a Wheatstone bridge or ratiometer circuit.
   b. a standing wave ratio (SWR) circuit.
   c. a thermocouple-type circuit.
   d. vapor pressure and a pressure switch.

6. When an aircraft altimeter is set at 29.92 in Hg on the ground, the altimeter will read
   a. pressure altitude.
   b. density altitude.
   c. field elevation.
   d. true altitude.

7. The doghouse of a turn-and-bank indicator represents a
   a. 1-min turn.
   b. 2-min turn.
   c. 2.5-min turn.
   d. 5-min turn.

8. The lubber line on the directional gyro is used to
   a. represent the nose of the aircraft.
   b. align the instrument glass in the case.
   c. represent the wings of the aircraft.
   d. indicate true north as opposed to magnetic north.

9. An aircraft magnetic compass is swung at specified operating intervals in order to determine the
   a. accuracy of the lubber line.
   b. compass precession.
   c. compass variation.
   d. compass deviation.

10. The pitot-static system provides what pressures to related instruments?
    a. Ram air pressure and ambient air pressure
    b. Cabin pressure and ambient air pressure
    c. Aerodynamic static pressure and ram air pressure
    d. Exhaust gas pressure and carburetor air pressure

11. The pitot-static system services what instruments?
    a. Altimeter, airspeed indicator, and directional gyro
    b. Airspeed indicator, directional gyro, and Turn and Back indicator
    c. Altimeter, airspeed indicator, and vertical-speed indicator
    d. Airspeed indicator, flux gate compass and intake manifold pressure

12. What does a reciprocating-engine manifold-pressure gauge indicate when the engine is not operating?
    a. Zero pressure
    b. The differential between the manifold pressure and the atmospheric pressure
    c. Corrected differential pressure
    d. The existing atmospheric pressure

13. Which statement is correct concerning a thermocouple-type temperature-indicating instrument system?
    a. It is a balanced-type, variable-resistor circuit.
    b. It requires no external power source.
    c. It usually contains a balancing circuit in the instrument case to prevent fluctuations of the system voltage from affecting the temperature reading.
    d. It will not indicate a true reading if the system voltage varies beyond the range for which it is calibrated.

Name _____

Date _____

14. Aircraft instrument panels are usually shock-mounted to
    a. absorb high-frequency, low-amplitude shocks.
    b. absorb low-frequency, high-amplitude shocks.
    c. permit the instruments to operate under conditions of major vibration.
    d. absorb high-frequency, high-amplitude shocks.

15. The number of shock mounts required for an original instrument panel installation is determined by the
    a. size of the panel.
    b. type of the panel.
    c. weight of the complete panel unit.
    d. number of instruments to be installed.

16. Which of the following instruments normally have range markings?
    (1) Airspeed indicator
    (2) Altimeter
    (3) Directional gyro
    (4) Cylinder-head temperature gauge
    a. 2 and 4
    b. 1 and 4
    c. 1 and 3
    d. 2 and 3

17. How would an airspeed indicator be marked to show the best rate-of-climb speed (one engine inoperative)?
    a. A white arc
    b. A red radial line
    c. A blue radial line
    d. A green arc

18. The green arc on an aircraft temperature gauge indicates
    a. the instrument is not calibrated.
    b. the desirable temperature range.
    c. a low, unsafe temperature range.
    d. a high, unsafe temperature range.

19. Who is authorized to repair an aircraft instrument?
    a. A certificated mechanic with airframe and powerplant ratings
    b. A certificated repair station approved for that class instrument
    c. An appropriately rated airframe repair station
    d. A certificated mechanic holding an inspection authorization

20. The minimum requirements for testing and inspection of instrument static pressure systems required by FAR Section 91.171 are contained in
    a. Type Certificate Data Sheets.
    b. Technical Standard Orders.
    c. AC 43.13-1A.
    d. FAR Part 43, Appendix E.

Chapter 18

1. A thermal-switch fire detection system is simply a circuit in which one or more thermal switches are connected in an electrical circuit with a _____ and an _____ to warn the pilot or flight crew that an overheat condition exists in a particular area.

2. If more than one thermal switch is in the circuit, the switches will be connected in _____ , so the closing of _____ will provide a warning.

3. A _____ is included in each fire detection system so the system may be tested for _____ .

4. The thermal switch, called a _____ , is designed so that when the detector is exposed to heat, the case becomes _____ and causes the _____ inside the case to be drawn together.

5. The thermocouple detection system, also called a _____ detection system, utilizes one or more thermocouples connected in _____ to activate an alarm system when there is a sufficiently high rate of temperature increase at the sensor.

6. A test circuit is provided for the system through the use of a _____ next to a thermocouple.

7. There are three types of tubular sensing devices, called _____ systems, commonly employed in modern aircraft for detecting overheat or fire.

8. The _____ sensor consists of a small, lightweight, flexible _____ tube with a pure _____ wire–center conductor.

9. When a Fenwal sensor is heated sufficiently, current can flow between the center wire and the tube wall because the _____ melts and its resistance _____ rapidly when the temperature reaches a given level.

10. The increased current flow between the nickel center wire and the tubing wall provides the signal, which is utilized in the _____ to produce the output signal that _____ .

11. The sensing element of the _____ system consists of an Inconel tube filled with a thermistor material.

12. In the Kidde sensing element the resistance of the thermistor material _____ when a high temperature is applied.

13. The change in _____ in the Kidde system is sensed by the electronic control circuit monitoring the system, and the control provides the warning signal to illuminate the fire warning light and activate the aural warning device.

14. The sensing element produced by the _____ is pneumatic in operation.

15. The _____ of the gas inside the Systron-Donner element is _____ by heat, and the increased pressure actuates a _____ inside the responder, which closes the circuit and provides the warning signal.

16. The continuous-loop (Kidde and Fenwal) and continuous-length (Systron-Donner) types of fire detection mechanisms are considered _____ to the spot and thermocouple systems where _____ , such as around a jet engine.

17. All sensing elements must be routed as described in the _____ .

18. Smoke-detection systems are usually installed to monitor the condition of the air in _____ and _____ , where considerable smoke may be generated before the heat level reaches a point to set off the overheat and fire warning system.

19. _____ (carbon monoxide) detectors are usually installed in cockpits and cabins, where the presence of the gas would affect the flight crew and passengers.

20. In a light-detection system, a _____ is placed in a location where it can ''see'' the surrounding area and produce a _____ of current flow when there is a change in the _____ or _____ striking the cell.

21. In a light-detection system, the _____ is used to activate an amplifier circuit, which produces the visual and aural alarm signals.

22. The light-detection system is activated only by an _____ .

23. In a _____ a light beam is passed through the detection chamber, and a photoelectric cell is placed in the chamber, where it is shielded from the _____ of the light source.

24. When smoke is introduced into the chamber of a light-refraction detector, the light from the particles of smoke is _____ into the photoelectric cell.

25. A change in the _____ of the photoelectric cell changes the _____ through the cell.

26. In an ionization-type smoke detector, a small amount of _____ is used to bombard the oxygen and nitrogen molecules in the air within the _____ .

27. If smoke is in the air, small particles of the smoke attach themselves to the oxygen and nitrogen _____ and _____ the flow of current.

28. When the current level is reduced by a _____ , the alarm circuit will be _____ to produce the visual and aural alarm.

29. The _____ type of smoke or toxic-gas detection utilizes two heated, solid-state _____ .

30. The composition of the sensors is such that ions of _____ or _____ will be absorbed into the solid-state _____ of the sensing element and change its _____ ability.

31. The commonly used agents for fire extinguishing are _____ , _____ , and _____ .

32. _____ is also an extinguishing agent but is primarily used in current systems as a _____ for one of the other chemicals.

33. _____ and _____ must not be allowed to come into contact with the skin because they will cause frostbite due to extremely low temperatures attained when the _____ .

34. Most modern aircraft extinguishing systems make use of _____ as the extinguishing agent.

35. The use of CO_2 is usually limited to _____ transports.

36. Dry-chemical extinguishing agents are not used for aircraft fire-extinguishing systems because they are _____ and _____ .

37. Some of the gaseous agents may be considered toxic while they are present in an area in large quantities because of the _____ of _____ .

38. Fire-suppression or fire-extinguishing systems usually consist of a fire-extinguishing agent stored in _____ , _____ to carry the extinguishing agent to areas that require protection, _____ , _____ , _____ , and associated components.

39. A discharge head containing an _____ is installed on one or both of the container necks to discharge the container by rupturing the disk when the cartridge is activated.

40. The _____ is the explosive charge that drives the slug through the disk.

41. When CO_2 systems are activated, the _____ rapidly discharge the bottles into the distribution lines.

42. Two methods are used to allow the pilot or technician to determine if the bottle has discharged thermally: the use of a _____ or the use of a _____ .

43. The conventional system fire-extinguishing system usually uses _____ as the extinguishing agent and makes use of a perforated ring and distributor-nozzle discharge arrangement.

44. When a conventional system fire-extinguishing system is activated, the CO_2 bottles are opened and the gas flows through the lines to the _____ and out of the perforated ring and distributor nozzles to _____ .

45. The _____ system uses Freon or Halon 1301 and spherical bottles actuated by explosive cartridges.

46. The discharge tubes of a high-rate-of discharge (HRD) system are configured to allow a _____ of agent into the fire area and _____ the compartment to eliminate the fire quickly.

47. If an electrical fire is most likely, extinguishing agents containing _____ must not be used, because water increases _____ and may cause more damage than good.

48. Oil or fuel fires should be smothered with a _____ agent or a _____ agent.

49. Mechanical parts of fire-extinguishing systems are examined for _____ , _____ , _____ , and _____ with technical and regulatory requirements.

50. Electrical control systems for fire-extinguishing systems are inspected in accordance with _____ for electrical systems and the special instructions given in the _____ .

51. An _____ prevents the formation of ice on the airplane, and a _____ removes ice that has already formed.

52. A Canadair Challenger 601 ice detector consists of a microprocessor circuit with an _____ and _____ extending into the _____ .

53. The probe normally vibrates at a frequency of 40 kHz; however, when ice starts to build on the probe, the _____ .

54. When the frequency has decreased to a preset value, the _____ will turn on a red annunciator light to advise the flight crew that the aircraft is in icing conditions.

55. For many years, various airplanes have utilized mechanical deicing systems consisting of

_____ formed to the leading edge of wings, struts, and stabilizers.

56. The deicing boots are attached to the leading edge of the airfoils by means of _____ and

_____ such as rivnuts, also called _____ .

57. Some aircraft use cement _____ for attaching the deicer boots to leading-edge surfaces.

58. The inflatable boots are usually constructed with several separate _____ or

_____ , so that some can be inflated while _____ are deflated.

59. The inflation of the boot is accomplished by utilizing the _____ from a vacuum pump for

inflation and the inlet side of the pump for _____ .

60. The control of the pressure and suction of deicer boots is accomplished by means of a

_____ , which rotates and periodically changes the flow of air to or from the

_____ of the boots or by flow-control valves.

61. The operation of the distribution valves results in alternate _____ and

_____ of sections of the boots, and this action _____ any ice that has

formed on the boots.

62. When the control switch for deicer boots is turned ON, the _____ energizes the pneumatic

pressure control valve.

63. The inflation sequence is controlled by the _____ and _____ located

near the deicer air inlets.

64. Deicer pressure is normally about _____ .

65. The inspection of pneumatic-mechanical deicer systems requires an examination of the deicer boots for

_____ , _____ to the protected surface, and condition of the

_____ of the boots.

66. Grease or oil found on the boots should be removed with an approved _____ , after which

the boots should be scrubbed with soap and water, then rinsed with clean water.

67. Deicer boots are provided with a _____ coating to prevent the buildup of

_____ on the boots.

68. During inspection and maintenance, the technician should determine whether the conductive coating is

_____ and _____ .

69. If the boots are cemented, the _____ should be consulted regarding the

_____ to be used for _____ and the procedure for

_____ .

70. If any of the tubes in the boots should fail to inflate in sequence or at the proper time, the air supply to that tube

should be checked for _____ .

71. _____ uses heated air flowing through passages in the leading edge of wings, stabilizers, and

engine cowlings to _____ the formation of ice.

72. The heat source for thermal anti-icing operation normally comes from _____ in

reciprocating-engine-powered aircraft and from _____ in turbine-powered aircraft.

73. From the heat source the hot air is distributed along the leading edge of the item being anti-iced by the use of a perforated air duct called a _____ or _____ .

74. When the air exits the piccolo tube, it is in contact with the leading-edge skin of the surface; the skin is heated and ice is _____ from forming.

75. _____ skins form the chordwise double-skin passages in the leading edges.

76. The items for smaller aircraft that need protection from ice buildup include the _____ and the _____ .

77. Larger aircraft require that additional items such as _____ be kept clear of ice along with _____ probes and _____ .

78. Probes are normally kept free of ice by the use of _____ .

79. When inspecting electric heating devices, the technician should be aware that even the units on small aircraft are capable of generating sufficient heat to cause painful _____ on the skin.

80. _____ touch one of these devices if its heater element is _____ .

81. The control of ice buildup on windshields may be accomplished by one of two basic methods: by _____ the windshield or by _____ a fluid on the windshield to remove ice and prevent the formation of any more ice.

82. The heating of windshields is the more common method and may involve the use of a _____ over the windshield surface, electric heater elements _____ , or the use of a flow of heated air _____ .

83. Anti-ice systems must be placed into operation by the pilot _____ any large ice buildup, because the unit is designed for anti-icing rather than deicing.

84. The following items should be checked when inspecting heated windshields:

    a. Check for any _____ in the windshield panels.

    b. Look for any _____ of the windshield and determine its cause.

    c. Any _____ that occurs during operation indicates that the conductive coating may be breaking down.

    d. _____ of the windshield is not normally a problem unless the optical quality of the windshield is affected.

85. When evaluating any of these types of damage to a windshield, follow the recommendations of the aircraft manufacturer. The basic guidelines are that the damage should not _____ the _____ , change the _____ of the windshield, or affect the _____ of the system.

86. Alcohol (isopropyl alcohol), which is used on some aircraft to provide for windshield deicing, is _____ on the outside of the windshield.

87. Care should be taken when inspecting the alcohol deicing system to be sure that all _____ and _____ are in good condition because in-flight fires have resulted from the alcohol line rupturing and spraying onto electrical equipment.

88. Rain may be removed by the use of _____ , _____ in combination with windshield wipers, or by _____ .

89. Windshield-wiper systems may be operated _____ , _____ , or _____ .

90. The rotary motion of the windshield-wiper motor is transmitted by the flexible shaft to a _____ .

91. The converter _____ the shaft speed and changes the rotary motion to an _____ of the windshield-wiper arm.

92. Hydraulically and pneumatically operated wiper systems are similar in that each requires a pressure supply to be directed to an _____ .

93. A control unit alternately connects a pressure or return line to _____ of the actuator, causing the piston to move _____ .

94. The actuator piston incorporates a _____ that operates a _____ at the base of the wiper and causes the side-to-side motion of the wiper.

95. During rain conditions, the windshield wipers are turned on, and a _____ is sprayed on the windshield.

96. The repellent is spread evenly by the _____ .

97. The rain repellent should not be sprayed on the windshield unless the windshield is _____ and the wipers are _____ , nor should the windshield wipers be operated on a _____ .

98. The effect of the rain repellent is to cause the water to form small _____ , which are quickly _____ by the rush of air over the windshield in flight.

99. When the pilot turns on the rain-removal system, _____ at a high temperature and pressure is directed to an outlet at the base of the windshield.

100. The water for drinking fountains or faucets is usually drawn from main _____ water tanks, passed through filters to remove any impurities and solids, cooled by dry ice or other means of cooling, and delivered to the faucets and/or drinking fountains.

101. Hot water for washing is provided by means of _____ located beneath the lavatory bowls.

102. A typical hot-water supply is contained in a 2-qt [1.89-L] tank, which includes the _____ heating unit to maintain the water at a temperature of 110 to 120°F [43.3 to 48.9°C].

103. Drain water from the lavatories can be drained overboard through _____ or can be drained into the toilet _____ .

104. The toilet system is designed so there is no possible _____ of the passenger water supply from the system.

105. The purpose of control-surface indicating systems is to allow the flight crew to determine if a control surface is in the _____ for some phase of flight and to determine if a flight control is _____ .

106. In some control-surface indicating systems, a cable is attached to the control horn of the trim tab, and as the tab moves, the cable pulls against a spring; as the spring is _____ or _____ by the movement of the trim tab, a _____ located where the cable connects to the springs moves along a _____ , indicating the trim-tab position.

107. Other position-indicating systems use a _____ in the trim-tab control wheel to cause a pointer to move, indicating the position of the trim tab.

108. When inspecting mechanical indicating systems, the technician should _____ that the _____ agrees with the _____ of the surface being monitored.

109. Large aircraft may make use of electric control-surface indicating systems in which _____ are located at each of the control surfaces.

110. The voltage inducted into the armatures by their _____ is used at the synchro _____ to position the indicator pointers.

111. The items that are checked by a takeoff warning indicator system are that the _____ is in the takeoff range, the _____ is in the 0° position, the steerable fuselage landing gear _____ , the _____ are at 10°, and the _____ are extended.

112. The exact aircraft configuration monitored by a takeoff warning system will vary, but the intent of each system is to prevent a takeoff with the aircraft in an _____ .

113. A stall warning indicator is designed to indicate to the pilot when the aircraft is close to the stalling _____ .

114. Most light aircraft have a stall warning system that uses a _____ on the leading edge of the wing to measure the aircraft's angle of attack.

115. Some light aircraft use a pneumatic stall warning indication system in which a _____ in the leading edge of the wing is connected to tubing _____ .

116. When the wing angle of attack increases to the point where a negative pressure exists on a slot stall warning system, air flows through the _____ and out the slot and creates an _____ stall warning indication.

117. Modern transport aircraft use stall warning computer circuits to activate the stall warning system; inputs to the computer include information about _____ , flap and slat _____ , and _____ on landing gear.

118. When the computer determines that a stall is imminent, a stick-shaker may start moving the control columns back and forth, an _____ warning may be sounded, or an indicator may _____ , depending on the specific system design.

119. To accommodate the needs of the aircraft on the ground for substantial amounts of energy while its engines are not operating, modern aircraft are equipped with _____ .

120. The APUs are _____ , using the aircraft's own fuel supply, which provide the power to run the attached generators.

121. In addition, the APU is typically large enough to provide sufficient _____ to start the aircraft's engines.

122. The APU operations panel usually includes controls for the APU _____ , _____ and _____ , and the fire extinguisher _____ .

123. The amount of airflow and its pressure are dependent upon the _____ and the _____ on (power being drawn from) the APU.

124. The _____ the load and/or ambient temperature, the lower the airflow and pressure.

125. The air-bleed valve should be closed during start-up and not operated until the APU is at approximately _____ power.

126. When the APU bleed valve, also referred to as the "load-control valve," is opened by placing its switch in the cockpit in the OPEN position, airflow is supplied to the aircraft's _____ .

Chapter 18

MULTIPLE CHOICE QUESTIONS

1. The thermocouple fire-warning system is activated by
   a. a slowly overheated engine.
   b. a certain temperature.
   c. a core resistance drop.
   d. a temperature increase at the sensor.

2. Why does the Fenwal fire-detection system use spot detectors wired parallel between two separate circuits?
   a. A control unit is used to isolate the bad system in case of malfunction.
   b. This installation is equal to two systems: a prime system and a reserve system.
   c. A short may exist in either circuit without causing a false fire warning.
   d. The dual terminal thermoswitch is used so that one terminal is wired to a bell, the other to a light.

3. The fire-detection system that uses two wires imbedded in a ceramic core within a tube is the
   a. Fenwal system.
   b. Lindberg system.
   c. thermocouple system.
   d. Kidde system.

4. After a fire is extinguished or an overheat condition removed in an aircraft equipped with a Systron-Donner fire detector, the detection system
   a. must be manually reset.
   b. automatically resets.
   c. sensing component must be replaced.
   d. must be recalibrated.

5. Smoke detectors that use a measurement of light transmissibility in the air are called
   a. electromechanical devices.
   b. photoelectric devices.
   c. visual devices.
   d. electromeasuring devices.

6. Which fire-extinguishing agent is considered to be least toxic?
   a. Carbon dioxide
   b. Monobromotrifluoromethane (Halon 1301)
   c. Dibromodifluoromethane (Halon 1202)
   d. Bromochloromethane (Halon 1011)

7. A fire-extinguisher container can be checked to determine its charge by
   a. attaching a remote pressure gauge.
   b. weighing the container and the remote-control valve.
   c. weighing the container and its contents.
   d. a hydrostatic test.

8. What method is used to detect the thermal discharge of a built-in carbon dioxide fire-extinguisher system?
   a. A discoloring of the yellow plastic disk in the thermal discharge line
   b. A rupture of the red plastic disk in the thermal discharge line
   c. The thermal plug missing from the side of the bottle
   d. A rupture of the green plastic disk in the thermal discharge line

9. A squib, as used in a fire-protection system, is a
   a. temperature-sensing device.
   b. device for causing the fire-extinguishing agent to be released.
   c. type of gauge for determining how much extinguishing agent remains in the tank.
   d. probe used for installing disks in extinguisher bottles.

10. How do deicer boots help remove ice accumulations?
    a. By preventing the formation of ice
    b. By melting ice formations
    c. By breaking up ice formations
    d. By allowing only a thin layer of ice to build up

11. What controls the inflation sequence in a pneumatic deicer boot system?
    a. Boot construction
    b. Vacuum pump
    c. Distributor valve
    d. Suction relief valve

12. When installing pneumatic surface-bonded-type deicer boots,
    a. apply high-grade tire talc between the rubber and the wing skin.
    b. remove all paint from the area to be covered by the deicer boot.
    c. apply a solution of glycerin and water between the rubber and the wing skin.
    d. apply a Silastic compound between the rubber and the wing skin.

13. Some aircraft are protected against airframe icing by heating the leading edges of the airfoils and intake ducts. When is this type of anti-ice system usually operated during flight?
   a. Continuously while the aircraft is in flight
   b. In symmetric cycles during icing conditions to remove ice as it accumulates
   c. At all times while the outside air temperature is below freezing
   d. Whenever icing conditions are first encountered or expected to occur

14. Three possible sources of hot air for the operation of a wing thermal anti-icing system are
   a. turbocompressors, air storage tank, and vacuum pump.
   b. engine bleed air, vacuum pump, and compressed air tank.
   c. engine bleed air, combustion heaters, and augmentor tubes.
   d. combustion heaters, augmentor tubes, and exhaust gases.

15. What is used to prevent ice formation on a pitot tube?
   a. An electric heating element built into the pitot head
   b. A ribbon heater installed around the pitot head
   c. A blanket-type heater installed on the pitot head
   d. A gasket heater installed at the base of the pitot head

16. What is the one check for proper operation of a pitot/static tube heater after replacement?
   a. Ammeter reading
   b. Voltmeter reading
   c. Visual inspection of all connections
   d. Continuity check of system

17. Arcing in an electrically heated windshield panel usually indicates a breakdown in the
   a. temperature-sensing elements.
   b. autotransformers.
   c. conductive coating.
   d. thermal overheat switches.

18. What is the principle of a windshield pneumatic rain-removal system?
   a. An air blast spreads a liquid rain repellent evenly over the windshield that prevents raindrops from clinging to the glass.
   b. A liquid repellent is sprayed onto the windshield and uses the raindrops as a carrying agent to carry away the rain, keeping the glass surface clear.
   c. An air blast forms a barrier that prevents raindrops from striking the windshield surface.
   d. A pneumatic rain removal system is a mechanical windshield wiper system powered by pneumatic system pressure.

19. The basic stall warning system generates a stall warning based upon the aircraft's
   a. gross weight.
   b. elevator trim-tab position.
   c. center of gravity.
   d. angle of attack.

20. The purpose of a gas-turbine auxiliary power unit (APU) is to
   a. provide extra electrical power during flight emergencies.
   b. reduce the aircraft's dependence upon limited energy sources and replace the need for ground power units (GPUs).
   c. provide supplemental power for takeoffs.
   d. recharge the aircraft's batteries.

Chapter 19

1. Troubleshooting is the process of identifying the _____ of a malfunction or discrepancy, determining its _____ , _____ , _____ discrepant components, systems, or structures, and finally, _____ .

2. The ultimate object of troubleshooting in aviation is to return aircraft to an _____ that offers a high probability that the malfunction or discrepancy _____ .

3. Whether the thought process is evident or not, the first step in troubleshooting is to identify the _____ of the discrepancy.

4. The second step in the troubleshooting process is to evaluate the reported discrepancy to determine if it has an _____ upon the _____ .

5. If the discrepancy adversely affects the airworthiness of the aircraft, corrective action must be taken _____ its next flight.

6. If the discrepancy does not affect the airworthiness of the aircraft, then the two major considerations are: Is the appropriate _____ and is there _____ available to perform the required activities properly?

7. The technician must use the information found in the text, _____ and _____ , and information in the _____ , _____ , etc., to identify the cause of the discrepancy.

8. Frequently, when manufacturers include a _____ chart in the maintenance manual, a written description of the actions to be taken is included.

9. It is important that the technician read the _____ and not refer solely to the graphic display.

10. Troubleshooting charts help identify _____ .

11. When experience does not suggest the point at which the troubleshooting should begin, the technician should use the _____ technique.

12. In the divide-and-conquer technique, the technician separates the system into _____ , either in regard to the _____ or in terms of a _____ , and then tests the operation of the system to that point.

13. The _____ of the system is then divided into two equal parts and the system is again tested.

14. The technician must be able to determine the _____ and _____ of the system at a given point.

15. Generally it is better for the technician to determine what is to be expected at any point _____ making the test.

16. The first step in troubleshooting intermittent discrepancies is to gather as much information regarding the _____ , _____ , and _____ of the discrepancy.

17. Analyze this information for _____ .

18. The final step in the troubleshooting process is the _____ that the analytical steps of the troubleshooting process were _____ .

19. The three most popular formats used to display troubleshooting logic are the _____ , _____ , and _____ formats.

20. The flow format begins with an _____ and then proceeds through a _____ .

21. A pick-type troubleshooting chart indicates the _____ , the _____ for the discrepancy, and the _____ typically required to correct the cause of the discrepancy.

22. Binary logic charts are used to troubleshoot systems that operate based upon a logic. This logic may be used when the status of two or more functions determines the _____ of another function.

23. Binary logic may be used in _____ , _____ , and _____ system applications.

24. Binary logic charts have six primary decision criteria called _____ .

25. If a signal exists, then it is said to be _____ .

26. The absence of a signal to a gate is said _____ to have input.

27. There are _____ basic decision gates, _____ invert gate, _____ complementary gates, and an infinite number of gate variations.

28. When the input meets the requirements of the decision criteria (gate), there is an _____ .

29. If the gate's input requirements are not met, there is _____ .

30. The three basic types of gates are

   a. The _____ gate has an output only when all inputs exist.

   b. The _____ gate has an output if any or all expected inputs exist.

   c. The _____ gate simply inverts (or changes) the output.

31. NOT gates are also referred to as _____ .

32. If there is no input to a NOT gate, there is _____ .

33. If input exists, the NOT gate has _____ .

34. The three complementary gates are slight modifications to or combinations of the three basic gates:

   a. The _____ gate has an invert (NOT) gate immediately prior to the AND gate.

   b. The _____ gate places a NOT gate immediately prior to an OR gate.

   c. The _____ gate operates in the same manner as the OR gate, except that if both inputs meet the decision criteria there is no output.

35. A _____ at an input places a NOT gate prior to the basic decision gate and as a result _____ the input.

36. The layout of all possible scenarios for a decision gate is called a _____ .

Chapter 19

Name _____

Date _____

1. The primary function of troubleshooting is to
   a. identify and replace a failed component.
   b. identify and correct the cause of a failed component.
   c. anticipate and avoid component failure.
   d. ensure that system failures will not occur.

2. If a discrepancy adversely affects the airworthiness of an aircraft,
   a. it must be corrected before its next flight.
   b. the FAA must be notified before the aircraft is released for normal flight operations.
   c. and if the discrepancy repair is deferred to a later date, the flight crew must be verbally notified regarding the discrepancy.
   d. the discrepancy repair must be of a replacement nature, rather than a repair.

3. Replacement of an aircraft component and subsequent release of the aircraft for flight, knowing that an abnormally high probability for repeated failure exists,
   a. may be the equivalent of releasing an unairworthy aircraft for flight.
   b. requires that the flight crew be notified both verbally and in writing.
   c. requires written notification to the FAA.
   d. is appropriate if the technician is instructed to do so by a supervisor or licensed mechanic with inspection authorization.

4. Manufacturer's troubleshooting charts
   a. must be followed.
   b. relieve the technician of the responsibility of identifying the cause of a discrepancy, if the procedures are strictly adhered to by the technician.
   c. contain all possible discrepancy-causal relationships that can exist.
   d. are one of many tools a technician may use in correcting a discrepancy.

5. When troubleshooting without a manufacturer's chart
   a. the technician should start at the point in the system nearest the power source and work outboard.
   b. the technician should start at the point in the system furthest away from the power source and work inboard.
   c. the technician should start in the middle of the system and work toward the portion of the system that contains the discrepancy.
   d. None of the above statements are true, because it is illegal to troubleshoot an aircraft without the use of a manufacturer's troubleshooting chart.

6. Often the key to identifying the cause of intermittent discrepancies is to
   a. start at the end of the system nearest the power source and change one component at a time until the problem is corrected.
   b. start at the end of the system furthest from the power source and change one component at a time until the problem is corrected.
   c. start in the middle of the system and change one component at a time, alternating inboard and outboard until the problem is corrected.
   d. look for patterns within the discrepancy profile.

7. Validation that a discrepancy has been correctly identified and corrected is accomplished by
   a. reviewing the aircraft's maintenance logbook after 10 h of in-service time.
   b. bench-checking the failed component to verify that it was discrepant.
   c. operationally checking the system.
   d. reviewing the appropriate troubleshooting chart to validate the cause-and-effect relationship between the discrepancy and the component involved.

8. Flow-based troubleshooting charts
   a. identify the most frequent cause for a discrepancy by frequency of occurrence.
   b. generally follow the system's function diagram (flowcharts).
   c. use binary logic to determine discrepancy causes.
   d. do not have any particular logic identified with them.

9. Pick-based troubleshooting charts
   a. identify the most frequent cause for a discrepancy by frequency of occurrence.
   b. generally follow the system's function diagram (flowcharts).
   c. use binary logic to determine discrepancy causes.
   d. do not have any particular logic identified with them.

10. When using a binary troubleshooting chart, if there are two inputs into an AND gate and only one input exists, the AND gate
    a. will have a normal output.
    b. will have half its normal output.
    c. will have a cyclical output, cycling rapidly between a normal output and no output.
    d. will not have an output.

11. An NOT gate is also called
    a. a supplemental gate.
    b. a bidirectional gate.
    c. an invert gate.
    d. a defiant gate.

12. The output of an OR gate
    a. exists if any or all expected inputs exist.
    b. exists if none of the expected inputs exist.
    c. is a variable depending upon the percentage of expected inputs that actually exist.
    d. has more than one type of output, each depending upon the combination of inputs that exist.

13. If the pictorial of an AND gate has a circle between the gate and its output,
    a. the output is doubled.
    b. there is no output if all expected inputs exist.
    c. the output is halved.
    d. a gate fault will exist.

14. A layout showing the combination of all possible inputs combinations and the resultant outputs is called
    a. a gate directory.
    b. a sequence table.
    c. a truth table.
    d. a branching table.

15. Binary logic troubleshooting charts may be used to depict
    a. an electrical system.
    b. a pneumatic system.
    c. a hydraulic system.
    d. all the above.

Chapter 1
STUDY QUESTIONS

1. most recent regulations; recommended practices prescribed by their employer; the associated equipment manufacturer's recommendations; the information provided by the manufacturers of any supplies being used
2. Consumer Product Safety Commission; the Food and Drug Administration; the Department of Transportation; the Environmental Protection Agency; the Occupational Safety and Health Administration
3. DOT
4. regulations of the EPA; environmental concerns; OSHA; safety and health
5. chemical agents; physical hazards; biological hazards
6. a. Flammable
   b. Corrosive
   c. Toxic
   d. Reactive
7. outside event; condition; substance
8. reactives; heat; gases
9. directly
10. skin; eyes; mucous membranes
11. poisoning
12. bloodstream; cause-and-effect
13. limit contact; exposure
14. heat exposure; impact
15. labels
16. ignite; catalyst; heat; sparks; flame
17. solid; liquid; gas
18. fuels; paint-related products; alcohols; acetone; toluene; metal filings
19. grounded
20. rinse; water
21. remove; store it in a proper container
22. compressed air
23. metallic surfaces; burning of the skin
24. battery acids; metal-cleaning solutions
25. liquid form; bases
26. water
27. separately
28. stored separately; attack
29. rinsing with fresh water (approximately 15 minutes)
30. DO NOT induce vomiting; drink large amounts of water; immediately
31. illness; injury
32. build up
33. remain in a human's system
34. a. solvents
    b. solids
    c. machine lubricants
    d. gases
    e. polymers, epoxies, and plastics
    f. sensitizers
    g. carcinogens
    h. reproductive hazards
35. minimal
36. cancer
37. capping
38. stored separately
39. LEAVE THE AREA IMMEDIATELY
40. react violently
41. violent explosions; heat; gases
42. oxidizers; water-reactive
43. peroxides; perchloric; chromic; halogens
44. hydrogen; explosive
45. physical hazards
46. X rays; microwaves; beta or gamma rays; invisible laser beams; high-frequency (ultrasonic) sound waves
47. pressurized
48. clearly marked; individuals exposed; proper safety equipment
49. illness; disease
50. contact
51. cargo; cargo (baggage) compartments
52. known hazards; chemicals; quantity
53. right-to-know
54. hazardous-communications
55. established; maintained
56. hazardous chemicals
57. stored; used
58. composition; health hazards; special handling instructions; proper disposal practices
59. training; rights; proper handling; labeling system used; detection techniques

60. present
61. hazardous material
62. a. Product Identification
    b. Hazardous Ingredients
    c. Physical Data
    d. Fire and Explosive Data
    e. Reactivity Data
    f. Health Hazard Information
    g. Spill, Leak and Disposal Procedures
    h. Special Protection
    i. Special Precautions
63. family; formula; I; Product Identification
64. name; address; telephone number
65. II; Hazardous Ingredients
66. personal exposure limits (PELs); threshold limit values (TLVs); toxicity data (TDs)
67. short-term exposure limit (STEL); 8-h time-weighted average (TWA)
68. the time periods for which these exposures apply are specified
69. parts per million (ppm)
70. III; Physical Data
71. IV; Fire and Explosive Data
72. IV; Fire and Explosive Data
73. flash point
74. lower explosive limit; leanest
75. release energy; heat
76. inhalation; skin irritation
77. VII; Spill, Leak and Disposal Procedures
78. VIII; Special Protection
79. handling; storage
80. location; approximate (or average) quantity in each area
81. never
82. clearly labeled; never be used to hold another substance
83. diamonds; another diamond
84. degree of hazard
85. health hazard; red; yellow; specific hazard
86. transferring; from one container to another
87. 1 (1%)
88. carcinogens
89. Environmental Protection Agency (EPA)
90. creators; identification; separation; labeling; packaging; storage; shipping; disposal
91. liquid; gaseous
92. is
93. evaluate; prepare
94. reporting
95. quantity or concentration

Chapter 1
MULTIPLE CHOICE QUESTIONS

1. a	5. d	8. a
2. d	6. d	9. d
3. b	7. b	10. c
4. b		

Chapter 2
STUDY QUESTIONS

1. carry
2. aerodynamic
3. high strength-to-weight ratio
4. one and one-half
5. load factor
6. total load supported; weight of the airplane and its contents
7. pull of gravity
8. type-certificated
9. normal category
10. 4.4
11. 6.0
12. Type Certificate Data Sheet; Airworthiness Certificate
13. permanent deformation
14. permanent distortion
15. maneuvering; gust
16. shorter duration; faster
17. landing loads
18. landing load factor
19. maximum certificated gross weight
20. horizontal; load factor (N)
21. fuselage; lifting surfaces; control surfaces; stabilizers; landing gear
22. compression; tension; torsion; bending; shear
23. compression
24. tension
25. twisting
26. compression and tension
27. shear
28. permanent deformation
29. stress analysis
30. reference lines; station numbers
31. zoning specifications
32. datum line
33. Type Certificate Data Sheet; Aircraft Specification
34. wing station; butt line
35. water line
36. reference lines
37. ATA-100 Specification
38. three
39. 100; 800
40. second
41. third
42. ailerons
43. airfoil
44. bulkhead
45. buttock line
46. cantilever
47. center section
48. circumferential
49. cockpit
50. control surface
51. cockpit
52. cowl panels

53. cowling
54. elevator
55. empennage
56. fairing
57. fin
58. firewall
59. leading edge flap
60. trailing edge flaps
61. frame
62. hat section
63. longeron
64. pressure web
65. rib
66. section
67. span
68. spar
69. stabilizer
70. station lines
71. longitudinal; spanwise
72. strut
73. vertical stabilizer
74. water line
75. web
76. fuselage
77. protect the passengers in the event of a crash; loads
78. truss; semimonocoque; monocoque
79. truss
80. bulkheads
81. bays
82. Warren truss
83. semimonocoque
84. formers; rings
85. stringers
86. all
87. inefficient
88. longerons; frames; bulkheads; stringers; gussets; possibly intercostal members
89. riveted
90. tail cone
91. semimonocoque
92. keel beams; shear ties; frames
93. keel beam
94. shear ties
95. frames
96. fail-safe
97. full
98. midsection
99. fuselage; wing
100. tail cone
101. is resistant to corrosion
102. lap type
103. butt-joint type
104. adhesive; mechanical fastener
105. an infinite range
106. strong; stiff; fatigue
107. deliberate fiber orientation; fiber content
108. reinforced areas
109. doubler; gusset plate

110. flight loads; increase its rigidity
111. forgings; castings; welded assemblies; heavy sheet-metal structures
112. integral; attached to
113. reach; operate
114. 23; 25
115. securely fastened
116. safety belt
117. plane of rotation; 5 in
118. inadvertently; mechanical failure
119. operational loads; around
120. plug; seats
121. larger; inside; outward
122. placard; weight
123. contour
124. bulkheads
125. types; methods; attachment
126. cantilever; semicantilever
127. inside; external bracing
128. struts and wires
129. monospar; two-spar; multispar
130. one; two spars
131. wing beam; spanwise
132. midpoint; airfoil chord line
133. leading edge; rear of the wing
134. wing rib; plain rib; loads
135. stiffeners; stringers
136. ribs; stringers
137. primary
138. inboard
139. drag wires; antidrag wires
140. two; intermediate; main
141. fuselage; engine pylons; main landing gear; flight surfaces
142. wing tips; leading edge; trailing edge
143. slats; leading-edge flaps
144. similar purposes
145. flight controls
146. spanwise stringers
147. wet wing
148. dry bays
149. longitudinal pitch stability
150. rear spar
151. longitudinal (yaw)
152. dorsal fin
153. ailerons; rudder; elevator
154. tabs; flaps; spoilers; slats
155. fixed; retractable; arrangement on the aircraft
156. reduce drag
157. conventional; tricycle
158. tailwheel located near the tail of the aircraft
159. tricycle
160. tricycle
161. engine nacelle
162. strut; pylon
163. isolated; firewalls; shrouds
164. sealed; close-fitting fireproof grommets; bushings; firewall fittings

165. fireproof; stainless steel; inconel; titanium
166. frame
167. cowlings
168. fairing
169. main rotor
170. steel-tube construction
171. semimonocoque; monocoque
172. composite materials
173. natural-path tape laying
174. equivalent stress
175. lower fuselage; upper fuselage
176. integral; structural
177. stabilizing surfaces; tail rotor
178. yaw; torque
179. forward; tail

Chapter 2
APPLICATION QUESTIONS

1. 5000 lb. *Note:* The total load is 10 000 lb, so the load caused by flight is 10 000 lb less the gross weight of 5000 lb.
2. 15 000 lb. *Note:* The general design safety factor is one and one-half times the anticipated load.
3. 20 000 lb. *Note:* G's are a function of the affective aircraft weight, including flight loads.
4. 2.5

Chapter 2
MULTIPLE CHOICE QUESTIONS

1. c
2. d
3. b
4. c
5. c
6. a
7. b
8. c
9. b
10. c
11. a
12. c
13. c
14. a
15. c
16. c
17. b
18. b
19. a
20. a

Chapter 3
STUDY QUESTIONS

1. softwoods and hardwoods
2. cellular structure
3. a. Sitka spruce
   b. Douglas fir
   c. Port Orford white cedar
   d. western hemlock
4. a. mahogany
   b. birch
   c. white ash
5. check
6. compression failures
7. moisture content
8. Sitka spruce
9. kiln-dried
10. quarter-sawed; edge-sawed
11. slope
12. six
13. 43.13-1A
14. plywood
15. same; large angle
16. casein
17. synthetic
18. weight; volume
19. air is not whipped
20. 4 to 5 h
21. prevents the glue from properly penetrating the surface
22. 8
23. warping; checks; strength
24. not adequately bonded
25. open assembly
26. closed
27. a. squeeze the glue into a thin, continuous film between the wood layers
    b. force air from the joint
    c. bring the wood surfaces into intimate contact with the glue
    d. hold them in intimate contact during the setting of the glue
28. light; heavy
29. large; small
30. curved laminated
31. double
32. water
33. 4
34. greater
35. veneer
36. perpendicular; 45°
37. solid
38. built-up
39. one; both
40. intercostals
41. box-beam
42. unrepairable
43. unrepairable
44. unrepairable
45. rib jig
46. cap strips
47. gussets
48. visible gap; more than a gentle push
49. gussets
50. rib cap strips
51. feathered
52. scarf
53. near the center; outward in both directions
54. single
55. double
56. 10
57. finished
58. two
59. final
60. more

61. crack; warp
62. 6893; 6894
63. plasticizers
64. rupture
65. dry rot and decay
66. must be rebuilt
67. compression failure
68. removed
69. inside
70. disassembled and repaired
71. any separations
72. twisting
73. powder flow

Chapter 3
MULTIPLE CHOICE QUESTIONS

1. c	6. d	11. c
2. b	7. a	12. b
3. c	8. a	13. d
4. c	9. b	14. c
5. a	10. d	15. b

Chapter 4
STUDY QUESTIONS

1. bias
2. bleaching
3. light cream
4. calendaring
5. nap
6. fill
7. mercerizing
8. selvage
9. sizing
10. threads per inch
11. warp
12. ounces per square yard
13. fill
14. 3806; FAA Technical Standard Order (TSO) C15
15. MIL-C-5643
16. 80
17. cellulose acetate butyrate
18. 70
19. MIL-C-5646
20. inorganic
21. 80; 84
22. 4; 135.6
23. gross weight; wing area
24. 3804
25. chemical processing
26. polyester
27. razorback
28. the same material that is being used to cover the airplane
29. reduce the tendency to ravel
30. reinforce the fabric covering at openings and fittings; protect and seal rib-attachment processes; streamline surface irregularities

31. fiber; yarn size; tensile strength; number of threads per inch
32. parallel
33. compound
34. larger; fill
35. reinforcing tape
36. MIL-T-5661
37. sewing thread
38. cords
39. twist
40. S
41. left-twist
42. right; left; left-twist; left
43. left; right; right-twist; right
44. structure
45. lacing
46. MIL-T-6779; MIL-C-2520A; MIL-T-5660
47. chafing strips
48. reinforce; drainage; lacing; inspection
49. cut out
50. punched out
51. not cut out
52. metal inspection cover or plate
53. rib lacing
54. beeswax
55. sealing; tautening; protecting
56. cellulose acetate butyrate; cellulose nitrate
57. aluminum oxide
58. bleeding
59. shrink
60. taut
61. polyester material
62. plasticizers
63. fire-resistant; shrinkage
64. fungus
65. fungicides; first
66. MIL-D-7850
67. thin
68. ultraviolet
69. pigmented
70. fabric rejuvenator
71. soften and penetrate
72. TT-T-266a; MIL-T-6094A
73. cellulose acetate butyrate dope thinner
74. acetone
75. thinner
76. blushing
77. retarder; retarder thinner
78. blushing
79. sealed
80. easel
81. trestles
82. minimum
83. V_{ne}
84. aircraft specification; Type Certificate Data Sheet; approved operator's handbook
85. 160 mph [257.5 km/h]
86. wing loading

87. aircraft specification; Type Certificate Data Sheet; approved operator's handbook
88. directly over the aircraft; any curvature on the surface due to airfoil shape
89. 9
90. no greater; intermediate-grade cotton
91. fiberglass; all
92. 20-44
93. selvage
94. STCs (Supplemental Type Certificates)
95. selvage; 1-yd
96. 0.91; 24 in; the center area; 18 in
97. fish wires
98. dope-proof paint; aluminum foil; cellophane tape; masking tape
99. plain overlap; folded fell; French fell; modified French fell
100. strongest
101. one end of the opening; just touch; ½; cut off
102. ¼; square; half hitch
103. baseball stitch
104. ¼ in [6.44 mm]; ¼ in [6.44 mm]
105. lockstitch; 6
106. modified seine knot; half hitch; the next stitch spacing
107. adhesives
108. 2 to 4 in
109. envelope
110. blanket
111. organic fabrics
112. 150; blanket
113. preshrunk; water
114. an electric iron
115. thin; fungicide; brush
116. second
117. rib-stitching; mechanical
118. 1
119. one-half
120. half-spaced
121. double loop
122. modified seine
123. modified seine; half hitch
124. application of surface (finishing) tape
125. all rib lacing; seams; leading and trailing edges; other points where reinforcement is necessary
126. dope; wet
127. all air bubbles
128. 200; 18
129. fire-safe
130. aluminum oxide
131. three
132. damage; dope-coat deterioration only
133. deterioration would be the most rapid
134. tensile
135. penetrates; strength
136. Maule
137. number of dope coats
138. punch
139. punch
140. Seyboth
141. 56
142. 46
143. minimum value; higher
144. tensile
145. sewing; doping
146. strength; finish
147. pigmented; aluminized; baseball
148. heavy; soften; scraping
149. 8 to 10; pinked-edge; doped
150. 1½
151. apex
152. 150
153. 16
154. 2
155. 8 and 16
156. 3
157. 150; 16
158. baseball; lock; 8; 10
159. 1½
160. 3
161. doped on
162. between the original
163. sewn-in
164. 3
165. flexibility

Chapter 4
MULTIPLE CHOICE QUESTIONS

1. d	6. a	11. c
2. b	7. d	12. a
3. b	8. c	13. c
4. d	9. d	14. b
5. c	10. d	15. c

Chapter 5
STUDY QUESTIONS

1. manufacturers
2. primers; wash primers; paint; lacquer; enamel
3. adhesion; corrosion-resistant
4. wash primer
5. P-15328C; C-8514(ASG)
6. zinc chromate primer
7. normal atmospheric conditions; conditions of high humidity
8. aluminum; aluminum-alloy; magnesium surfaces; iron or steel
9. toluene
10. red iron oxide
11. lacquer-type; colored lacquer; synthetic enamel; acrylic lacquer
12. finish coats
13. corrosion-inhibiting; fast-drying; heavy-duty; chemical- and solvent-resistant; amine-cured
14. catalyst
15. polyurethane

16. steel; zinc-coated metals; aluminum; fiberglass
17. pot life
18. pot life
19. methyl ethyl ketone (MEK); reducer
20. pigment; binder; solvent; additives
21. pigment
22. binder
23. solvent
24. additives
25. speed drying; prevent blushing; improve chemical resistance; higher gloss
26. lacquer; enamel
27. compound; polish
28. more slowly
29. metal; wood
30. fuel-resistant; MIL-L-7146; clear coating for aluminum; MIL-L-006805; acrylic nitrocellulose lacquer
31. acrylic enamel
32. more care during application; a longer drying time; special precautions
33. polyurethane finishing
34. strong chemical agents
35. drying or ''hardening'' process
36. waxed
37. thinners; reducers
38. temperature; humidity
39. temperature
40. fastest
41. cold; wet; humid
42. faster
43. slower-drying
44. cold
45. orange peel; blushing; overspray
46. sags; runs
47. may not mix with the thinner; prevent the paint from drying; attack the coats of paint beneath the coat being applied
48. static charges
49. respirators
50. air transformer-regulator
51. pressure drop
52. increase
53. smoothness
54. increase
55. airless
56. hydraulic pressure
57. pressure pot; pressure-feed tank
58. pressure regulator
59. shell; clamp-on lid; fluid tube; fluid header; air-outlet valve; fluid-outlet valve; air-inlet valve; safety relief valve; agitator; pressure regulator; release valve; pressure gauge
60. electrostatic
61. high-voltage
62. air
63. fluid adjusting screw; spreader adjustment valve; air-valve assembly; an air cap; a fluid inlet; air inlet
64. quality; pattern
65. size of the spray pattern
66. holes in the cap
67. wider
68. fluid volume
69. air pressure
70. 6; 10
71. runs; sagging
72. excessive paint buildup
73. heavy paint buildup; runs in the center portion of the pass
74. Zahn viscosity cup
75. seconds
76. tack cloth
77. no wax; oil
78. heavier film; light covering
79. dirty air cap
80. highly volatile
81. thick cream
82. acrylic lacquer
83. nonmetallic; MEK; acetone
84. cracks; crevasses; metal joints or seams
85. wax
86. Plexiglas windows; fiberglass parts; fabric; other plastic or porous materials
87. adhesive-bonded
88. nonabrasive plastic beads
89. distance; air pressure; media selection
90. wet; dry
91. clogged
92. rinse away the removed material
93. wet
94. filiform
95. metal; finish
96. moisture in the air; wash primer
97. 57; 49
98. distilled
99. 30; 40
100. phosphoric acid etch; wash primer
101. conversion coating
102. compatible
103. preventing corrosion; microscopically roughen
104. phosphate film
105. chromic acid etch
106. washed off with water
107. wash primer
108. corrosion-inhibiting pigments
109. bare metal; conversion coating
110. thin
111. improved bonding; corrosion protection
112. MIL-P-8585A
113. toluol; phosphoric acid solution; conversion coating
114. no phosphoric acid will be trapped against the metal
115. urethane; polyurethane
116. steel; aluminum; magnesium; fiberglass
117. wash primer
118. 24 h
119. 5 h; preferably overnight

120. two-part; 6; 8
121. flat; smooth; being repelled from areas of the surface
122. oil
123. quick-drying
124. dry dust-free
125. dust-free spray booth
126. dust coat
127. mist coat
128. immediately
129. nitrate thinner; reducer
130. cellulose nitrate dope; lacquer
131. epoxy; urethane; acrylic
132. MEK
133. feather
134. interaction; avoided
135. soften
136. immediately prior to
137. templates; chalk lines
138. not; pencil; pen
139. not; solvents
140. Propylene fine-line
141. rubbing compounds
142. polishing compounds
143. smooth out; remove fine scratches
144. gloss
145. an improperly adjusted spray gun; holding the gun too close; moving the gun too slowly
146. too far away from the surface; moved too rapidly; improper gun adjustment
147. far away; air pressure
148. blisters or bubbles
149. too soon
150. blushing; evaporating
151. fine splits; small cracks; air temperature
152. craterlike openings
153. improper surface cleaning or preparation
154. irregular surface
155. improper air pressure; too far away from the surface; insufficient thinning of the paint
156. peeling; the surface not being properly cleaned and prepared
157. pinholes
158. insufficient drying time between coats; paint or trapped solvents or moisture in the finish
159. FAR Part 45
160. nationality and registration marks
161. permanent
162. contrast
163. ornamentation; other markings or insignia adjacent to them
164. N
165. limited; restricted; experimental; provisional airworthiness
166. 2; 6
167. vertical tail surface; fuselage
168. outer surfaces
169. bottom surface of the fuselage; cabin; left

170. 12
171. two-thirds
172. equal to
173. one-sixth
174. one-fourth
175. 2

Chapter 5
APPLICATION QUESTION

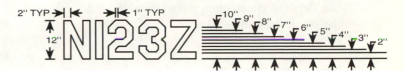

Chapter 5
MULTIPLE CHOICE QUESTIONS

1. b
2. a
3. c
4. c
5. c
6. d
7. c
8. b
9. a
10. d
11. c
12. a
13. a
14. c
15. d
16. c
17. a
18. b
19. d
20. a

Chapter 6
STUDY QUESTIONS

1. fusion
2. oxyacetylene (or oxyfuel) welding; electric-arc welding; inert-gas arc welding
3. properly balanced
4. electric-arc welding
5. low-voltage, high-amperage
6. blankets; oxidation
7. spark test; chemical test; flame test
8. ferrous metals
9. spark patterns; spark pattern
10. the volume of the spark stream; the relative length of the spark stream; the color of the spark stream close to the grinding wheel; the color of the spark streaks near the end of the stream; the quantity of the sparks; the nature of the sparks
11. chrome-nickel corrosion-resisting steel; nickel-chromium-iron alloy
12. flame test
13. joint
14. butt joint
15. plain butt joint; flange butt joint
16. tee joint
17. plain tee
18. penetration
19. lap joint
20. sheet; plate; loading is not severe
21. same plane
22. both parts joined

23. the corner of a rectangle
24. heavier-gauge sheet metals
25. face
26. root
27. throat
28. toe
29. added above the surface of the base metal
30. leg
31. fusion zone
32. bead
33. the depth of penetration; the width of the bead; the height of the reinforcement
34. one-fourth
35. two and three
36. not less than one-half
37. undercutting of the base metal at the toe of the weld; not enough penetration; poor fusion of the weld metal with the base metal; trapped oxides, slag, or gas pockets in the weld; overheating of the weld; overlap of the weld metal on the base metal
38. tensile strength; ductility; yield point
39. lower
40. melting point; heat conductivity; rate of expansion and contraction
41. Heat
42. British thermal units (BTUs)
43. distortion; breakage
44. coefficient of thermal expansion
45. shrinking
46. expansion; contraction
47. whole
48. thermal conductivity
49. rate of conductivity
50. flammable; colorless
51. greater
52. 15; 29.4
53. 15
54. acetone
55. 250
56. tare; gross; multiplied
57. oil; grease
58. 11.203
59. safety-valve assembly
60. reduce the high pressure; containers; constant pressure; volume
61. two pressure
62. in the cylinder; gases flowing to the torch
63. mix; correct proportions
64. volumes
65. burning conditions
66. the balanced-pressure type; the injector type
67. heat; flame; kind; thickness
68. source of the acetylene gas
69. low
70. high
71. velocity; draw
72. diameter of the orifice
73. heat

74. temperature; mixing head; velocity of the gases
75. low; backfire
76. orifice
77. red or maroon; left-handed; groove cut
78. green; right-handed; no
79. additional metal
80. fuses
81. compatible; heat-treatment process
82. flux; copper; rusting
83. the same as
84. heat; ultraviolet; infrared
85. an igniter; friction lighter; safety lighter; spark lighter
86. a cigarette lighter; matches
87. carbon dioxide
88. cracked
89. side; behind; dirt; propelled; defective; burst
90. test for leaks
91. soapy water
92. lighted match
93. one complete turn; all the way
94. acetylene; three-quarters of a turn; spark lighter
95. well-shaped bluish-white inner
96. second outer cone; envelope
97. neutral
98. 2½; 1
99. 1/1
100. 6300°F
101. acetylene; oxygen
102. nickel alloys; Monel; Inconel
103. oxygen
104. brass
105. soft flame; low speed
106. high speed; harsh flame
107. backfire; out; come on again
108. there may be dirt or some other obstruction in the end of the welding tip; the gas pressures may be incorrect; the tip may be loose; the tip may be overheated; the welder may have touched the work with the tip of the torch; allowed the inner cone of the flame to touch the molten puddle
109. flashback
110. disappears entirely; return
111. shrill hissing; squealing
112. needle valves; torch
113. a. Close the acetylene needle valve on the torch to shut off the flame immediately.
    b. Close the oxygen needle valve on the torch.
    c. Close the acetylene cylinder valve.
    d. Close the oxygen cylinder valve.
    e. Remove the pressure on the regulators' working pressure gauges by opening the acetylene valve on the torch to drain the acetylene hose and regulator.
    f. Turn the acetylene-regulator adjusting screw counterclockwise (to the left) to relieve the pressure on the diaphragm, and then close the torch's acetylene valve.

g. Open the torch oxygen valve, and drain the oxygen hose and regulator.

h. Turn the oxygen-regulator adjusting screw counterclockwise to relieve the pressure on the diaphragm; then close the torch's oxygen valve.

i. Hang the torch and hose up properly to prevent any kinking of the hose or damage to the torch.

114. cleaned; sandpapering; wire brush
115. mill scale; rust; oxides; other impurities
116. excessive amount of heat
117. flange; tapered; U
118. pencil
119. hammer
120. puddle
121. intermingle
122. placing the filler rod
123. control the motion of the puddle; consistent
124. at all times
125. semicircular; crescent; circular
126. reducing the pressures
127. increase
128. increasing
129. forward
130. in front of
131. backhand
132. between
133. flat
134. vertical
135. horizontal
136. overhead
137. a. The seam should be smooth and of a uniform thickness.
b. The weld should be built up to provide extra thickness at the seam.
c. The weld metal should taper off smoothly into the base metal.
d. No oxide should be formed on the base metal at a distance of more than ½ in [12.7 mm] from the weld.
e. The weld should show no signs of blowholes, porosity, or projecting globules.
f. The base metal should show no sign of pitting, burning, cracking, or distortion.
138. distribute the heat more evenly; put a smaller amount of heat into the weld ; use special fixtures to hold the metal rigidly in place; provide a space between the edges of the joint
139. contraction
140. stagger welding; center; end
141. skip
142. fixture
143. spacing; butt
144. tack
145. step-back; back-step
146. cooled evenly and slowly
147. heat treatment
148. filed
149. filled
150. old weld metal
151. an old weld
152. brazed
153. parallel; top; line of the weld
154. inert-gas welding
155. heated
156. burns with a very bright flame
157. completely
158. 1100; 3003; 4043; 5052
159. heat treating
160. soft; reducing
161. low-voltage; high-amperage current
162. electrode
163. $\frac{1}{16}$; $\frac{1}{8}$
164. heat; arc
165. gap
166. is attached to the welding machine; ground cable is attached to the welding machine
167. to the electrode holder; electrode; across the arc
168. anode; cathode
169. plasma
170. excited gas atoms
171. ions
172. voltage drop
173. the type and amount of electrical power; the distance between the anode and cathode; the type of atmosphere or gases between the anode and cathode
174. slag; cooling
175. flux coating on the electrode
176. dcsp; dcrp; ac
177. direct current, straight polarity
178. direct current, reverse polarity; positive
179. make no difference
180. dcsp
181. dcrp; lessened
182. dcrp
183. chemical coating
184. the arc
185. filler metal
186. arc steadier; increases the arc force; provides a shield of smokelike gas around the arc to keep oxygen and nitrogen in the air away from the molten metal; provides a flux for the molten pool, which picks up impurities and forms the protective slag
187. AWS; tensile strength; best welding position; flux-welding current recommendations
188. letter
189. core material
190. E; mild steel
191. tensile strength
192. six
193. recommended welding position
194. any position
195. horizontal fillets; flat-position welding
196. flux coating; power source
197. slightly less
198. being maintained

199. too short an arc gap
200. too large an arc gap
201. shield the arc; molten metal
202. nonconsumable
203. sustain
204. thickness
205. argon; gas cup
206. surrounds; directs
207. gas metal-arc welding (GMAW)
208. metal inert-gas (MIG)
209. electrode
210. at a constant distance
211. carbon dioxide
212. restricted; at an increased speed; higher temperatures; improved concentration
213. carbon tetrachloride; trichlorethylene; tetrachloroethylene
214. form a toxic gas
215. 100 percent
216. ⅜ and 1 in
217. filler rod
218. ½ in
219. reinforcement
220. filler rod
221. thickness of the material; size of the weld desired
222. welding current
223. no filler rod
224. cooling; water system
225. backing
226. heat sink; drawing away
227. direct current, straight polarity (dcsp); direct current, reverse polarity (dcrp); alternating current, high-frequency stabilized (achf)
228. achf or dcrp
229. dcsp
230. much higher
231. dcrp
232. one-half
233. larger diameter electrode
234. a narrow, deep weld
235. wide; shallow
236. oxides; scale; dirt
237. Dcsp; dcrp
238. rectification
239. high-voltage; high-frequency; low-power
240. collet; collet body; tungsten electrode; lens; flow; gas cup
241. compatible
242. argon/helium
243. argon
244. helium
245. 1 to 1½
246. postflow timer
247. oxidation; cooling
248. does not have to
249. actually touch
250. on a heavy piece of copper or scrap steel
251. snapped quickly
252. wandering
253. low electrode-current density; carbon contamination of the electrode; magnetic effects; air drafts
254. 75°
255. 15°; 1
256. perpendicular
257. bottom; leading edge
258. ¼
259. thickness of the material; current-carrying capacity of the equipment involved; assembly being fabricated
260. a root weld; complete fusion
261. electrode is consumable; fed
262. spray-arc; short-circuit
263. arc; by gravity
264. constant-voltage direct current; reverse polarity
265. 1; 2; stabilization
266. touched
267. high amperage
268. dcrp; constant voltage supply
269. amperage
270. SVI; slope; voltage; inductance
271. voltage; amperage
272. slope; power source
273. changes
274. resultant current
275. leave the electrode
276. violent fashion; splattering
277. low voltages
278. inductance
279. decreased
280. less
281. less; heat; fluidity; splatter
282. flat; inductance
283. 20; 30; higher; splatter
284. steep; upper half
285. too great
286. burn back
287. beginning; ending
288. approximately an inch from the end of the joint
289. about 1 in over the newly welded joint
290. 70°; 85°; forehand
291. plasma-arc welding (PAW)
292. plasma section of the welding arc
293. the directional stability of the plasma arc; the focusing of the arc by the orifice; minor changes in the torch's stand-off distance
294. melt-in; keyhole
295. an ionized column of gas that passes from the anode to the cathode
296. tungsten
297. adversely affect
298. argon; helium; argon-helium; material; material thickness; current; type of welding technique employed
299. electric circuit
300. the plasma gas
301. transfer; nontransfer

302. include
303. exclude
304. direct; accelerate
305. cathode
306. no longer needs be part of the electrical circuit
307. magnetizing; magnetic induction
308. round; concentric
309. not extended
310. 20°; 60°
311. pilot-arc
312. positioning
313. 25°; 35°
314. forehand

Chapter 6
MULTIPLE CHOICE QUESTIONS

1. a	11. d
2. a	12. a
3. c	13. c
4. a	14. a
5. b	15. c
6. d	16. c
7. d	17. d
8. b	18. b
9. c	19. c
10. a	20. b

Chapter 7
STUDY QUESTIONS

1. chromium-molybdenum; chrome-molybdenum or chrome-moly
2. 4130
3. outside; wall thickness
4. joint
5. cluster
6. match
7. do not
8. fixtures
9. oxyacetylene
10. inert-gas welding
11. magnetism
12. degausser
13. tack-weld
14. welds
15. quarters; warping
16. load
17. single thickness; one wall
18. supporting members; more than
19. the main member; both walls
20. brace members
21. fingers; brace members
22. hot linseed oil; petroleum-base oils; corrosion
23. an epoxy primer; tube-sealing solutions
24. thoroughly dried
25. protective coating
26. zinc chromate primer; aluminum-bronze powder
27. tape; dopeproof paint
28. 10 power
29. proper alignment; evidence of deformation; cracking
30. secondary damage
31. transmission of loads
32. small hammer
33. bottom; lower; internally
34. dye-penetrant; fluorescent-penetration; magnetic-particle; X-ray; ultrasonic; eddy-current
35. same
36. secured
37. inclusions; contamination
38. steel wire
39. thickness
40. crack
41. structural failure
42. welding (filler) rod
43. heat-treatable
44. dissipation
45. draw
46. old weld
47. forbidden; hidden
48. removed
49. brazed area; removed
50. expansion; contraction
51. weight; expansion; contraction
52. annealed; brittleness
53. 1150; 1200; very slowly
54. welding; rivets are driven
55. progressive welding; reducing strains
56. the tubing having the damaged fitting attached to it should be removed; a new section and fitting should then be installed
57. cracks
58. dented; crushed; kinked
59. one-twentieth
60. pushed out; air pressure
61. carefully removed; original
62. spreading
63. completely around
64. 1½
65. does not
66. tube diameter; one-quarter
67. middle third
68. temporary purposes; permanent repair
69. cracks; dents; gouges
70. patch plate; finger plate
71. thickness; cover the damage
72. diameter of the brace tube; at least 1½ times that of the diameter
73. remove; partial replacement tube; entirely new section of tubing
74. external replacement; next-larger; internal or external
75. same diameter; reinforcing sleeves
76. external replacement tube
77. diagonal (scarf); fishmouth
78. butt
79. fishmouth weld

80. tubular joint
81. scarf joint; 30°
82. reduction joint
83. telescope joint
84. scarf-butt splice
85. one; two
86. butt; scarf splice; direct cross section
87. continuous members; different diameters
88. different diameters; direct cross section
89. bending stresses
90. straight line; break; vibration; shock
91. not; middle third
92. one
93. entirely new web member
94. avoid; too close
95. rosette weld
96. inner reinforcing; outer member
97. one-quarter; outer tube
98. diagonal
99. middle third
100. wall thickness; diameter; ¼
101. wall thickness; equal; inside; 1½; original tubing; replacement tubing
102. ¹⁄₁₆
103. weld
104. smooth
105. telescope
106. 2½; 4½
107. square
108. wall thickness; ¹⁄₁₆
109. fishmouth; 30°
110. 1½
111. least
112. outside-sleeve
113. braced; correct alignment
114. before
115. ream
116. a. round tubing
     b. split sleeve
     c. inside sleeve
     d. splicing method
117. cracking
118. slip over
119. checking the alignment
120. rewelding the ring; gusset or a mounting
121. not
122. heat; fire
123. creased; folded
124. streamlined wires and cables; brazed or soldered parts; steel parts; heat-treated
125. heat-treated again
126. stainless steel; Inconel; inert-gas welding
127. clean; bright; stop-drilled
128. purged
129. live steam; 3 min
130. inert-gas
131. by welding
132. welding flux
133. nitric; sulfuric; 1 h
134. silver nitrate; white precipitate; not
135. inert-gas welding
136. brazing; hard soldering
137. capillary action; very small clearances
138. tinned
139. neutral flame; slightly carbonizing
140. tinned
141. fluxes
142. wetting
143. not
144. rosin; nonacid paste
145. wiped off
146. tin and lead
147. tin; lead
148. not; fuse
149. iron; tin; copper; brass; galvanized iron; terneplate
150. heat-treatable
151. silver soldering
152. bronze; copper; stainless steel; brass
153. brass-type
154. low-melting-point

Chapter 7
APPLICATION QUESTIONS

1. a. ¼ in
    b. 1 in
    c. ⅞ in
    d. ½ in

Chapter 7
MULTIPLE CHOICE QUESTIONS

1. c	11. b
2. d	12. d
3. c	13. c
4. b	14. b
5. d	15. a
6. c	16. d
7. a	17. a
8. c	18. c
9. b	19. a
10. b	20. b

Chapter 8
STUDY QUESTIONS

1. structural; nonstructural
2. transfer; absorb
3. do not
4. 25 percent
5. accept the forces; neighbor components
6. anticipates their growth; inspection discipline
7. safety factor
8. design
9. margin of safety
10. stress
11. kinetic energy; overcome; resistance

12. potential energy
13. bearing stress
14. strain
15. fatigue
16. retention
17. stress risers
18. cross-sectional area; rises
19. 3; 6; 20
20. distance; reduced
21. reamer
22. gradual
23. stress corrosion
24. transmit; one; to another
25. original material; the fasteners; from the fasteners; patch material; fasteners on the opposite side of the damage; balance of the original material
26. not
27. load-carrying
28. pure tension
29. pure compression
30. 70 percent of the UTS
31. torsion; compression; shear; tensile; tearout; bearing
32. diameter
33. tensile
34. fastener holes
35. shortest distance
36. area of contact
37. fastener shear area
38. tensile area
39. tearout area
40. bearing area
41. ultimate shear strength
42. tensile load; ultimate tensile strength
43. tearout load
44. sheet bearing load
45. minimum
46. less
47. tension; compression
48. neutral axis
49. 44.5
50. inside radius
51. thickness of the metal; radius of the bend; degree of the bend
52. bend tangent lines; bend allowance
53. bend angle
54. angle of bend
55. closed angle
56. mold-line dimensions
57. outer mold point
58. mold-line angle; angle of bend
59. X-dimension
60. setback
61. length of the flat portion
62. setback
63. radius of the bend; thickness of the sheet material
64. K-factor
65. $K \times (R + T)$
66. that angle; adjacent column

67. mold-line dimension; setback
68. developed width
69. developed length
70. circumference; $2\pi \times R$
71. neutral axis; halfway; $(R + 0.5T)$
72. portion; bend angle; $N/360$
73. $0.445T$; known
74. tables
75. working surface
76. layout fluids
77. zinc chromate; bluing fluid; flat white paint; copper sulfate solution
78. need not
79. must be removed
80. water
81. iron; steel
82. must not be
83. measurements
84. finished part
85. reference lines
86. base lines
87. scratches; nicks
88. finished part
89. no pencil lines
90. planishing hammers
91. hand nibbling
92. hole saw
93. chassis punch
94. hand rivet set
95. rivet set
96. set sleeve; retaining spring
97. retaining spring; always
98. pliable
99. 1X
100. shank
101. cupped head
102. regulator adjustment; position
103. bucking bar
104. is flat
105. 1 lb
106. expanding bucking bars
107. sheet fastener
108. locking wires; spreader
109. hole finder
110. rivet cutter
111. squaring shears
112. perpendicular
113. gap-squaring shears
114. slitting shears
115. throatless shear
116. rotary slitting shears
117. scroll shear
118. A Unishear
119. rough edges
120. bar-folding machine
121. pipe-folding
122. cornice brake; leaf brake
123. thickness of the material that is to be bent

124. box and pan brake
125. forming roll
126. turning machine
127. beading machine
128. crimping machine
129. combination rotary machine
130. metal-cutting blades
131. stake
132. drill press
133. template
134. straight; left; right
135. directly below
136. sight line; directly below
137. gage line
138. bend line
139. mold-line dimensions
140. heat-treating
141. across the grain
142. lengthwise
143. aligned
144. joggle
145. stretching; shrinking
146. inside
147. bumping
148. bucked head
149. rivet part number; diameter; positioning; dimple and countersink information; fastener length; spot weld
150. drilling; reaming; deburring
151. larger
152. outer cutting edge
153. slower
154. pilot
155. drill fixture
156. perpendicular; steady
157. by hand
158. deburring tool; countersink
159. 7
160. conical depression
161. countersink; dimpling
162. 99 percent of its thickness
163. dimpling
164. subcountersunk; dimpled
165. coin dimpling
166. few blows
167. shank
168. 1.5D
169. 0.65D; 0.50D
170. rivet shaver
171. one size smaller; no further; base of the rivet head
172. snap
173. pin punch
174. next larger

Chapter 8
APPLICATION QUESTIONS

1. 50 000 psi
   (40 000 = X/(1 + 0.25), X = 40 000 * 1.25 = 50 000)
2. 50 percent
   MS = 75 000/50 000 − 1 = 1.5 − 1 = 0.5 = 50 percent
3. a. 2368 lb (with safety factor 1888 lb)
   b. 2124 lb
   c. 50 percent
   The original design with a safety factor of 25 percent allows 472 lb for safety. The scratch resulted in an ultimate loss of load-carrying capability of 236 lb (235/472 = 0.5 = 50 percent).
4. a. 0.007 in^2
   Remember that the diameter of rivet is the diameter after driving the rivet, or the hole size. The drill bit used for a 3/32 rivet is a no. 41 drill bit, 0.0960-in diameter.
   b. 0.040 in^2
   c. 0.025 in^2
   (1 − (0.0960 * 4)) * 0.040 − 0.0246
   d. 0.007 in^2
   2 * (6/32 − 0.0960/2) * 0.040
   e. 0.004 in^2
   (0.0960 * 0.040)
5. a. 217 lb
   (0.007 in^2 * 30 000 lb/in^2)
   b. 2368 lb
   (0.040 in^2 * 59 000 lb/in^2)
   c. 1454 lb
   (0.025 in^2 * 59 000 lb/in^2)
   d. 271 lb
   (0.007 in^2 * 37 000 lb/in^2)
   e. 1859 lb
   (0.004 in^2 * 121 000 lb/in^2 * 4)
   Note that there are four (4) holes; therefore the bearing strength is factored by 4.)
6. a. 0.040 in
   b. 0.165 in
7. 4.285 in
   K-factor for 90° = 1.000
   2.020 leg = 2.020 − K * (0.48 + 0.040) = 2.020 − 1 * 0.520 = 1.50
   2.520 leg = 2.520 − K * (0.48 + 0.040) = 2.520 − 1 * 0.520 = 2.00
   BA = 2π(0.480 + 0.040/2)*90/360 = 2π* .5/4 = 0.785
   1.5 + 0.785 + 2.0 = 4.285
8. 5.047 in
   K-factor for 120° = 1.732
   Each leg = 2.90 − K * (0.48 + 0.400) = 2.90 − 1.732 * (0.520) = 2.00
   BA = 2π(0.480 + 0.040/2)*120/360 = 2π*0.5/3 = 1.047
   2.00 + 1.047 + 2.00 = 5.047

9. 7.333 in

Note this figure uses the same basic dimensions as the previous two figures, except one leg (the 2.52-in leg) of the first drawing is removed.

2.020 leg = 1.50 in.

2.900 leg = 2.00 in

3.420 leg = 2.00 in

(Note the setback from the right angle is 0.520 in and from the mold point of the 120° angle is 0.900 in)

BA 90° = 0.785

BA 120° = 1.047

1.50 + 0.785 + 2.00 + 1.047 + 2.00 = 7.333 in

10. 6.833 in

The distance from end *A* to end *B* is the flat-pattern layout total distance and the distance from end *B* to the center of the hole is 0.500 in. Subtract 0.500 from the flat-pattern layout total distance. Or subtract 0.500 from the 2.90 leg dimension and calculate as done in the previous question.

Chapter 8
MULTIPLE CHOICE QUESTIONS

1. c	11. a
2. d	12. c
3. b	13. b
4. a	14. a
5. a	15. c
6. d	16. a
7. b	17. d
8. b	18. a
9. a	19. c
10. c	20. b

Chapter 9
STUDY QUESTIONS

1. naked eye; magnification
2. 10X
3. before
4. dye-penetrant; developer; bright red line
5. fluorescent-penetrant; developing powder
6. magnetic-particle; magnetized
7. alternating-current field coil
8. X-ray
9. high-frequency sound waves
10. eddy-current
11. failing that; approved data
12. major repair
13. original strength
14. two lap; pickup; return
15. plug; doubler
16. does not
17. loads are transferred
18. negligible; repairable; replacement
19. does not
20. if not repaired
21. practically repaired; prohibited
22. cause
23. attribute or attributes
24. not; rigidity; strength
25. flexibility
26. the FAA
27. not; approval
28. same
29. original
30. next-larger rivet
31. three; heavier sheet
32. pitch; gauge
33. edge distance
34. two
35. three; four
36. two; 2½; countersunk
37. 24
38. twice
39. stop-drill
40. round
41. equal to
42. parallel; perpendicular
43. perpendicular
44. equal
45. repairable
46. larger
47. actual; minimal rivet diameter
48. width; layout rivets; minimum; edge distance; number of fasteners required
49. twice
50. one
51. next whole number
52. length; number of fasteners in
53. operational stresses
54. major repairs; approved
55. not
56. bearing load
57. shear load – carrying; rivet
58. sheet-bearing; sheet
59. tear out; bearing
60. increases
61. shear; rivets; tensile
62. lowest cross-sectional area; perpendicular
63. width; diameter
64. adjusted width
65. least cross-sectional area; most
66. shear load for each fastener; bearing load of the sheet; least
67. lap joint; twice
68. wider
69. width; less the diameters of the fastener holes; thickness of the material
70. sum of the diameters of the fastener holes; outside the damaged area
71. type; diameter; thickest
72. a. thickness
    b. material thickness
    c. AN-3 bolts
    d. type; size

e. rivet diameter
f. notes; engineering notes
g. per inch
73. per lap joint
74. row; different load
75. the most load
76. maximum; less
77. actual load
78. transferred
79. multiple shear planes
80. carries over
81. two planes
82. significantly lower
83. aircraft manufacturer
84. ultimate strength
85. no; perpendicular; application of the load
86. first choice; 43.13-1A & 2A; MIL-HDBK-5E
87. must; FAA Form 337
88. prior to

Chapter 9
APPLICATION QUESTIONS

1. 0.044 in thickness
   1.09 * 0.040; note that if the thickness was greater than 0.063 the factor is 1.10.
2. $^3/_{16}$ in diameter
   3 * 0.063 = 0.189, which is approximately equal to $^3/_{16}$ in.
3. 1.375 in
   Note that the rivets are countersunk and therefore 2½D edge spacing is recommended.
   $^4/_{32}$ * 2.5 = 0.3125
   $^4/_{32}$ * 3 = 0.375
   Edge distance + gauge distance + gauge distance + edge distance
   0.3125 + 0.375 + 0.375 + 0.3125 = 1.375
   Also note that in the above equation each plus sign (+) represents a row of rivets.
4. 2.064 in
   Note that although $^4/_{32}$ rivets will be used, the layout is for $^6/_{32}$ rivets.
   $^6/_{32}$ * 2.5 = 0.469
   $^6/_{32}$ * 3 = 0.563
   Edge distance + gauge distance + gauge distance + edge distance
   0.469 + 0.563 + 0.563 + 0.469 = 2.06
5. This question may not be answered using the table identified because MS20426 rivets are countersunk rivets and the table applies to protruding head rivets.
6. 10 rivets
   6.2 rivets per inch of width are required.
   6.2 * 2 = 12.4
   Only 80 percent are required per table note a.
   12.4 * 0.8 = 9.92 or 10 rivets
7. 24 rivets
   7.7 rivets per inch of width are required.
   7.7 * 2 = 15.4

Only 75 percent are required per table note c.
15.4 * 0.75 = 11.5 rivets or 12 rivets per joint. However, a patch consists of two lap joints, so this figure must be doubled: 2 * 12 = 24
Note: The reference to a single lap sheet joint refers to the number of sheets in the joint, not the number of lap joints. That is, if two sheets are used in a lap joint, there is one shear plane. If three sheets are used in a lap joint there are two planes of shear (referred to as double shear) and this type lap joint would require all rivets specified by the chart.

Chapter 9
MULTIPLE CHOICE QUESTIONS

1. a   11. c
2. c   12. c
3. c   13. c
4. c   14. a
5. d   15. b
6. d   16. b
7. c   17. c
8. a   18. b
9. c   19. a
10. d   20. a

Chapter 10
STUDY QUESTIONS

1. thermosetting
2. bonding materials; resinous
3. thermoplastic
4. form
5. transparent plastics
6. acrylics; cellulose acetates
7. replaced
8. P-6886; P-8184; P-5425
9. visual; burning
10. clear
11. yellow
12. clear flame
13. heavy black smoke; pungent odor
14. white
15. softens; does not affect its clarity
16. milky; acrylic
17. masking paper
18. aliphatic naphtha
19. clean water
20. racks; on flats
21. excessive stress
22. slowly
23. does not dissipate
24. cooling
25. air stream; cutting fluid
26. less
27. hollow ground; sufficient side clearance
28. feed; speed
29. scribe; under; both sides
30. 60°; zero

31. depth-to-diameter; 90°
32. 118°
33. exits the plastic
34. high; light to moderate
35. 180
36. heat
37. hot oil bath; a heater strip; a hot air chamber; a heat gun
38. oil bath
39. heater strip
40. gradually; proper size
41. drops below the minimum
42. stress
43. heat gun
44. preshrunk; unshrunk
45. shrinkage
46. unshrunk acrylic plastic
47. full
48. melting; chemically
49. specific type of plastic
50. plastic shavings; cement
51. vertical surfaces; bottom of surfaces
52. full
53. full contact
54. softening
55. heat
56. harden
57. internal stresses; dimensional stability; resistance to crazing
58. prior to
59. final
60. before
61. soaking; slowly
62. fresh water
63. clean soft cloth
64. wax; antistatic component
65. polish
66. fine scratches; improve the visual clarity
67. high speed; heat
68. should never; crazing
69. fine cracks
70. solvents; sand blasting; trialene soap
71. cyclohexanone
72. paint remover; crazing
73. acrylic-based paints
74. ¼
75. heat gun; installation stresses
76. padding of rubber or felt
77. 1⅛; ⅛; expansion and contraction
78. ⅛; expansion and contraction
79. just; one full turn
80. Micro-Mesh process
81. replaced
82. replacement
83. stop-drilled; patched
84. same thickness; ¾; fully; tapered
85. stop-drilled
86. tapers outward
87. thicker; more severe; heated and pressed; adhesive

Chapter 10
MULTIPLE CHOICE QUESTIONS

1. d
2. b
3. d
4. c
5. b
6. a
7. d
8. b
9. c
10. c

Chapter 11
STUDY QUESTIONS

1. greater
2. holes
3. stress concentrations
4. ''glued''
5. exothermically cured
6. chemical; physical
7. chemical reaction; agents
8. cold bonding
9. hot-bond
10. imbedded; matrix
11. AC 43.13-1A & 2A
12. urethane
13. inhomogeneous; synthetic
14. homogeneous; retain
15. fibrous; matrix
16. thermoset
17. thermoplastic
18. preimpregnated
19. transverse; direction; transfer loads
20. same direction
21. transferred; matrix; lowest
22. greater
23. low sensitivity to sonic vibrations; reduced weight; high corrosion resistance; high deterioration resistance; smooth surface; aerodynamic; parasitic
24. solid laminate; honeycomb/rigid foam sandwich
25. bonding; several layers
26. high-density laminate; low-density filler
27. reinforced paper; Nomex; fiberglass; aluminum; carbon
28. strength-to-weight
29. mechanical principles
30. S-glass; E-glass
31. advanced composites
32. particles; flakes; fillers
33. hollow fibers; noncircular cross section; solid, circular cross-sectional fibers
34. solid, circular cross-sectional
35. orientation; length; shape; composition
36. volume; particular direction
37. bidirectional; unidirectional
38. resin-impregnated
39. flat; irregular-shaped

40. individual
41. tows
42. directly
43. twisted; yarns
44. fill; perpendicular
45. weave
46. selvage
47. warp tracers
48. over; under
49. several successive; one
50. crowfoot satin-weave
51. four; one
52. seven; one
53. same lengthwise
54. plastic-based; encapsulates; between
55. thermosetting; thermoplastic
56. completeness; increase strength; relieve stress
57. thermal; electrical
58. one-part polymer; two-part liquid mixture; sheet-film adhesive; preimpregnated reinforcement
59. two-part liquid mixture
60. weight; volume
61. A
62. shelf life
63. pot life; gelling
64. 6 months
65. B
66. honeycomb
67. voids; improper fit
68. preimpregnated
69. kept frozen
70. adhesive
71. C
72. increase strength
73. syntactic foam
74. non–gas
75. edges; corners
76. isotropic; no specific orientation
77. less density
78. mold
79. mold
80. open molds
81. closed molds
82. coefficient of thermal expansion
83. different
84. room temperature
85. release agent; release film; prevent
86. vacuum bag; heat source
87. autoclave; under pressure
88. parallel
89. directional relationship
90. 0° plane
91. 0° position
92. warp orientation
93. warp clock; four
94. orientation; direction of rotation
95. plus; negative
96. unidirectional; anisotropic
97. more than one direction
98. bidirectional
99. quasi-isotropic
100. cross-ply stress
101. all directions; not truly
102. delamination
103. spade; long tapered
104. high-speed, low-feed
105. specially ground; sheared
106. carbide; diamond
107. coarse
108. nondestructive inspection
109. voids; delaminations
110. dull
111. couplant
112. airtight
113. moisture; corrosion
114. corrosion; disbonding
115. surface patch
116. abrasives
117. chemicals; weakening
118. tapered; stepped
119. ½-in
120. four
121. 1 in
122. adhesive
123. impregnated
124. smallest; largest
125. align; warp direction
126. vacuum; thermocouples
127. rise; soak; drop-off
128. wet lay-up; pre-preg
129. release film
130. porous film; bled
131. high-temperature nylon release film
132. high-temperature; course-weave; nonporous
133. breather-bleeder material
134. air; volatiles; solvents
135. vacuum port; breather-bleeder
136. nylon plastic bagging film
137. 23 in Hg; wrinkles
138. plastic squeegee
139. breather-bleeder
140. heated; after
141. initially; out-gasing; air bubbles
142. constant and controlled level of heat
143. must be removed
144. bridges
145. undercut; anchor
146. syntactic
147. scarfing; stepping; router
148. adhesive mixture (viscous slurry)
149. same orientation
150. sheet foaming adhesive
151. cavity
152. sealed
153. moisture condensation
154. proper orientation

155. external plate; blind pull riveted
156. air hammers; bucking bars; not

Chapter 11
APPLICATION QUESTIONS

1. a. The 14-in diameter should be fabricated to 14.2951 in.
   b. The 10-in diameter should be fabricated to 10.2089 in.
   c. The depth should be fabricated to 4.0837 in.
   Note: The number of degrees used is 530°F. (600°F less the standard temperature of 70°F).

2. a. Layer 3 removal should have a diameter of 1 in.
   Layer 2 removal should have a diameter of 2 in.
   Layer 1 removal should have a diameter of 3 in.
   b. Surface layer should be cut to a diameter of 5 in.
   Layer 3 should be cut to 1 in.
   Layer 2 should be cut to 2 in.
   Layer 1 should be cut to 3 in.
   c. The warp of layers 3 and 5 should be in the 12 o'clock–6 o'clock plane.
   The surface layer and layer 4 warp should be in the 9 o'clock–3 o'clock plane.

Chapter 11
MULTIPLE CHOICE QUESTIONS

1. a	11. a
2. b	12. b
3. b	13. d
4. d	14. a
5. a	15. c
6. c	16. a
7. b	17. c
8. c	18. b
9. b	19. c
10. a	20. d

Chapter 12
STUDY QUESTIONS

1. a. type; size
   b. proper direction
   c. safety mechanism
   d. head up; forward
   e. force; without checking
   f. cables; hoses; tubing
   g. safety precautions
2. attaching hardware
3. installed
4. tapered drifts
5. distort; overstress
6. cause
7. jig; fixture
8. well padded; reinforced position; bulkhead; former
9. fixed components; control surfaces
10. before
11. each other
12. cable length; cable tension; push-pull rods; bell cranks; cable drums
13. level attitude
14. components
15. longitudinal; lateral
16. plumb bob; target; specified structural member; centered
17. permanently
18. supports
19. not; structurally weak area
20. symmetry; angular
21. alignment checks
22. leveling; measuring
23. vertical symmetry
24. reference point
25. amount
26. mounting point; reference
27. alignment
28. straight and level
29. increased
30. wings; ailerons
31. dihedral; angle of incidence; washin; washout
32. dihedral
33. longitudinal
34. angle of incidence
35. washin
36. washin; 1°
37. washout
38. counteracting
39. decreases
40. increases
41. washed in; washed out
42. stagger; angle of incidence; dihedral angle; decalage
43. stagger
44. positive
45. decalage
46. positive
47. cradle; jacks
48. movement; not
49. ailerons; elevators or stabilators; rudder or rudders
50. three
51. lateral (roll) control; longitudinal
52. balancing mechanisms
53. aerodynamic balancing; static balancing
54. hydraulically
55. yaw
56. adverse yaw
57. vertical axis
58. flutter
59. lateral
60. unbalanced; balanced
61. stabilator
62. ruddervators
63. same
64. opposite

65. flaperons
66. full-span flap
67. primary surfaces; reduce
68. bending; zero-control
69. rudders; ailerons
70. elevator
71. mechanically; electrically; hydraulically
72. flight controls
73. deflects
74. returning a surface
75. pitch trim; neutral trim
76. hydraulically
77. camber
78. plain flap
79. split flap
80. Fowler flap
81. slotted flap
82. gap; extended
83. leading-edge flap
84. forward; down; increase
85. high angles of attack
86. reduce; improve
87. slats
88. slot
89. spoilers
90. flight spoilers
91. ground spoilers
92. slowing
93. drag panels
94. symmetrically
95. cables; pulleys; turnbuckles; push-pull rods; bellcranks; quadrants; torque tubes; cable guards; fairleads
96. carbon fiber; corrosion-resistant steel
97. pulleys
98. turnbuckles
99. push-pull rod; torque arms
100. bellcrank
101. quadrant
102. torque
103. cable guards; guard pins
104. fairlead
105. 3°
106. air-pressure seals
107. a. level; jacks
     b. before
     c. reinstallation
     d. label
     e. three threads
     f. neutral
     g. neutral; neutral
108. cable tensions; synchronization; control surfaces; range
109. a. neutral position
     b. rig; tension
     c. check; adjust
     d. secure
     e. position locks

110. position
111. tensiometer
112. universal protractor; digital protractor
113. 2 in [5.08 cm]
114. static balance; flutter
115. wear; corrosion
116. wear; cracks; alignment
117. deflection
118. pulley bearings; bearing bolts; bushings; clevis pins
119. Type Certificate Data Sheet
120. operational check
121. cyclic control; antitorque control; throttle and collective control
122. cyclic control
123. laterally; longitudinally
124. antitorque pedal; rudder pedals
125. angle; heading of the aircraft
126. increase; decrease
127. fully articulated; semirigid; rigid
128. independent
129. flapping
130. lead-lag
131. feathering
132. semirigid
133. central hub
134. teetering
135. rigid; feather
136. follow the same path as the other blades; low-frequency
137. yawing
138. torque; heading
139. collective-pitch
140. cyclic-pitch control; plane or disk
141. different values
142. 90° after; gyroscopic precession
143. rises
144. antitorque rotor (tail rotor)
145. sideward thrust
146. extremely low frequency
147. shock mounting
148. low-frequency; main rotor; vertical; lateral
149. up and down; up; down
150. spanwise; chordwise
151. heavier
152. trailing edge
153. medium
154. high-frequency
155. follows; path
156. magnetic pickup; interrupters; retroreflective targets; accelerometers electronic balancer; Phazor
157. coil of wire
158. Strobex light; interrupter
159. azimuth; clock angle
160. physical motion; voltage; amplitude
161. retroreflective target
162. balancer; accelerometers; magnetic pickup
163. flag-tracking; relative vertical

164. one
165. pitch-link assembly

MULTIPLE CHOICE ANSWERS

1. b	11. c
2. d	12. c
3. b	13. d
4. b	14. b
5. b	15. c
6. a	16. b
7. a	17. c
8. a	18. d
9. a	19. b
10. a	20. b

Chapter 13
STUDY QUESTIONS

1. operation; components
2. backup
3. landing gear; gear doors; flight controls; brakes; high power; quick action; accurate control
4. area
5. force
6. pressure; pounds per square inch (psi); kilopascals (kPa)
7. stroke
8. displacement
9. definite
10. hydraulic fluid
11. expand; cooled
12. increase
13. force
14. pressure
15. area
16. incompressible
17. volume; area; length
18. equal
19. equal; every; every
20. friction
21. fluid flow
22. differential pressure; restrictor
23. loss of energy
24. subtracted
25. multiplied
26. proportional
27. distance
28. pressure regulator; relief valve
29. vegetable-base fluids; mineral-base fluids; phosphate ester–base fluids
30. blue; blue-green; clear
31. red; 5606
32. less corrosive
33. red; 83282
34. fire resistance
35. synthetic rubber; leather; metal
36. very; not
37. IV
38. low density; high density
39. butyl synthetic
40. soften; dissolve
41. a. marked; type of fluid to be used in the system
    b. Never
    c. do not use it
    d. become mixed
    e. heat; flames
    f. (i) soap; water
       (ii) water; anesthetic
       (iii) inhaled
       (iv) eye; inhalation
    g. gloves; face shield; lines that are under pressure
42. hydraulic reservoir
43. hydraulic reservoir
44. standpipes
45. standpipe; the bottom of the tank
46. in-line; integral; pressurized; unpressurized
47. not; air space; expansion of the fluid
48. dipstick; remote indicating system
49. separate components
50. lower altitudes; ground operations
51. pulled; pushed
52. foam; air bubbles
53. pressurized
54. positive feed; foaming
55. spring pressure; air pressure; hydraulic pressure
56. 10; 90
57. turbine engine bleed; venturi-type aspirator
58. manifold
59. sight glass
60. relief-and-bleed
61. air breather
62. atmospheric impurities
63. pressure head
64. combined
65. relief valve
66. particles
67. wear of operating components
68. inlet; outlet; reservoir; pump outlet
69. micronic filter
70. porous metal filters
71. pressure; return
72. bypass valve
73. clogged filter
74. O ring
75. pressure
76. contamination
77. downstream
78. heat exchanger
79. temperature rises
80. pumpcase drain return lines
81. transferring
82. ram air; engine bleed air
83. volume
84. hydraulic cooler
85. hydraulic pumps
86. reservoir; check valve; cylinder

87. one direction
88. piston-displacement
89. positive-displacement; given
90. gear-type
91. vane-type; positive-displacement
92. volume
93. gerotor pump
94. axial multiple-piston
95. at an angle
96. side of the cylinder block; toward
97. inlet; outlet
98. fixed delivery
99. volume
100. stroke
101. cam-type piston; parallel
102. cam-type piston; wobble plate
103. angle
104. cam-type piston; hanger
105. shear; prevent further damage
106. ram air turbine (RAT)
107. speed; variable-volume pump
108. pressure switches; pressure regulators; relief valves; pressure-reducing valves
109. system; set limits
110. pressure
111. range
112. unloading valves
113. relief valve
114. exceeds
115. return line; reservoir
116. highest-pressure; descending
117. thermal relief; trapped; higher temperatures
118. above
119. pressure-reducing; debooster; higher
120. force; pressure; area; surface exposed
121. surface area; length of the stroke; moves
122. differential area
123. inverse proportion
124. accumulator
125. dampen; supplement; store power; supply
126. three; separate
127. diaphragm; bladder; piston
128. compressed air; inert gas
129. under pressure
130. preloaded; charged
131. one-third
132. very small; pressure gauge; air chamber
133. air side
134. accumulator air pressure
135. hydraulic system pressure
136. bladder-type accumulator; air; hydraulic fluid
137. air chamber; outside
138. collapses
139. less space
140. hydraulic pressure; removed; before
141. nitrogen; dry air
142. before; all; relieved
143. leak

144. selector valves
145. rotary; poppet; spool; piston; open-center-system
146. directly; electrical or electronic control; hydraulic pressure; pneumatic pressure
147. opposite
148. poppet valves
149. open-center selector
150. automatically
151. reservoir
152. automatic-operating control
153. prevent; restrict
154. orifice
155. restrictor
156. variable restrictor
157. rate of flow
158. more slowly
159. check valve
160. direction of flow
161. arrow
162. orifice check valve
163. metering check valve
164. adjustable; not
165. prevents further flow
166. sequence valve; timing valve
167. alternate; emergency
168. priority valve; unrelated
169. flow equalizer
170. two equal
171. both directions
172. dual acting
173. constant-flow; reverse flow
174. mechanical motion
175. actuating cylinder
176. direct; positive
177. intermediate positions
178. feeds back
179. cyclic; collective
180. one direction
181. return spring
182. double-acting
183. internal-lock
184. an actuating cylinder; a multiport flow-control valve; check valves; relief
185. pressure; load
186. without significant
187. prevent leakage
188. packings; gaskets
189. between two parts
190. two stationary parts
191. O-ring seal; chevron seal; universal gasket; crush washer
192. both directions
193. colored dots; colored stripe
194. system; fuel systems only; hydraulic; pneumatic; oil systems only; white
195. Skydrol
196. new
197. not

198. correct size; installed without
199. same type
200. threads; sharp corners
201. twisted condition
202. used alone; 1500 psi [10 342.5 kPa]
203. backup rings
204. away from the pressure
205. two sets of seals
206. a. one ring at a time
    b. shim stock
    c. adjustable packing gland nut
    d. firmly but not squeezed; loosen
    e. by hand
    f. the manufacturer's instructions
207. power section; flow; limits pressure; carries fluid
208. actuating section; operating units
209. open; closed
210. open-center valve; power-control valve; pump-control valve
211. open position
212. time-lag; resistance
213. bypass
214. pressure regulator; power pump; pressure switch
215. under pressure
216. removed; pressure regulator; integral control valve; idle
217. open system
218. pump-control; power-control; block; force
219. operated; relief valve
220. one subsystem
221. closed system
222. constant volume; variable-volume pump
223. not in operation
224. manifold
225. Powerpak
226. more power
227. three separate
228. modular unit
229. return line
230. separate; parallel; continuously
231. 11; engine-driven pumps; air turbine motor–driven pumps; power-transfer units; a ram air turbine; electrically operated pumps
232. one
233. three; two; utility
234. parallel
235. pressure
236. compressible; gradually
237. store
238. filters; liquid separators; chemical air driers
239. moisture
240. return lines
241. engine-driven air compressor; engine compressor bleed air
242. emergency
243. nitrogen; carbon dioxide
244. charging; control valve
245. correct type of fluid

246. color; smell
247. closed
248. clean
249. fill the reservoir; purge the system of air; FULL
250. air
251. flushing
252. approved limits
253. twisted
254. play
255. leakage; preload; position
256. sheared pump shaft; defective relief valve; pressure regulator; unloading valve; lack of fluid in a hydraulic system; check valve installed backward
257. hold pressure
258. worn; leaking
259. pressure regulator; unloading valve; obstruction
260. straighten; change
261. template
262. capped; plugged
263. seals; leaks; loose parts

Chapter 13
APPLICATION QUESTIONS

1. a. 4 in³   (2 in² * 2 in = 4 in³)
   b. 120 lb   (60 lb/in² * 2 in² = 120 lb)
2. 108 strokes and 138.9 lb
   The large piston has an area of 113 in². Dividing 5000 lb by 113 in² yields a pressure need of 44.2 psi. Since the large piston's stroke travel needed is 6 in, the volume of fluid required for the large piston is 113 in² * 6 in = 678.5 in³. The small piston is 3.14 in² and a full stroke of 2 in yields a volume of 6.28 in³. Dividing the large piston volume (678.5 in³) by the small piston volume (6.28 in³), the number of strokes needed is 108. To produce 44.2 psi using a 3.14-in² piston requires 138.9 lb of force. (44.2 lb/in² * 3.14 in² = 138.9 lb).
3. 270 lb
   The pressure leaving the master cylinder is 38.2 psi. At the brake each piston exerts 67.5 lb of force. Since there are two pistons both exerting 67.5 lb, the force at each brake is 135 lb. Since there are two wheel brakes, the total force is 270 lb.

Chapter 13
MULTIPLE CHOICE QUESTIONS

1. b		11. b
2. b		12. d
3. c		13. a
4. c		14. d
5. a		15. b
6. b		16. d
7. c		17. c
8. c		18. c
9. b		19. c
10. a		20. d

1. tricycle; conventional
2. nose wheel; main gear
3. conventional-geared
4. dampens vibrations; cushions the landing impact
5. main
6. tail; nose
7. dissipate
8. rigid landing gear
9. shock cord
10. spring steel; composite material
11. metering
12. structural members; bolts
13. hydraulic; electric
14. amphibious; floats; hull
15. wheels
16. along with
17. common
18. trunnion
19. strut
20. outer cylinder
21. piston
22. snubber valve
23. metering pin
24. wiper ring
25. dry, clean air; nitrogen
26. snubbing
27. centering cams
28. torque links
29. truck
30. drag link
31. side brace link
32. overcenter link
33. downlock; jury strut
34. swivel gland
35. shimmy damper
36. piston-type shimmy damper
37. vane-type dampers
38. small aircraft
39. steering arms
40. electrically operated
41. air bottle; mechanical system; separate hydraulic system; release the UP locks
42. pneumatic bungee
43. "squat switches"; gear retraction
44. below-cruise-power; warning horn
45. antiskid system
46. ground-sensing control
47. low-frequency vibration
48. ground resonance
49. tuning forks
50. wear; deterioration; corrosion; alignment
51. age; fraying of the braided sheath; narrowing (necking) of the cord; wear
52. advisable
53. color-coded
54. 5 years
55. leakage; smoothness of operation; the moving parts; play
56. springs
57. all air pressure is removed
58. the smoothness of operation; locks; warning horn; indicating systems; in wheel wells; landing-gear doors
59. camber; toe
60. vertical
61. positive
62. horizontal axis
63. toed in
64. closer together
65. shim washers
66. shim plates
67. toed out
68. torque links; spacer washers
69. corrosion
70. removed; examined
71. shear forces; shoulders; lower sidewalls
72. ply rating
73. greater
74. does not; plies in the tire
75. balance marks
76. FAR 37.167; Technical Standard Order (TSO) No. C62b
77. brand name; size; ply rating; serial number; qualification test speed; skid depth; reinforced; TSO number
78. 160 mph [257.6 km/h]
79. three; prefix
80. width; rim width; base
81. outside
82. nominal width
83. "R"
84. steel wire beads
85. plies
86. apex strips; flippers
87. chafers
88. air seal; chafing
89. breakers
90. tread
91. mounting surfaces
92. bead heel
93. bead toe
94. tread
95. chine or deflector
96. ozone
97. vertically
98. four high
99. traction
100. fusible plugs
101. two pieces
102. deflated
103. even; tire bead
104. protected area
105. tire talc

106. yellow strip; red dot
107. give it shape
108. denatured alcohol
109. light coat of grease
110. alternating tightening sequence
111. 25 percent; increments of 20 to 25 percent; alternating torque sequence
112. inflation cage
113. 12 to 24 h
114. should not
115. overinflated; reduced
116. underinflation
117. generally
118. peeling tread; thrown tread; deep damage across the tread; removed from service
119. blisters; bulges
120. deceleration; turning
121. replaced
122. the cord is not exposed or damaged
123. five
124. permanently marked
125. sequential
126. FAR 37.167 (TSO-C62)
127. month; year; name
128. static unbalance
129. chafing; thinning; elasticity
130. disassembled; paint; grease; dirt; corrosion
131. flexibility
132. fluorescent penetrant; dye penetrant; eddy-current; ultrasonic methods
133. assembly bolt holes
134. wear; discoloration; roughness; rotate freely
135. bearing drag; one serration
136. one-way or single-servo; two-way or dual-servo
137. adds
138. one direction; either direction
139. brake frame; expander tube; return springs; brake blocks
140. expander tube; blocks
141. pistons; brake linings; disk
142. pistons; pressure plate; rotating; stationary
143. wear indicators
144. stationary; high-friction-type brake linings
145. gap; lining sections
146. carbon composite
147. indicated airspeed; gross weight; density altitude
148. thrust reversers; reduced
149. self-contained; independent
150. atmosphere
151. air
152. energizing unit; foot-operated; single-action
153. mechanical linkages
154. toe; heel
155. balance; equal force
156. main hydraulic system
157. closed; opened
158. brake debooster valve
159. antiskid systems
160. wheel torque; maximum braking effectiveness
161. wheel-speed-sensor; control-box; servo valves
162. rate of change; wheel speed
163. select; hold; adjust; best
164. pressure bias-modulation
165. comparator amplifier; servo valve driver
166. wheel-speed transducers; axle
167. deactivate; nonautomatic
168. fully cured
169. pitting; grooving
170. distorted; clips are broken
171. wear indicator pin
172. correct type
173. swelling; sponginess; leakage; wear
174. dragging brakes
175. grabbing brakes
176. fading brakes
177. worn brakes; lack of fluid in the brake system; air in the system; improperly adjusted mechanical linkages
178. piston seal
179. bleed; air
180. spongy brakes; drag
181. bleeder fittings
182. operated
183. forced; back to the reservoir

Chapter 14
MULTIPLE CHOICE QUESTIONS

1. a
2. c
3. b
4. c
5. a
6. b
7. a
8. c
9. b
10. d
11. c
12. a
13. b
14. b
15. c
16. d
17. b
18. d
19. d
20. b

Chapter 15
STUDY QUESTIONS

1. uniform flow; constant pressure
2. rate; pressure
3. power interruption
4. independent
5. for each engine; shutoff valve
6. two vents
7. incorrect installation; loss
8. atmospheric pressure
9. FUEL; type; minimum grade
10. ignition; fuel vent outlets
11. gravity-fed
12. 125 percent
13. 100 percent
14. 20 s
15. automatic

16. overfilling
17. interconnected tank outlets
18. vapor lock
19. fuel starvation; bubble
20. automatic shutoff
21. bypassing
22. emergency control
23. aluminum alloy; fuel-resistant synthetic rubber; composite materials; stainless steel
24. 3½
25. sumps
26. FUEL; minimum grade; capacity
27. 0
28. fuel screens
29. inlet
30. integral fuel tank
31. baffles; reduce sloshing
32. "wet wing"
33. rigid removable
34. bladder fuel
35. empty; overflow; fuel spillage
36. alternative
37. fuel pumps; gravity flow
38. boost pump; scavenge pump; cross-feed pump
39. sliding
40. varying; constant
41. around; starting the engine; emergency operation
42. balanced relief valves
43. diaphragm
44. loosened
45. center inlet; impeller
46. submerged pump
47. ejector pump
48. returned
49. venturi
50. pressure drop; drawn
51. the engines are running
52. finger strainer; master strainer; carburetor; fuel-control unit
53. fuel-tank; fuel-metering device; engine-driven positive-displacement
54. lowest; water trap
55. extremely fine
56. bypass valves
57. bypass warning
58. accumulated moisture
59. the fuel flow; the tank; transferring fuel; one or more
60. fire protection; shut
61. fuel heaters
62. engine compressor bleed air; engine oil
63. no sharp bends; three
64. vertical bends
65. flexible hose assemblies
66. bonded
67. the force of gravity
68. high enough
69. pump
70. parallel
71. fuel boost
72. primer
73. fuel vent
74. ambient atmospheric
75. surge tank; vent compartment; vent box
76. pressure buildup; spilling overboard
77. ambient pressure
78. flame arrester
79. fueling station; truck
80. fueling-control panel
81. any fuel tank; any engine
82. fuel jettison
83. continous fuel jettison manifold
84. oil dilution
85. fueling receptacle
86. flow-limiting
87. positive closing
88. fueling-level-control shutoff valve
89. fueling-level-control pilot valve
90. motor-driven valves
91. to each engine
92. should be checked
93. leaks; corrosion; microorganism growth
94. venting
95. obstructions
96. routing
97. effectiveness; accuracy
98. operational check
99. normal level-flight attitude
100. artificially inducing
101. stain; seep; heavy seep; running leak
102. in an enclosed area
103. outside; away from
104. fire hazard
105. all
106. growth of microorganisms
107. checked for corrosion
108. never
109. as it is drained
110. welding
111. riveting
112. sealing compound
113. soldering flux; solder beads
114. sloshing
115. tightening the metal seam
116. sealing compound
117. condition
118. nonabsorbent
119. excessive corrosion
120. sharp edges; protrusions

Chapter 15
MULTIPLE CHOICE QUESTIONS

1. d
2. d
3. b
4. d
5. c
6. a

7. d
8. b
9. a
10. c
11. a
12. b
13. a

14. d
15. b
16. a
17. a
18. d
19. a
20. d

Chapter 16
STUDY QUESTIONS

1. heater muff; air scoop; ducting; valve
2. heat; transferred
3. control; transfer
4. cannot; cabin
5. compressed air
6. combustion heaters; surface combustion heaters; airplane fuel
7. vented; drained
8. whirling action; stable
9. ducting; chamber; condition; gap; operation; airflow; fuel system; individual; complete
10. inside of
11. bleed air
12. mixed; ambient; recirculated air
13. closed; freon
14. compression; expansion; lower
15. latent
16. emits; same amount
17. increases; decreases
18. lower
19. two
20. evaporator
21. condenser
22. liquid; gas
23. push; under pressure
24. refrigerant; atmosphere
25. liquid
26. expansion valve
27. heat; gas
28. decreased
29. Refrigerant 12
30. temperature; pressure
31. receiver-dryer-filter
32. sight glass
33. low
34. high; condenser
35. subcooled; premature vaporization
36. evaporator; slugging
37. thermal expansion valve; variable
38. outlet; inlet
39. evaporator
40. leaving the evaporator
41. evaporator; condenser
42. compressor; thermal expansion valve; thermal expansion valve; inlet side of the compressor
43. high side; low side
44. temperature; sight glass

45. water
46. service manifold; test pressures; add refrigerant; purge; evacuate; recharge
47. vacuum pump; closed container
48. compressor oil
49. capped immediately
50. receiver-dryer
51. air; attendant moisture
52. boiling point
53. odorless; nontoxic; displaces
54. toxic; high temperatures
55. open area
56. eye and skin damage
57. amount; type
58. upright
59. service fittings
60. cooling
61. heated; cooled
62. heat exchangers; ram air; expansion turbine
63. cooling air
64. air-cycle machine (ACM)
65. primary heat exchanger
66. compressor inlet
67. secondary heat exchanger
68. expansion turbine
69. air temperature
70. heat energy; expansion
71. water separator
72. dried, cold air
73. not required
74. 8000 ft [2438 m]
75. rapid pressure changes
76. cabin differential pressure
77. ambient outside; inside
78. type of engine
79. supercharger
80. turbocharger
81. bleed air
82. too much
83. mixing valve
84. outflow valve
85. escape
86. pneumatic pressure; electric motors
87. safety valve; positive pressure-relief valve
88. positive pressure-relief valve; higher; outflow valve
89. overpressurized
90. maximum pressure setting
91. higher altitude
92. automatic
93. 0.3 psi [2.3 kPa]
94. dump valve
95. landing-gear squat switch
96. open; equalizes
97. release cabin pressurization; does not
98. spring
99. rate; altitude change; cabin pressure altitude
100. gasper system
101. cabin altitude

102. isobaric-control
103. hypoxia
104. stored-gas; chemical; solid-state; liquid oxygen
105. 1800 psi [12 411 kPa]
106. green color
107. yellow
108. safety disks
109. lower pressure
110. demand; continuous-flow
111. airtight seal
112. inhalation; flow of oxygen
113. ambient air
114. constant-flow mask; cabin air
115. exhales
116. phase-dilution; deflated
117. chemical oxygen generator
118. candle
119. water; oil; grease; solvent contamination
120. Teflon fluorocarbon resin tape
121. no; aluminum-alloy flared fittings
122. coupling sleeves; outside flares
123. first three threads
124. sparkless
125. designation number
126. DOT-3AA-1800; ICC-3AA-1800; hydrostatic testing
127. 5 years
128. DOT-3HT-1850; 3 years
129. 24 years; 4380 filling cycles
130. composite cylinders
131. 15 years; 10 000 filling cycles
132. an entry in the aircraft logbook
133. stamped; shoulder; neck
134. tested for leaks; purged
135. leak detector
136. purging
137. aviator's breathing; MIL-0-27210
138. not assume

Chapter 16
MULTIPLE CHOICE QUESTIONS

1. b	11. b
2. b	12. a
3. d	13. a
4. c	14. c
5. a	15. a
6. d	16. d
7. c	17. b
8. b	18. c
9. a	19. a
10. a	20. c

Chapter 17
STUDY QUESTIONS

1. pressure instruments; altitude and airspeed; engine oil pressure
2. bourdon tube
3. straighten out; sector

4. diaphragm; bellows type
5. corrugated concentrically; sealed
6. converted
7. cylindrical capsule
8. ambient; absolute zero; [pounds per square inch differential (psid)]
9. above or below ambient pressure
10. gauge pressure
11. absolute zero; actual pressure
12. psia
13. ram air pressure; differential pressure indication (psid)
14. concentrated around the rim
15. its axis; same plane
16. increased; speed of rotation
17. rings; free gyro
18. gimbal rings
19. precession
20. pneumatically or electrically
21. direct-indicating
22. Wheatstone bridge
23. ratiometers
24. altimeter
25. decreases; pressure
26. nonsensitive altimeter
27. in series
28. adjusted
29. installation; position error
30. particular
31. temperature changes
32. encoding altimeters
33. through the air
34. movement of the diaphragm
35. differential pressure
36. impact pressure; expand
37. indicated airspeed
38. calibrated airspeed
39. temperature; pressure altitude; window
40. various operating speeds
41. red radial line
42. normal operating range
43. yellow arc
44. flap operating range
45. best-rate-of-climb
46. face card
47. slippage
48. airspeed-angle-of-attack
49. segment rotating
50. indicated airspeed
51. temperature; altitude
52. Machmeter
53. true airspeed; speed of sound
54. altitude
55. rate; climbing or descending
56. atmospheric pressure; atmosphere
57. lag
58. capillary restrictors
59. sensitive vertical-speed indicators

60. total energy
61. accelerometer; acceleration loads
62. gravity
63. independently operating
64. direction
65. magnetic; true
66. not; variation
67. deviation; airplane
68. north-south; deviation
69. ''swinging''; compass rose
70. simulated level flight conditions; doors are closed; flaps are in the retracted position; engines are running; throttles are set at cruise position; electrical switches; alternators; radios
71. a. zero
    b. magnetic north; adjust
    c. magnetic east; east
    d. one-half of the error
    e. one-half the E-W error
    f. successive magnetic 30° headings; record the compass readings; deviation card
72. $+10°$
73. radio equipment; other equipment
74. at the annual inspection
75. radios; electrical circuits
76. vertical-dial direction
77. desired course
78. Gyro Flux Gate
79. earth's magnetic field
80. directional gyro
81. particular heading
82. heading of the aircraft; spin axis of the gyro
83. rigid; motion of the aircraft
84. heading indicator
85. gimbals
86. tumbled
87. caging
88. jets of air
89. horizontal situation indicator
90. flags
91. artificial horizon; attitude indicator; attitude gyro
92. horizon; aircraft
93. actual position; natural horizon
94. vertical plane
95. turn-and-bank
96. rate
97. inclinometer; coordinated
98. rate gyro; proportion
99. doghouses
100. standard-rate turn; 3°
101. one-half; 4 min
102. turn coordinator
103. vacuum pumps
104. pitot-static system
105. static pressure
106. dynamic air pressure; static air pressure
107. perforated static buttons
108. all water

109. register false readings
110. flag; visible; not being supplied
111. filtered
112. venturi; restricted
113. sidewall pressure; reduced
114. wet-pump; dry-pump
115. engine
116. low friction; proper sealing
117. ambient air; aircraft speed
118. tachometers
119. percent of rated rpm
120. mechanically; electrically
121. bourdon tube; gear segment
122. electrical; mechanical
123. thermocouples; exhaust gases
124. current
125. amplified; adjusted
126. engine pressure ratio; thrust
127. manifold pressure
128. cylinder head
129. inverted float gauge
130. rotating dial
131. upright float
132. sight-glass gauge
133. magnetic direct-indicating
134. resistance-type
135. capacitance fuel; weight
136. dielectric constant
137. fuel-pressure gauge
138. red limit
139. direct indication; power output
140. blue; AUTO LEAN; green; AUTO RICH
141. diaphragm; pair of bellows
142. fuel-flow gauges
143. increase; higher
144. 8-day
145. 5 s per day
146. no condition
147. brass; iron
148. curve
149. a computer
150. symbol generator
151. electronic attitude director indicators; electronic horizontal situation indicators; monitoring and alerting displays
152. electronic attitude director indicator (EADI)
153. electronic horizontal situation indicator (EHSI)
154. electronic centralized aircraft monitor (ECAM); engine indicator and crew-alerting system (EICAS)
155. mounting screws; circumferential clamps; brackets
156. nonmagnetic screws
157. brass; mounting nuts
158. internal stops
159. air pressure; suction; electrical power
160. force
161. covered; protective caps; plugs; protected
162. tagged
163. dirt and dust; stored

164. aircraft operations manual; maintenance manual; Type Certificate Data Sheet/Aircraft Specification
165. red radial line
166. normal operating range
167. yellow arc
168. critical vibration range
169. slippage mark
170. controlled
171. comparing
172. must not be applied
173. adjustments; aircraft's permanent maintenance record
174. regular schedule
175. FAR 43; Instrument Flight Rules (IFR)
176. negative pressure; airspeed indicator
177. static system
178. are connected
179. static system
180. before
181. glass faces; range markings; cases; case vent filters; mounting; connections
182. looseness
183. gyro erection; noise
184. bearing wear or damage is indicated; foreign matter
185. tubing; hose; hose clamps; fittings
186. suction pressure (vacuum)
187. disconnected
188. instrument end; static vents or pitot head

Chapter 17
MULTIPLE CHOICE QUESTIONS

1. a
2. b
3. d
4. c
5. a
6. a
7. b
8. a
9. d
10. a
11. c
12. d
13. b
14. b
15. c
16. b
17. c
18. b
19. b
20. d

Chapter 18
STUDY QUESTIONS

1. warning light; aural alarm unit
2. parallel; any one switch
3. test circuit; operation
4. spot detector; longer; two contacts
5. rate-of-rise; series
6. heater
7. "continuous-loop"
8. Fenwal; Inconel; nickel
9. eutectic salt; drops
10. electronic control unit; actuates the alarm system
11. Kidde
12. decreases rapidly
13. resistance

14. Systron-Donner Company
15. pressure; increased; diaphragm switch
16. superior; large areas must be covered
17. aircraft maintenance manual
18. cargo; baggage compartments
19. toxic-gas
20. photoelectric cell; change; visible light; infrared radiation
21. change in current flow
22. open flame
23. light-refraction detector; direct light
24. reflected
25. resistance (conductivity); flow of current
26. radioactive material; detection chamber
27. ions; reduce
28. predetermined amount; triggered
29. solid-state; detecting elements
30. carbon monoxide; nitrous oxide; coating; current-carrying
31. carbon dioxide (CO_2); Freon (a chlorinated hydrocarbon); Halon 1301 (monobromotrifluoromethane—CF_3Br)
32. Nitrogen (N_2); propellant
33. liquid Freon; Halon; liquid evaporates
34. Halon 1301
35. older reciprocating-engine-powered
36. toxic; corrosive
37. displacement; free oxygen
38. pressurized containers; tubing; control valves; indicators; control circuitry
39. explosive cartridge
40. squib
41. flood valves
42. pressure gauge; "blowout" disk
43. CO_2
44. selected engine; smother the fire
45. high-rate-of-discharge (HRD)
46. rapid release; flood
47. water; electrical conductivity
48. foam-type; dry-chemical
49. damage; wear; security of mounting; compliance
50. approved practices; manufacturer's instructions
51. anti-icing system; deicing system
52. aerodynamic strut; probe; slipstream
53. frequency will decrease
54. microprocessor
55. inflatable rubber "boots"
56. cement; fasteners; bootnuts
57. only
58. air passages; chambers; alternate chambers
59. output pressure; deflation
60. distributor valve; different sections
61. raising; lowering; cracks off
62. time module
63. time module; solenoid-operated valves
64. 18 psig [124 kPa]
65. condition; adherence; surface
66. solvent

67. conductive neoprene; static charges
68. intact; effective
69. manufacturer's instructions; type of solvent; dissolving the cement; applying the solvent
70. obstruction or damage
71. thermal anti-icing; prevent
72. combustion heaters; engine bleed air
73. piccolo; spray tube
74. prevented
75. chem-milled
76. pitot mast; stall warning indicator
77. static ports; total-air-temperature; angle-of-attack indicators
78. electric heaters
79. burns
80. never; operating
81. heating; spraying
82. heated panel; inside the windshield structure; between windshield surfaces
83. prior to
84. a. delamination (separation of the layers)
    b. scratching
    c. arcing
    d. discoloration
85. decrease; strength of the windshield; optical quality; normal operation
86. sprayed
87. lines; fittings
88. windshield wipers; chemical repellents; a flow of air
89. electrically; hydraulically; pneumatically
90. converter
91. reduces; oscillating motion
92. actuator
93. opposite sides; back and forth
94. rack; pinion gear
95. repellent
96. wiper blades
97. wet; operated; dry windshield
98. globules; blown away
99. bleed air
100. pressurized
101. electric water heaters
102. thermostatically controlled
103. drain masts; waste tanks
104. contamination
105. correct position; moving properly
106. stretched; released; pointer; scale
107. spiral groove
108. verify; indicator; position
109. synchro transmitters
110. exciter windings; receivers
111. elevator trim; speedbrake (spoilers) handle; is centered; wing flaps; leading-edge wing flaps
112. unsafe configuration
113. angle of attack
114. sensor vane
115. slot; routed to the cabin area
116. reed; audible

117. angle of attack; position; weight
118. aural; illuminate
119. auxiliary power units (APUs)
120. gas-turbine engines
121. pneumatic power
122. start and stop; fire-protection test; indicating; manual discharge
123. ambient temperature; load
124. greater
125. 95 percent
126. pneumatic power-distribution system

Chapter 18
MULTIPLE CHOICE QUESTIONS

1. d
2. c
3. d
4. b
5. b
6. b
7. c
8. b
9. b
10. c
11. c
12. b
13. d
14. c
15. a
16. a
17. c
18. c
19. d
20. b

Chapter 19
STUDY QUESTIONS

1. cause; severity; eliminating the cause; replacing or repairing; returning the aircraft to service
2. airworthy condition; will not recur
3. cause
4. adverse effect; aircraft's airworthiness
5. before
6. equipment available; sufficient time
7. personal experience; training; maintenance manuals; service bulletins
8. troubleshooting
9. associated information
10. common malfunctions
11. divide-and-conquer
12. two equal parts; number of components; linear measurement
13. discrepant half
14. inputs; outputs
15. prior to
16. nature; frequency; duration
17. patterns
18. validation; properly interpreted
19. flow; pick; binary
20. assumed condition; series of checks
21. nature of the discrepancy; possible causes; corrective action
22. operational condition
23. electrical; pneumatic; hydraulic
24. gates
25. input
26. not

27. two; one; three
28. output
29. no output
30. a. AND
    b. OR
    c. NOT
31. invert gates
32. an output
33. no output
34. a. NAND
    b. NOR
    c. EXCLUSIVE-OR
35. circle; reverses
36. truth table

Chapter 19
MULTIPLE CHOICE QUESTIONS

1. b
2. a
3. a
4. d
5. c
6. d
7. c
8. b
9. a
10. d
11. c
12. a
13. b
14. c
15. d

NOTES AND CALCULATIONS

NOTES AND CALCULATIONS